# Bad Marxism

# Bad Marxism

## Capitalism and Cultural Studies

John Hutnyk

Pluto Press

LONDON • ANN ARBOR, MI

First published 2004 by Pluto Press
345 Archway Road, London N6 5AA
and 839 Greene Street, Ann Arbor, MI 48106

www.plutobooks.com

British Library Cataloguing in Publication Data
A catalogue record for this book is available from the British Library

ISBN 0 7453 2267 0 hardback
ISBN 0 7453 2266 2 paperback

Library of Congress Cataloging in Publication Data applied for

10 9 8 7 6 5 4 3 2 1

Designed and produced for Pluto Press by
Chase Publishing Services, Fortescue, Sidmouth, EX10 9QG, England
Typeset from disk by Newgen Imaging Systems (P) Ltd, Chennai, India
Printed and bound in the European Union by
Antony Rowe Ltd, Chippenham and Eastbourne, England

# Contents

# Acknowledgements

This book is to be blamed in part on Anne Beech, who suggested I write it after I made an intemperate, obvious and not very original comment at a conference in Stoke-on-Trent in 1996.* My comment had to do with the fact that it was not Marxism that fell with the Soviet Union, but only 'sausage-and-three-veg' versions (the phrase is from Ian Wilson) of something that was not (was no longer) recognisable as communism insofar as that means participation of all the people in decisions about how they will live. The suggestion was that there was now an opportunity to kill off the opportunists, to sort wheat from chaff, and other metaphors I did not really use with restraint or style. Instead of dismissing or celebrating an end of communism – a polarisation of two identical pathological and morbid stupidities – I thought we might attend to an even worse Marxism, an ever contrary, ever renewed, ruthless critique of everything, party of the new type, open polemic kind of rampant Marxist intelligence.† The form of this book was conceived in the notorious Pink House in Puri with Ben Rosenzweig, Cassandra Bennett and Elizabeth Wong. They know what strange forces shaped the plan; I hope they are not too surprised at its execution. This book now works through some of that motivation in the fields of anthropology, philosophy and cultural studies that govern my days in the regime that is Goldsmiths College. I owe my colleagues and students there much more than I can say. They know who they are if I don't list them all.

In addition to those already mentioned, parts of this writing were also read by Saul Goode, Seth Lazar, Imogen Bunting, John Gledhill,

---

* Many years earlier, before returning to school as a 'mature' student, I had worked as a packer for a pottery importer in Australia. Most of our wares – hideous Toby Jugs – came from Stoke-on-Trent. I just had to get this in – my family still has the mugs – Hi Dave, Marie-ann, Cheryl, Darren, Kim, Keri, Joshua, Henry, Daisy (meow), Ella, Lily, Mabel and Megan.

† In 1996 this book was provisionally called *Bad Marxism, Lousy Leninism and Mad Maoism – To the Barricades or the Book Arcades?* Luckily it got a bit more focused since then. Early or partial versions of the core sections are referenced in the bibliography as Hutnyk (1997a, 1997b, 1998b, 1998c, 2002b, 2003).

Victor Alneng, Howard Potter and Steve Wright. Everyone knows that writing acknowledgements is not the last thing to be done before packing the manuscript off to the publishers; it is an accretion and cumulative record, updated haphazardly, but I hope without too many omissions, of debts and gratitudes. Given idiosyncrasies of style, thanks are often overwrought when claiming reciprocity and obligation, but without exchanges with, influences, and gifts in kind, awesome and terrible, there would be no book: Gayatri Spivak, Mick Taussig, George Marcus, Nicola Frost, Carrie Clanton, Penny Harvey, Javier Taks, Sheila Robinson, Anthropology Departments (Manchester, Goldsmiths), Reading Groups (Charterhouse, Translasia, Marx, Heidegger, Adorno), Angie Mitropoulos, Danny Sullivan, Peter Phipps, Nikos Papastergiadis, Atticus Narrain, Julian Henriques, Elena Papadaki, the Centre for Cultural Studies at Goldsmiths, Scott Lash, Yin Shao-loong, the staff and students of the Department of Intercultural Studies at Nagoya City University, Masahiko Tsuchiya, Kaori Sugishita, Klaus Peter Koepping, Ashis Nandy, Don Miller, Scott McQuire, Malcolm Crick, Virinder Kalra, Alexander Bard, Tim Youngs and Sophie Richmond. For assistance in getting early parts published I thank Vijay Prashad, Amitava Kumar, Gareth Stanton, Stephen Nugent (*Critique of Anthropology*), Peter Wade (*Manchester Anthropology Papers*), Geert Lovink (*Nettime*), Abdul Karim Mustapha (*Rethinking Marxism*), Joost van Loon, Rob Shields (*Space and Culture*), Stephen Clarke (*Travel Writing and Empire*), Bobby Sayyid (*Contemporary South Asia*).

# Introduction: Cultural Studies as Capitalism

What is the point of polite erudition? A frisson of enthusiasm in the service of coffee shop chats and glossy publishing houses? Books on Marxism are legion and justifications for adding to this corner of the culture industry are few. Arguing that contemporary cultural theory has opportunistically failed in its take-up of the philosophy of praxis, or effectively to engage any kind of politics, persuasion or purpose that matters, is hardly going to endear me to my well-read betters. Nonetheless, I read recent encounters with Marxism in order to clear a path to something more. Ruthless critique of everything is the credo, relentless and dutiful, focus the procedure. The writings gathered here engage with Marx's latter-day culturalist epigones as promoted in the marketplaces of cultural theory. I ask you, what is this Marx that we are offered up now, just when we need him more than ever?

The approach of this book is to mark out a double strategy that (a) critiques the work of influential theorists – James Clifford, Jacques Derrida, Antonio Negri – who have had substantial impact in the last ten years with versions of Marx that are eclectic and often diverting, but substantially misconstrued. Second, (b) the book presents the study of culture through these figures as a wider concern than that usually identified as cultural studies proper – that is, cultural study is also about geo-politics, theory, war, capitalism. The book approaches cultural studies on a global scale, such that the influence of Georges Bataille, Frankfurt School critical theory, post-structuralism, reflexive anthropology, Gayatri Chakravorty Spivak, Subaltern Studies, Slavoj Žižek, Samir Amin and 'even' that three-headed beast 'Marx-Lenin-Mao' are also relevant in a mode of inquiry that should not be parochially defined.

Despite the expansiveness of the above list, I do not presume to address all studies of culture or all 'cultural studies'[®]. Rather, the task is to ask if the theoreticians that cultural studies draws upon, as well as those in anthropology and related socio-cultural disciplines, offer an adequate theorisation, and a politics, commensurate with the circumstances in which those theorists are read. Such questioning presumes a clear notion of the circumstances, of the coordinates, of contemporary social and political life, and of the moment of culture and politics today. All manner of debates could be had here – is it possible to name the evils of our time? Does the war machine, the corporate machine, the environmental crisis, the legitimation crisis, the predicament of culture, the credibility gap, the generation gap, the identity and difference over diaspora and belonging gap, the two camps, the in-between camps, the razor wire detention camps, the party question, the international divisions, the crisis of diplomacy, the crisis of identity, the nuclear stand-off, the arms trade, the terror raids, the occupying armies, the Hiroshima memorials, the police question, the 64 million dollar question – does any of this demand theorising that performs better than cultural studies has offered hitherto? My suggestion is yes and no, and this book attempts only to look to how certain theorists influential in the cultural studies tradition have used Marx as a name for these 'problems'. I will ask, has this use been up to par? I will not expect to hand out gold stars (or even red ones), nor to engage in cynical sectarianism (too often). Not very ambitious then. The book will be serious, playful and droll, at times frivolous or angry, both fair and unfair – the point is to show how theory reading is an ongoing lived critical political practice, warts and all, and to make it matter. Possibly wrong-headed at times, the readings here are subjective, personal and now public offerings in a community of criticism. Is this the best way that cultural studies contributes to culture?

I take cultural studies as the study of culture in the widest possible sense encompassing, but not limited to, anthropology, sociology, media studies, politics.[1] Wanting to think generously, I do not restrict it to any approach based wholly on that which sprang fully formed from the heads of Stuart Hall, Theodor Adorno, Bronislaw Malinowski or even Marx – despite impressive and unavoidable contributions from each. Cultural studies here is both expanded and reduced: more than the usual names are included, though fewer of them are examined in detail – those that are, obsessively so. Thus the book examines four topics as representative 'areas of contest' or exemplars of debate: the notion of travel as metaphor for our times; the work of Derrida on Marx and the party; the origins of capitalism, and anti-capitalism, in the scene of the first Indian revolution; and the history of anti-war communism as a critique of fascism and liberal charity. These are obviously not the only issues that could be raised, and capitalism is not simply the target of culture. Capitalism is clearly diverse and dissembling, and as a mode of production now consuming the planet, I have to take it, too, in a broad and narrow sense; late, early, global, changing (filtered through charity, travel, exotica, music, race).[2] While I do not imagine for a minute that the theoretical work discussed here will wipe this mode of production away, I am also sure it cannot last forever. I do think it is far better that we do away with it before it does away with us, and so this little book (I have tried to keep it small enough to be portable) adds another voice to the clamour that most tunefully harmonises in the international movements that fight for the alternatives that are its (distant) context.

In the struggle against the idea that 'there is no alternative', aimless flailing about of an anti-capitalism without theory is no better than a congealed orthodox politics of parliament or sect. Neither is viable or adequate to the situation in which we find ourselves, born to make history in circumstances some other rich bastard has chosen (to 'badly' paraphrase Marx in a style I will return to in Part 1). Instead, this book looks for the ways that recent academic Marxism, itself a strange beast, might be dragged kicking and screaming into anti-capitalist mobilisation. Too many academics, sequestered in their alcoves and chambers, have not yet heard about this movement. They seem unwilling to listen to the complaints of their students; the old left press has been displaced by digital retailers selling academics as 'stars'; and photocopiers are displaced by text messaging as the technology that stumps them. Fashionable designer anarchism is not much more effective either, now that it dominates the militant sections. Contemptuous of theory and methodically bizarre, the critique of books has taken the form of a refusal to open them rather than a drive to learn. This book fights on both fronts to add its voice to a renewed theory and practice.

The very idea of a book on 'Capitalism and Cultural Studies' should draw dubious looks; even a bad etymology would know that anything that started with 'cult', studied it, taught it for export profits, and sold it from super-book-market shelves, was bound to lead serious politics astray. Should we wander about then? I think that debate about the value of cultural studies is left unspoken insofar as it is the legacy of Marxist criticism, for and against, which is at stake. Cultural studies could still be the theorising of anti-capitalism, as this would befit its tradition(s) well. However, its success within the commodity sector that is education today teeters on the brink of co-option and complicity, always threatening a more radical take – not quite able to deliver. Ever more glossy readers and bumper selections of the same few articles and authors adorn the shelves (in somewhat similar circumstances, Theodor Adorno, in a 1968 lecture, once recalled Auguste Comte's contemptuous dismissal of philosophers as 'the blowers of bubbles' [Adorno 2000]). More urgent matters insist that a narrowing rehash of the discipline is not the only option. The anti-capitalism that cultural studies theorising might aspire to should also not be just that critical scholarship released in the wake of the Birmingham school, itself soon shorn of its anti-racist, anti-imperialist foci in favour of commercial, symbolic consumption and audience studies (however important they remain). The competition over the heritage of Marxism – be it Gramscian, Trotskyite, orthodox economism or a critical theory 'of everything' – does not in itself animate a renewal of cultural studies. The grounds of debate, if not explicit, are there in many happy returns – Derrida to Marx, Žižek to Lenin, even Dirlik [or Hutnyk] to Mao. The few studies presented in this book offer a preliminary step in a larger Marxist history of cultural studies that will debate its heterogeneity as heritage, as present and as future. A spectre *is* haunting Europe. And abstract, Eurocentric, complicit theorising should quake. Much of this book, then, is an examination of what we ought not to do, so as to keep on doing, so as to work through the negative implications and conceits. This may perhaps be the wandering path towards ever more creative and capable Marxisms, and Marxists who act.

What sort of action? (Stifled yawn: 'What is to be done?') In this book I intermittently defend the idea of the Leninist party. Paradoxically, this party is not something I can join – but I have to defend it from – even as I applaud with fascination – the rogue intelligence that seems set to always undermine it. Is this the continuous revolution? I am not sure. An idea from Avital Ronell indicates where the problem lies, in that while supporting the party and the necessary sublimation of intellectual freedom that the goals of the revolution entail, the revolutionary thinker cannot let go of the 'narcissistic disorder' (Ronnel 2002:25) that insists on that freedom, from party, responsibility, discipline, whatever.

Sick with anger, watching death-news-war-destruction on the television, I know there seems little I can do, and everything remains to be done. This is not to say that I won't continue to try to untangle these thoughts – about war, philosophy, culture; books, reading, scholarship – but it is also an analysis provoked by despair and dismay that can only be resolved by joining with others in something like the party. Mute before devastation, only the individual can be a coward; to join with others is the way out, forward, upward, away …

Party: ✓. Type: emergent. There is far too serious a tone in the grim pretensions of social theory; taking itself as profound, it also wants immortality. As usually does the Left party theorist. Not much of that here I'm afraid (said with smirk). I can only wish for a rush of profundity, do not attain it. Nor, practically, is this likely to be all that much help in the struggle for (the) 'struggle' – how does seriousness recruit to seriousness if it presents seriousness as absolute? No need to be sad to be militant, as we shall see Foucault write. 'Redness of tomatoes, redness of manifestoes', in Michael Healy's mischievous phrase (Healy 1986).

Cultural studies in the narrow disciplinary sense does often seem to take on only a bleached form, especially in its little England and North American manifestations, appearing to reinforce the centrality of WASP culture long after the rest of the world has become more interesting than suburban Britain, and popular culture in America has become hip hop. In the disciplinary corral where I have most often worked, anthropology 'at home' seems also to enact a nostalgic assertion of the 'importance' of the white supremacist homelands, but apparently 'unlike' the foundation of cultural studies, the rush home was a reaction to being exposed as voyeuristic abroad. In so many ways the division of anthropology and cultural studies[3] is bound up with a specific global imperial moment – it is no accident that one emerged at a time of 'decolonisation' and one crashed in crisis. I take the two together as broken pieces of the same heritage, still unable to cope with the necessary anti-capitalism inherent in a parallel but more enabling tradition – Marxism. That the belated take-up of a reading of Marx in the theorists who inform anthropology and cultural studies today has gone horribly astray comes as no surprise. This book details the shocks.

The deviations I wish to show in contemporary theorising have a long pedigree. Cultural studies, in its disciplinary UK version, can be traced to the group of ex-Communist Party historians and fellow travellers who started the journals *Universities and Left Review* and *The Reasoner*, merged later as *New Left Review* under the initial editorship of Stuart Hall. Cultural studies harks back as well to the Workers' Educational Association teachers Raymond Williams and

Richard Hoggart (a future warden of Goldsmiths College), both of whom came from working-class socialist backgrounds but gained scholarships and took degrees at Cambridge and Leeds (see Dworkin 1997:83). Similarly, social anthropology can primarily be taken as an inquiry into 'other modes of life' founded by UK-based scholars, but with far wider international variants that cannot be ignored, and beginning as an academic enterprise variously in the service of colonialist administration or as a critique of this and its assumptions (Gledhill 2000).[4] Certainly Malinowskian anthropology has sought to work a conceit that goes 'look at these people who seem strange and incomprehensible. I, the anthropologist will show you that if we look closer they are not so strange at all.' The premise that social anthropology has moved on from its early primitivism is tempered by its transformation into a culture industry, marketing postgraduate degrees and fieldwork method for dollars and yen, where scholarship or thinking can take a secondary place. I suspect it is possible to show that when method is taught and sold, it is the heritage industry of colonial era Malinowski that is mass produced, and thereby distributed throughout the world.

Although it may seem a bizarre question for someone obsessed with theorists, to explain how social science method has been commercialised I think it should be asked why anthropology and cultural studies would need 'Theory' at all these days. Many practitioners seem to do fine with the most minimal or haphazard versions. As a brutal obsession with abstracted minutiae seems to have captured social research of many kinds, observation and extrapolation is now taught as 'discipline', but theory seems to be a free for all. The hyper detail hunting I have in mind is not just concerned with the empirical, but fetishises the object or discrete item with a gathering-mentality that smacks of a curator's cast – contextualised with the briefest docketing and citation. Scholars of repute increasingly limit their interest to the collection and contemplation of trinkets and factoids with the most eclectic and incidental assertions of theory as, at best, a hardly necessary, accompaniment. Much deconstruction, fieldwork, audience studies and interpretation shrug off philosophical and political doubts in favour of a contained discourse on method. This makes 'doing theory' more of a fashion, fad or window-dressing, than an intrinsic component of intellectual analysis. Method as theory is now packaged in fee-paying postgraduate courses within the teaching factory, where problems of research become just a programme of study, competitively priced in the global education marketplace and labelled as 'research training', accredited and approved by committee. Fieldwork, for example, in the Malinowskian mode, is the carefully tended mythic and protective final crutch of a disciplinary demarcation with outdated colonial foundations – the old allocation of the 'primitive' and the 'Third World' to anthropology, industrialised society to sociology and pop culture to Birmingham. For anthropology departments, despite acknowledgement that Malinowski's fieldwork was never as methodical as he said it was, a distinct programme is often now packaged as research training in fieldwork and debates in ethnography to maintain the brand-name viability of British social anthropology as such. Thus anthropology departments as separate entities in the university sector and, to a diminishing degree, in the bookshops, are secured as well.

Other disciplines look on 'fieldwork' with envy, as it was never so easy to 101-ify methods in the fine arts or design. British cultural studies, for example, in its least overtly political forms, seems keen to do the same packaging trick with audience studies, though the method here is less strict – the rite of passage of a year in a tent in the jungle is not replicated in front of the TV. Psychoanalysis has done better in terms of thinking about and codifying method as philosophical problem – though having to pay for the cure seems to ignore economic difference. In the section on Derrida (Part 2) there will be reason to consider how new technologies might influence the empirical scene on the couch. The same sort of question with regard to fieldwork and media might be usefully raised. New media anthropology too has been sufficient cause for new programme expansion in the departments, where visual anthropology is an increasingly popular option (and a good little earner). But rather than complain about the commercialisation of higher education teaching (I have done much of that elsewhere) I want to ask what all this means for theorising, in this institutional and market-driven context? There is much to be said here. We might just note that within method as 'Method Course 101', a foreshortened Marx is relegated to one of many theories the prospective researcher must fill up with – must get under their belt, jump through the hoops. Here credentialism makes a mockery of thinking; impoverished and perverse. Adorno once said, again in his lecture series of 1968, that whenever social scientists do not understand something they start talking about method. The security this brings is deceptive (2000:69).

It can also be comic. A student in one of my classes at Goldsmiths College wrote a gloss on the eleventh thesis: 'The point was to change the world, not just to entertain it' – and oftentimes the indulgence of high theory within the apparatus of the teaching factory seems a very long way from action. But this is not the place to parody critical thinking – it is not about a Derrida broadcasting from inside the head of Donald Duck, or a Marx relayed back via the miserly mutterings of Uncle Scrooge (but see Dorfman and Mattelart 1971). The academic game is not just about star turns and celebrity names. In a marketplace where promotion and hype is said to be more important than production, a blinkered view of the productive process prevails, obscuring distributed assembly sites and misrecognising the struggle for valorisation in near-monopoly conditions. The entertainment industry of theory in cultural studies has become hegemonic, glossy covers and all (and I fall for that every time). This does not excuse an avoidance of the makings of the disciplines and the forces that constitute them, alongside their ideological role.

*   *   *

The chapters in this book were written consecutively over several years, and betray circumstantial marks of particular debates, but also a constant obsession. There is in academic Marxism often a doubled play that seems to me to be a kind of refusal or denial of Marx. It is both a reluctant acknowledgement but also a tendency to dissociate, to go past, to rework or to revoke Marx, oftentimes in the name of an academic interest in Marx. This then is generalised in other discourses into a blind rejection, an automated reaction that turns away with a 'not relevant to us'-type shrug. The love–hate relation often seems to be pretty hateful, and Marx is a scratch disk bogey for all sorts of projects, though this itself is no surprise. What does seem surprising is that otherwise comradely activist types can be lazy in their thinking, too quick to throw out the bathwater with the baby, falsifying one and so all, arrogant accusations, retributions, delusions of grandeur. There are too many dismissals and avoidances of particular Marxisms blown up into rejection of Marxism as such for this not to betray a pathology. Refusals look plain silly in the cases where the protester protests too much (or rather does not go to protests enough) and small objections to specific Marxisms are taken as the collapse of the whole. The quiet fear and anxiety that the most important social scientist ever still provokes is itself worthy of close attention; it seems to govern the intellectual and emotional production of entire disciplines. The idea here is not to simplify with cynicism. The readings of this book seek to learn much from the epigones. And there is plenty to learn, and I am not prepared to give up on this practice.

This is my defence against a pessimism that would make it impossible to think that a critical mode of thought, pillaging theory and honed in debate, cannot still prevail over greed, stupidity and oppression. Making this defence seems worthwhile, doesn't it?

The less hurried reading advocated here also looks back to old texts – Marx, Malinowski, Bataille – and long-faded history – the East India Company, communism in 1930s France – and as such might also draw the charge of conservatism. New-fangled this is not; but then taking the time to critically assess and evaluate with a wider frame and timeline might offer ways to counter and perhaps avoid the kind of thinking that hastily capitulates to a vicious instant buccaneering which renders entire populations expendable, and leaves regions and cities abandoned to asset-stripping plunder and remorseless destructive sell-off.

Slow it down. This book is a kind of record of reading. It is a time-consuming process for me, obsessed with detail and correspondences – no doubt there are more. I know I miss much. Careful readers will find their own ways; here are mine for comparison.

Anthropological fieldwork works on the premise that you should go (travel) and have a look for yourself. With this in mind, the material, even geographic, underpinnings of West Coast academic pronouncements exemplified in the work of James Clifford are made evident in the first chapter of Part 1, which considers his work alongside that of the ever intrepid Malinowski. Issues of land ownership, rent, anxieties about cultural belonging, mix and control are not the only themes in Clifford, but there is a symptomatic concern here – what I diagnose as Clifford's uncertainty belongs to a tendency in cultural studies that finds justifications for prejudice and xenophobia in progressive-sounding concepts and trendy formulas. Travel is the one I look at closely, with Marx in mind. This is not to say that the metaphor of 'travelling theory' is without merit, but it certainly can be criticised, and it is no excuse for sloppy theorising. In the second chapter I show how Clifford gets Marx wrong and reverses key parts of the Marxist critique, with dire consequences. If this were just a matter of an error of interpretation it would be of small significance, but Clifford has influenced a version of cultural studies and anthropology in important ways. I want to characterise this as a commodity fetish fieldworking version of trinketisation – the advent of a collecting 'empiricist' dilettantism in theory, that can be found in later sections of this book too. Clifford has been an inspiring writer in many ways, but what particularly bugs me among the new concepts offered up by the sort of flash thinking that rushes to declare paradigmatic breakthroughs is a kind of rapid-fire self-important trend-setterism. Clifford is one for buzzwords in the same way that Malinowski wanted to establish his name and career. And so, one of the big themes in this book has been the promotion of the concept of hybridity. This appears in Part 3 (on *Empire* and Subaltern Studies), but Clifford, too, is well enamoured of hybridity. I have set out why the hyping of this term by cultural theory is problematic, showing how anxiety over miscegenation and racial mixture, the urbanisation-causes-hybridity thesis, and an avowedly anti-essentialist politics that confirms exactly the romantic traditionalism that it professes to decry, all show hybridity theory as the latest in a series of book publishing buzzwords that are more marketable than coherent. I think the same can be said of diaspora, whiteness, identity and community (see Hutnyk 1998a, 2000a; Kalra et al. 2004). The sometime progressive, relativist, racist, Malinowski was part of the land grab that was the colonial project in the South Seas; Clifford is part of the latter-day version of the same project, this time glossed as globalisation by neoliberal ideology, and a reading of Marx against Clifford shows where this goes wrong.

I wanted to describe how Clifford's interest in fieldwork and travel works as a set of exchanges at the beginning of the book, as it reflects something like the interfacing of Freud, Derrida and Marx in Part 2. A productive tension in exchange that rests at the heart of Malinowski's obsession with things – the kula – is only the first appearance of an obsession with trinkets that continues throughout the book and allows what I mean by bad Marxism to emerge. That the meaning of this term morphs as the exchanges turn to fetish objects, quotations, citations and glossy publications – and even gifts by the end – only underlines the theme. But another thread running throughout questions the purposes and protocols of research, and the commercial imperative of 'disciplinary' applications of method. In Clifford's work this means fieldwork and history; in Part 2, on Derrida, it pertains to Marx on telecommunications and time, alongside Freud's and Heidegger's comments on speed.

Derrida's influence upon cultural studies has been profound. First in literary theory and filtered through careful readings by Gayatri Spivak (though on Marx she has earned his ire [Derrida 1999]), later through a punishing (for readers) schedule of publications which no-one can deny has been impressive – at least one book a year since the late 1970s, or at least as long as I have been reading him. For the purposes of my work the reading focuses primarily on Derrida's mid-1990s 'return' to Marx. This is read through Freud and the question of technology. I will argue that the *arriviste* technology of cyber-capitalism has Derrida in its sway. In Chapter 4 I tamper with Derrida's ten-word telegram on the 'plagues' of contemporary capitalism, and in Chapter 5 – after reading Derrida's prescriptions on the International – the question of communism and the party is broached, and philosophy found wanting.

The density of information in the so-called information society does not necessarily imply the transformation of everything, despite what some enthusiasts, and some sceptics, seem to think (see Bard and Söderqvist 2002). What needs to be examined when evaluations are made of the take-up of telematic forms of communication like email (the chapters on Derrida in Part 2), or of finance capital land speculation on the West Coast of America (the chapters on Clifford in Part 1), or the network capabilities of global Empire (the chapters on Hardt and Negri in Part 3), are the socioeconomic conditions that govern such innovations. This is neither to dismiss technology (though the rise of technological determinism is a dangerously simplifying development) nor to insist on the final instance of the economic (the old vulgar orthodox Marxist reading of base and superstructure has ignored the dialectical dance of these shorthand terms by Marx).[5] The point is that there is no avoiding issues of profit, gain, price fixing, competitive advantage, commercial fakery and super-exploitation in explaining why a technology such as email should be promoted as somehow new, providing text transfer between two distant sites at speed. How new is this? For text transfer the fax was capable of doing the same many years before (from 1843 to be precise – with Alexander Bain's invention, followed 20 years later by Giovanni Caselli's 'pantelegraph' which was operational in the early 1860s as Marx was writing *Capital*; AT&T were sending photographs over the wires by 1924). In terms of putting human beings in instantaneous touch with each other, the telephone proper was capable of this long long ago – clearly the idea that email is new, quick and shiny has to do with profit. In banking, the idea of speed has certainly had an astonishing effect – but the time of money flow still relies upon banks. In the end profits and vaults are part of the supporting infra-structure. Various material units of computing equipment – modems, machines, connections – are also sold. Telephone and transfer charges, and the structure of telecommunications as industry, have more to do with commercial imperatives than facilitation of communication between here and there. These matters are taken up in the chapters on Derrida, where the reading is displaced by the idea that time is social and not fixed in singularity forever; its operation, conception and even duration change with history.

*Empire* is the paradigmatic publishing sensation that captured a *zeitgeist*. More successful than any other academic book for many years, much debated and discussed, already plenty has been said in the salons of theory here. My take then is selective and angular; I read *Empire* alongside other Marx-influenced theoretical moves on colo-nialism. Hardt and Negri posit a break in capitalism at its opening that mistakes the role of the state and colonialism. Along the way they erase good Marxisms, as do later readings of subaltern resistance. If paralysis, uncertainty and undecidability are the results of lazy readings of very late capitalism (in Clifford and Derrida), the possible alternatives explored in the latter chapters of *Empire* also paralyse with an obtuse terminological optimism. Hardt and Negri's *Empire*, and its notion of multitude, offers a publishing sensation but no organisation (or is at best parasitical on the back of other attempts to organise). The book weighs in with historical disingenuousness com-mensurate with an activist paralysis – seeming to want to do things but unable to broach the 'how to' of them – and so there is good rea-son to worry. This is where the craze for hybridity returns as farce. In the founding texts of Subaltern Studies and a certain postcolonial criticism I detect a shying away from Mao, and the organisational politics of peasant struggles against capital. Homi Bhabha's reading of Ranajit Guha at the same 'moment' of colonial conflict examined in *Empire* becomes the site of a calculated erasure. I do not think this is merely terminological, but am prepared to be wrong. So it goes.

The Marxisms of the academy seem to lead theorising in cultural studies more and more to a space marked by institutionalised qui-etism. Perhaps only the maverick thought of Georges Bataille escapes this, but perhaps not – even if the discussion of his work in the context of war suggests possible militant paths, there is no guar-antee except in struggle. I think Bataille is more relevant today than he has ever been, and more misread, ignored or dismissed than he deserves. In the four chapters of Part 4 offered here his experience of the First World War and his syphilitic father are considered as context for his engagements with Surrealism, Communism and Fascism. His anti-war sentiment, somewhat ambivalent, is mediated through his notions of expenditure and sacrifice and his post-Second World War studies of the gift. These offer material that I think might be worth considering in the light of contemporary political questions. With a new global war emergent from the unexamined limits of liberal charity and 'Third Way' governance, an experimental and extravagant, even excessive bad Marxist, application of Bataille might provoke rethinking. I see this writing as antidotal and want it to suggest a turning, from a focus upon late Bataille mysticism to a more critical re-engagement. The gift is not a neutral 'theme of discussion' suitable only for cultured contemplation of peoples who live far away (in the Trobriands, say), nor is Bataille to be dissociated from sharp political conflicts and communist politics by restricting interest in his work to esoteric topics. Sacrifice and transgression cannot be read as if they had no connection with or impact upon the political and the problems of the present. I do not want to 'operationalise' Bataille (bad Marxism), but the conceit of asking about the uses to which he may be put is provocative in a way I find helpful.

A brief explanation of bad Marxism is possibly in order (there will be more in the conclusion). In some ways, bad Marxism is only the impoverished intellectual background to the lackadaisical analyses of late capitalism that dominate the publishing game today. Anticapitalism has been undermined by the privatisation of critique – naff and dull tracts from 'popular' critics; slated name stars without social(ist) organisation; glamour theorists wracked with guilt at having knowingly, but secretly sold their souls (I have in mind the neos, the retros and the exes, the tears, the rethinking). God-botherers all, the entertainment of society has replaced the struggle to change it.

Bad kinds of Marxism would, not least by their ongoing mutation, be too numerous to list, amounting in any case to a microhistory of the sectarian struggles and accusations cum pogroms of actually existing Marxisms from Stalin to the Trotskyite cults. It is enough to acknowledge the versatility, and diversity, of bad Marxist accusation, since this gives adequate indication of a living, lively and intensely real-world legitimacy of struggle. I would argue that this is evidence that there is something of great importance for the ideas and the politics at stake, which other philosophies, disciplines or creeds do not confront, cannot contain. That many Marxists might be appalled at this defence of diversity within Marxism – as a kind of twisted tolerant liberalism or a demotic diverse democratism – worries me about as much as the conceit of my first book, which conjoined Heidegger and Marx over the table of representation and technology (see Hutnyk 1996: ch. 1). If it is not possible to debate the meanings and nuances of phenomenology, psycho-socio-economic ethnography or of poetry within Marxist texts then we have certainly lost the plot. Bad Marxism would also be that moment in which everything is up for grabs once again – for a ruthless critique of everything as the slogan goes.

So, as a bad Marxism that retains both the critique of deviations and the right to deviate as method, I feel there is no requirement that I say exactly what a progressive cultural studies Marxism might be – the point has been to demonstrate that an open debate is preferable to pronouncements of truth that have not been tested in struggle. No twelve-point plan, then. Despite acknowledging the need, bad Marxism cannot be that programmatic – this book seeks merely to criticise the take-up of an academic and sanitised Marx, not to confuse the study of culture with the revolution. It is reading only, there must also be acts; some guidelines for which are of course humbly suggested at the end (six of them).

In this corner of the publishing game we are just reading and teaching; it is not yet the revolution.

Bad Marxism is a critique of Marxism from within; it is not anti-Marx. In fact what I want to show is where the name of Marx is sometimes taken up in the name of a not-Marx, or of a Marxism that is, for one reason or another, nothing of the sort. Or maybe not nothing, but certainly drifting out there in the realms of unexpected versionings. In various ways the works read here are good deviant creative Marxisms, raising important points, offering new, even unforeseen, perspectives and increasing our comprehension of the world and our efforts to change it. The trouble is that we can never just think that this could be OK. Bad Marxism would not rest, it continues to demand more; it persists. Wicked, mischievous, dissembling Marx – while the ruthless critique of everything has not yet won, there can be no truck with Marxisms that do not deliver 'more'. These do, and don't – this book explores the good and bad in social criticism, and asks what reading Marx badly means. Thus, to move in several directions at once does away with the cult of the correct line, without becoming only a cosy debating school; the plan is to discuss everything every which way and then come to decisions. This requires not that we learn to debate, nor learn to shut people up – the rhetoric of the louder voice – but that we learn to listen and reply. To and fro – the social co-constitution of ideas – for open airways. Too often intellectual pedagogy has amounted to telling people to be silent – the practice has been that of demagogy not democracy.

I expect accusers will adopt 'bad Marxism' and turn it back on the readings offered here, but this will be a response of those who cannot countenance the simultaneity of fun and seriousness in critique. Mockery of that police action is the joy of thought-crime. Of course this thought-crime is also a necessary component of the fight against the spurious, calculated, erasure and trinketisation of Marxism as the first transnational opposition to capital. To miss the point that Marxisms must be defended from the narrowing that reduces history to orthodox line management or the shibboleth of orthodoxy as dominant tendency is just as dull.

So, happily, I expect to be taken to task by other Marxists (precious keepers of the flame) and by cultural theorists (keep flaming precious) and the expectation is as welcome to me as ongoing polemic must always be. A book is a bus stop on the way from here to there and the destinations are not foretold. Or at least the ticket is an all-day pass (public transport should be free).

What the book attempts to offer, through fast and loose, slow theory reading, is some sort of composite picture of the culture of capitalism today. Through Clifford's travelling theory and routed predicaments, Derrida's ten-point telegram, Hardt and Negri's *Empire* and Bataille's library, there is an accumulation of trinkets arranged in a way that I believe amounts to a – bad Marxist – analysis of where we are now. This is never conclusive and always open. Sometimes contradictory, privileging some notions over others, some themes over all, the party question and the school … but always a reading practice open to change – the point being that, and more … I hope it is of interest; I hope it will be read; at least gnawed.

# Part 1
# Clifford's Ethnographica

# 1
# Clifford and Malinowski

'The institutionalisation of fieldwork in the late nineteenth and early twentieth centuries can be understood within a larger history of "travel" ' (Clifford 1997:64). As James Clifford retells the founding narrative, prior to Malinowski's 1915–19 adventures in the South Seas, anthropologists stayed at home. Only with the professionalisation of the discipline – and strictly keeping science separate from colonial administration (they liked to think) – did anthropologists begin to move.[1] Where did they go? Famously, much has been said about rhetorical fabulations in Malinowski, and elaborate commentary is given over to photographs of him in the Pacific, his tent on the beach, himself in his tent, and Clifford sees the tent as an icon of 'deep' fieldwork. But he would also have it that Malinowski travels, that he was a 'displaced person' (Clifford 1988:95) and 'shipwrecked' (1988:10). The reference here is to the English-language difficulties of a Polish migrant, but by association the nautical tone deposits the 'founding' father-figure of fieldwork in a South Sea Island scene. Big reputations have been made in this potlatch of metaphor – Clifford himself came to fame editing the agenda-setting text *Writing Culture* with George Marcus (Clifford and Marcus 1986), and the attention paid to ways of writing has enriched ethnography and extended the discipline ever since. In the process, however, Malinowski has become a cartoon character. Good to think with, conjured here and there, turned every which way and moved about at will, he struts the Trobriand beach frightening postgraduate students with a year stuck in a tent reading trashy novels. As a rite of passage and ritual incantation, reading Malinowski has become, via Clifford and others, overdetermined.

It is important to note that the circumstances of the paradigmatic deep fieldwork scene are more mobile than is often glossed. Malinowski travelled back and forth between several islands, between the Islands and Australia, and between the villages and the huts of traders, missionaries and magistrates. George Marcus has called Malinowski's years in the Trobriand village one of the initial examples of 'multi-site' ethnography (Marcus 1995:106), although Michael Young has a different view of Malinowski's predicament, saying that travel 'was simple in theory, difficult in practice' and that boat-bereft as he was, it was easier for him to stay put (Young 1984:23). It might also be wondered just how often the other 'travel' aspects of Malinowski's book, the circulation of kula shells and fascination with canoes, are stressed when the iconic text about 'staying put' to do fieldwork is taught to students in anthropology departments everywhere today.[2] Malinowski travels, but with what degree of attention?

Clifford has praised Marcus's advocacy of 'innovative forms' of multi-locale research in more than one place (Clifford 1997:27, 57; Marcus and Fischer 1986:94, 186n). Given that multi-site ethnography has become fashionable for advocates of the new experimental moment (which seems to be dragging on and on, unable to consolidate), it is no surprise that Clifford celebrates travel as a metaphor for anthropology. In *Routes: Travel and Translation in the Late Twentieth Century*, Clifford sees 'fieldwork as a travel practice' (Clifford 1997:8). *Routes* elaborates moments of his earlier book, *The Predicament of Culture* (1988), which was subtitled *Twentieth-century Ethnography, Literature and Art*. The shift in the titles is indicative of a larger move, from twentieth-century modernism (albeit in postmodernist forms) to the 'late' twentieth century (global and local, dwelling and travelling). From 'predicament' (as in 'stuck'?) to 'on the move' in less than a decade. Now the concerns are with translation, postcolonialism and, allegedly, post-exoticism. It is my argument that the more Clifford discusses travel, the more stuck and stationary he becomes.[3] The diary form that dominates the later book does not move beyond Malinowski, it does not offer a renewal of anthropology, it is – in my assessment – inferior to the earlier work and, most disappointing of all, it offers no adequate response to the 'predicament' of our, however late, twentieth-century condition or that of the twenty-first. The present commentary is an exploration of these concerns, but one that also seeks to show what can be retained and what is worth reading in this set of texts.

It seems to me that nearly all recent complaints about Clifford mouthed by anthropologists – and there is even more mouthed than written – are often so much sour grapes. It is the case that Clifford's work has shaken the more staid anthropologies, for good or ill it has inspired many, it has raised a host of questions and brought questions raised by others to wider attention. My own problem is largely with the context in which these questions are asked, or rather, with the necessity to seek out a more radical questioning – one that takes place in a context that matters. The Clifford project, as I view it, is not so disruptive of anthropological modalities as the staid types fear, nor is it so revolutionary as the 'inspired' might think. We can learn much from Clifford, but there is little to it if there is not a programme that will transform the ways we write, read, think and live. The criticisms of Clifford come thick and fast: for collecting (Strathern 1991); for getting surrealism wrong (Price and Jamin 1988); for rehashing Geertz (Whitten 1991); for 'not being an anthropologist' (Nugent 1991:130) (really? by what criteria?); for patronising women (almost everywhere, but most significantly in the 'companion volume', *Women Writing Culture* [Behar and Gordon 1995; see also Babcock 1993]); and for promoting a reflexive dialogic anthropology that is insufficiently aware, or perhaps not capable of escaping its own artifice, and in danger of being not much more than another 'elitist, intellectualist and essentially Western paradigm for academic knowledge production' (Gledhill 1994:224).[4] Yet there may be something to thank Clifford for: a generation of readers, who might have ignored anthropology, now find it intellectually, even politically, stimulating. Another kind of travel connection. Even though the critique of anthropology has its own long history (Hymes, Asad and, tangentially, Said), it was Clifford who helped put the debates on a wider curriculum and awoke other disciplines, like history and literature, to matters of theoretical importance. It's good copy, Clifford's stuff, whatever limitations there also must be – 'wrong on any number of things' as Ben Ross might say. Similarly, many new and contemporary anthropological readers might not have found a way to Bataille, Leiris, the College of Sociology, as part of the social sciences, if he had not been such a good publicist (whatever he makes of that history). Even where he is wrong, simplifies or exaggerates, Clifford has the merit, at least, of bringing me back to the debate to try to distinguish, differentiate and to supplement and extend. This is a much more preferable response than endlessly arguing that anthropological truth claims are fiction, or not, or that authority tropes rule the page, or don't.[5]

But travel as a metaphor for anthropology, culture, translation and the predicament of contemporary life deserves evaluation. Let us check the visa requirements.

Clifford begins with travel as a way of bringing the borderlands of ethnography to attention. Certain aspects of the construction of anthropological texts had consistently slipped out of the frame. He offers a list:

> (1) The means of transport is largely erased – the boat, the land rover, the mission airplane. These technologies suggest systematic prior and ongoing contacts and commerce with exterior places and forces which are not part of the field/object. The discourse of ethnography ('being there') is separated from travel ('getting there'). (2) The capital city, the national context is erased. This is what George Condominas has called the *préterrain*, all those places you have to go through and be in relation with just to get to your village or to that place you will call your field. (3) Also erased: the university home of the researcher. Especially now that one can travel more easily to even the most remote sites and now that all sorts of places in the 'First World' can be fields (churches, labs, offices, schools, shopping malls), movement in and out of the field by both natives and anthropologists may be very frequent. (4) The sites and relations of *translation* are minimised ...
>
> (Clifford 1997:23)

Admittedly Clifford calls this a partial list. And certainly some of his points might be extended and stressed. The erasure of the university context for anthropological research might especially be noted, as the anthropologist takes the university with him/her in the tent,[6] and carries also the institutional apparatus, and entire global network of centres, conference circuits, publishers, bookshops, course guides, canonical texts, disciplinary affiliations, careers and tenure, etc., etc., along into this 'field'. Clifford's point, however, is sound. The 'field' was never a discrete and bounded scene, however much 'being there' was privileged over 'getting there', or even 'being there on the shelf'.[7]

But can travel be the keyword that will open up the various contexts of cultural codification that are hidden in ethnography's realist narratives, and increasingly surrealist inspired ones if we are to follow Clifford? Already in his first chapter of *Routes* he finds it necessary to point out that certain forms of travel have not counted as 'proper travel', and he singles out the need to 'know a great deal more about how women travel' in various traditions and histories (Clifford 1997:32).[8] As well, we need more on crosscultural travel, travel that avoids the hotel–motel circuits, immigration, servants who accompany travellers, explorers, guides and, later in a footnote, 'another area of specification I am not yet prepared to discuss: diasporic sexualities and/or sexualised diaspora discourses' (1997:367n [Why not?]). His brief intro comments on domestic workers from South Asia, the Philippines and Malaysia, whose 'displacement and indenture have routinely involved forced sex' (1997:6) do not succeed as Clifford struggles 'never quite successfully to free the related term "travel" from a history of European, literary, male, bourgeois, scientific, heroic [and] recreational meanings' (1997:33). Just considering the absurdity of including the racist violence and atrocity of the slave trade under any revamped notion of 'travel' would be sufficient to show the likely inappropriateness of generalising extensions of the travel trope in its Euro-American modes. Referring to 'transatlantic enslavement' as one of the harsh conditions of travel, 'to mention only a particularly violent example' (Clifford 1997:35), he gathers deportation, uprooting and other terms under the more inclusive 'diaspora' to which he devotes a useful essay (although still wanting to 'sort out the paradigms' [1997:247]). If it were not for several returns to the governing trope and the ambition to found a 'travelling theory' and a renewed anthropology on the term, perhaps there would be something gained in the association of all those diverse movements under travel: asking if the violence of slavery was travel does at least raise questions about the violences underlying all travel, including that which enables ethnographic projects, such as the colonial power that makes the world safe for ethnographers and tourists.[9]

I think it is worth attempting an evaluation of the general trajectory of this travel trope. Clifford's musings have deservedly come in for some serious scrutiny. Theorising travel has itself become an industry of sorts. And Clifford has become something of an avatar for dispersed members of the cultural studies writing corps. Among others, bell hooks is one who most clearly shows this double gift when she praises Clifford's essay 'Notes on Travel and Theory' (Clifford 1989), for 'his efforts to expand the travel/theoretical frontier so that it might be more inclusive' (hooks 1995:43). She is also unsparingly critical, showing that the answers to the questions Clifford poses about travel require a 'theory of the journey that would expose the extent to which holding on to the concept of "travel" as we know it [and as Clifford does] is also a way to hold on to imperialism'. She also makes the stark point that ' "Travel" is not a word that can be easily evoked to talk about the Middle Passage, The Trail of Tears, the landing of Chinese immigrants, the forced relocation of Japanese Americans, or the plight of the homeless', and – though it should be noted how far hooks' own examples are 'American' ones – that theorising disparate journeying is 'crucial to our understanding of any politics of location' (hooks 1995: 43). This is no game however, as hooks points out that 'playing' with the notion of travel may not be exactly the best way to narrate experiences of travel that are about encounters with the terrorism of white supremacy (hooks 1995:44).

Clifford wants to 'hang on' to the term travel because of its very 'taintedness' – its 'associations with gendered racial bodies, class privilege, specific means of conveyance, beaten paths, agents, frontiers, documents, and the like' (1997:39). A vocabulary of apparent sin – gender and class as 'tainted' – which redeems travel is akin to what Kaplan calls a 'theoretical tourism [which] constitutes the margin as a linguistic or critical variation, a new poetics of the exotic' (1996:93). As Kaplan presents it, this is a 'utopian process of letting go of privileged identities and practices [requiring] emulation of the ways and modes of "modernity's" others' (1996:88) and this 'repeats the anthropological gesture of erasing the subject position of the theorist and [perpetuating] a kind of colonial discourse in the name of progressive politics' (1996:88). Perhaps this is also at play in the theoretical advocacy of the travel trope in Clifford, although I would also go further to read a more pervasive 'anthropological gesture' here, in the usurping of the 'other's' place of representation as Clifford becomes spokesman (gender intended) for those writers of diaspora and politics of 'travel' he so usefully promotes (this is important in light of Clifford's readings of Paul Gilroy [1993] and Avtar Brah [1996] in his 'diasporas' essay – the institutional and disciplinary overview question is: why is it that Clifford is the one so well placed, resourced, and circulated to provide the global survey of best new work in the field?). When it comes to presentation of progressive postcolonial, post-exotic Others, Clifford's text does not fall for any of the old ways of representing difference, his version of anthropological ventriloquy occurs through representing himself, and his predicament, *through* that of the other. That this is done on the basis of explicit self-reflexive post-structural high theory credentials may be all the more troublesome.

* * *

I want to put Clifford in the fieldwork scene for a moment (there will be justification for dress-ups later). Clifford comments often on photographs; he loves instamatic anthropology. Especially shots of the photogenic Malinowski. In *Routes*, the much conjured with scene of Malinowski's tent on the beach in the Trobriands is evoked again (Clifford 1997:20, 54; see also Clifford 1990). The technology of the tent as a marker of presence, in the village, as well as 'its mobility, its thin flaps, providing an "inside" where notebooks, special foods, a typewriter could be kept' (Clifford 1997:20), also provokes Clifford to ask who is being observed, natives or anthropologist, hiding away behind the canvas (see Dube 1998). He is interested too in the shots of Malinowski in the field in *Coral Gardens and Their Magic*: dressed in white, surrounded by black bodies, in a posture, attitude and style that reminds Clifford of those colonial Europeans dressing formally for dinner in hot sweaty climes (Clifford 1997:74). Malinowski is not 'going native' here. In *Writing Culture* Clifford takes up the photograph of Malinowski inside his tent: 'Malinowski recorded himself writing' (Clifford and Marcus 1986:1), but curiously the position of the photographer is not interrogated when Clifford asks 'who speaks? who writes? when and where? with or to whom? under what institutional and historical constraints?' (Clifford and Marcus 1986:13). Surely attention to these questions should teach us to read such scenes in a multi-locale way, to see the traces of other travelling Europeans, and of the international extension of the means of representation, at least, in this scene from early twentieth-century Trobriana. The photographs in question must have been taken on a day when Billy Hancock or some other European neighbour was visiting Malinowski (most likely it was Hancock as some of his photographs, better than Malinowski's, were used in *Argonauts*).[10] Yet, whoever the photographer was for sure, we have no guarantee that this was everyday attire and that Malinowski is got up in gear for a sweaty colonial dinner. Well, perhaps; but what is served by such questions? (Then again, what did he get up to? After reading the letters [Malinowski and Elsie Mason, in Wayne 1995] there is perhaps reason to suspect that the taboo subject of sexual activity in the field, as signalled, but never confirmed, in the 1967 publication of his secret Trobriand jottings: *A Diary in the Strict Sense of the Term*. This has become the hidden controversy of Malinowski's stay.)[11]

Whatever the case, how the Trobriand books have travelled. Annette Weiner, who also did her fieldwork on Kiriwina in the Trobriands, says 'No other ethnography has had a more lasting impact' (Weiner 1988:140), and it has never been out of print. As I have argued in 'Castaway Anthropology', the voyaging of kula structures the book (Hutnyk 1988:46). 'Argonauts' is the most obvious clue, and Malinowski's thinking can be discerned from the published correspondence between himself and his first wife, Elsie Mason: Jason/Malinowski imagines he would make 'a nice penny' out of the 'golden fleece' of his text (Wayne 1995, Bronio to Elsie 21.12.1921, 4.4.1922). The influence of Malinowski's Trobriand text has travelled in many directions and justice could not be done in a single essay to the disciplinary ramifications alone, leaving aside the political, social, economic and psychological consequences of the work's itinerary. Malinowski and his *protégés* came to establish their brand of anthropology worldwide – departmental intrigues there must be – but it very much depended upon the initial success of the *Argonauts*. If he hadn't managed to get *Argonauts* published, Malinowski had decided he was going to go into the margarine business (Wayne 1995:162, Bronio to Elsie 4.6.1918). So the text had to be a success and was compared from the beginning to almost every other book: Boon quotes Frazer's preface comparison of *Argonauts* with Cervantes and Shakespeare (Boon 1983:133), while Conrad, Joyce, Zola, Freud, Kipling and Frazer are recruited in other commentaries (Ardener 1985; Clifford 1986; Rapport 1990; Stocking 1985; Strathern 1987; Thornton 1985). Already in the letters Elsie Masson was filling Malinowski's head with grand ideas. She imagines the two of them together on a sea voyage: 'You know how Robert Louis Stevenson used to cruise around the South Sea Islands in any old ship, and carry out his work all the while, and wring such a lot of romance and interest besides health out of his life' (in Wayne 1995:40). Malinowski accepts and appropriates the comparison (Wayne 1995, Bronio to Elsie 17.1.1918), and also likens his 'writing diary'[12] to the writing of the *Arabian Nights* (Wayne 1995:18). The momentum of *Argonauts* (as vehicle for various debates) was recharged with the publication of the *Diary*. The literary complex multiplies. Clifford takes the *Diary*, with its day-to-day minutiae of novels read, anxieties, prejudice against 'the nigs' and fantasies of sex, and the carefully polished and public *Argonauts* together as one text, without forgetting that both are constructed and selective works. Despite the 'unintended for publication' tag attached to the *Diary*, and the hostile or cautiously indifferent reception it received from anthropologists at the time of its release, it has now become, 70 years after it was written, another part of the 'complex intersubjective situation' (Clifford 1986:145) which also produced *Argonauts, The Sexual Life of Savages, Coral Gardens*, as well as other eruptions of matters Trobriand into anthropological discourse. 'It is I who will describe or create them' Malinowski says (1967:140), and still in 1935, 20 years after his first visit, he was writing: 'Once again I have to make my appearance as the chronicler and spokesman of the Trobrianders' (Malinowski 1935:v). It would be impossible comprehensively to track the extent to which these texts have now travelled through the various global circuits of discipline, publishing, libraries and gossip.

Of all Malinowski's travel books though, it is the diary which most appeals to Clifford when he claims it as a heteroglot text: 'Malinowski wrote in Polish with frequent use of English, words and phrases in German, French, Greek, Spanish and Latin, and of course [!] terms from the native languages [of which] there were four: Motu, Mailu, Kiriwinian and Pidgin' (Clifford 1986:53). Yet celebrations of heteroglossia, especially when found in rehabilitations of previously discarded texts, seem somewhat forced. The current fashion for hybridity and multi-vocal dialogue (Malinowski talking to himself in the jungle) does not exclude the anthropologist, or later the commentator, from the controlling position of authorship as Clifford so often seems to want. Pluralities and multiplicities do not necessarily subvert established orthodoxies of publication and reception. The diary, in Clifford's hands, becomes a record of a fragmenting dissociated self attached, in a process of functionalist therapy, to the *Argonauts* ethnography written several years later (in the Canary Islands): 'One of the ways Malinowski pulled himself together was by writing ethnography. Here the fashioned wholeness of a self and of a culture seem to be mutually reinforcing allegories of identity' (Clifford 1986:152). This, presumably, is to be contrasted to the 'special poignancy' of the last words of the diary: 'Truly I lack real character' (Malinowski 1967:53). Clifford adds: 'the arbitrary code of one language, English, is finally given precedence' (1986:53). Later he calls *Argonauts* a 'lie', or rather a 'saving fiction' (1988:99) and suggests that 'To unify a messy scene of writing it is necessary to select, combine, rewrite (and thus efface)' (1988:110).

\* \* \*

Much of Clifford's own work takes on the diary form. In a chapter of *Routes* called 'Palenque Log' Clifford offers a travel report of a visit to the site of some Mexican ruins in the state of Chiapas. It is perhaps the influence of Michel Leiris that gives Clifford cause to include weather reports, the news that he has dropped his camera on the bathroom floor, breakfast details and bus itineraries at the beginning of his narrative. Clifford has been reading Leiris for a long time. In *The Predicament of Culture*, the chapter 'Tell Me About Your Trip: Michel Leiris' is devoted to the ethnographic documentation of everything. Leiris' African ethnography from the Mission Dakar-Djibouti tells of both beauty and of the gloriously satisfying morning shit (see Koepping 1989). But more than 60 years later why is this still 'experimental'? Hasn't the convention of travel writing invaded creative ethnography as well, introducing predictable and pedestrian routine to what once were curious or exotic revelations? Is it too demanding to wonder if both travel writing and ethnography need sometimes to be rendered more seriously? Clifford visits the 'jungle walk' at the 'Temple of Inscriptions' and his text documents, in 15-minute segments, his 'trip'. Why should we care? (And although his dropped camera jams up, he still manages to take a photograph, it is included in his book, how? Later he writes: 'I'm glad I can't take pictures' and 'Everywhere I glance, it seems, someone is pointing a camera ... hundreds of photos per hour' [Clifford 1997:224]. I hope this is only an ironic rehearsal of the photogenic self-loathing peculiar to tourists today.)

We should care about Clifford's trip, not because he is illustrating that the 'ethnographer' is little different from a tourist on a tourist bus snapping happy snaps and buying souvenir t-shirts, but because of the context. Here is Clifford, the producer of books, telling us about his travels in, not insignificantly, Chiapas, in an experimental 'post-exoticist' (1997:90) ethnographic text offered as illustration of contemporary anthropological writing, and he leaves out all but the most trivial reference to politics. At the same time that this report is published, the consequences of a military crackdown on the people of Chiapas, initiated just a few months after Clifford's 'Palenque Log' adventure, visits death and destruction upon the indigenous people, farmers and peasants of the region. Clifford's only substantial comment on the Zapatista 'rebellion' is that it interrupted travel to the ruins at Palenque 'temporarily'. No elaboration on what force was needed to ensure this temporary interruption, no report on the military repressions there, or for that matter the more disturbing actions in nearby Geurrero,[13] nor of the US support for the Mexican regime et cetera. Surely at some point the political and military force that enables travel narratives and ethnography should be examined by the self-reflexive scholar who has made a career of telling us that anthropology is founded on power and authority? Later Clifford comments on the exchange value of a fax machine for SubComandante Marcos, and how it is 'not surprising' that the Zapatista uprising was timed to coincide with the implementation of the North American Free Trade Agreement (1997:322) – this is at least better than some romantic reports on the Zapatistas which suggested that the date was chosen because it coincided with indigenous harvest rituals – but Clifford draws no conclusions beyond noting the 'mysterious' equivalences made between corn in Mexico and corn in Kansas by way of the international market: 'the fact still does not compute' (1997:323).[14] This is not to say that the 'independent traveller' (Clifford identifies himself this way three times in the chapter) should have noticed at the time – six months before the uprising – that Zapatista organisers were working among the people (and had been for some years), but certainly pointing to privileges of position – as independent traveller – or even as critic – and noting incongruities and contradictions, does not yet amount to an adequate politics. It may be bordering on churlishness to wonder at the timing of Clifford's visit to Chiapas and to link this also to the (un)computed facts of power that include NAFTA, research visas, social science, military control and market trickery. We do not know if he has returned to the troubled region again, but certainly this resonates with other timely anthropological visitations – there will be reason to consider especially Malinowski in the South Seas during the 1914–18 imperialist world war.

Echoes of other famous monographs on time: Lévi-Strauss is evoked when Clifford wonders when was the best time to visit (1997:232); the Palenque arrival story could have come from any of dozens of scene-setting ethnographic scenes – Firth arriving at Tikopia, Evans-Pritchard 'on the heels of a punitive expedition', Geertz invisible in Bali (Clifford 1997:237).[15] After a day full of minutiae reported as if anyone's day would be available for rendering, only Clifford, professor and author, armed with the resources of publishing industry, Harvard University Press, past authorisations, the history of anthropology, institutional affiliation with 'hist-con' (the History of Consciousness Programme at the University of California), in the West, in the 1990s, gets into print.[16]

* * *

The front cover photograph of *Routes* deserves attention, since photographs are the icons of travel stories. Necessary accoutrements, markers of real presence (more so than postcards of the very same scenes).

The 'subject', James Bosu, has been cropped for the cover, although remaining curiously 'hybrid' with traditional 'mind-boggling' headdress and necktie. Clifford 'gravitates towards the incongruous detail' (Clifford 1997:178), but Bosu's stubbie of beer is kept for the inside enlargement. This doctoring – not necessarily by Clifford, but by design – may well change readings of the image, and it is not without significance that the cover evokes a schoolbook with its background map of the world (or rather, of the West Coast of North America, Clifford's institutional base). In the context of a debate about his Mashpee study in *Predicament*, Clifford has written that the 'invented differences' he values 'are very similar to the products of a transnational capitalism that feeds on impurities, mix and match, unconstrained juxtaposition and import-export' (1991:146). This important point is not countered, however, by fascination with the very mix and match 'invented differences' so denounced. The review of the 'Paradise' Wahgi (Highland Papua New Guinea) exhibition, curated by Michael O'Hanlon, that constitutes the chapter 'Paradise' in *Routes* also includes a photograph of the woman Kala Wala, though Clifford mistakenly identifies her earrings as beer-can rip-tops when they are in fact clearly not can but stubbie tops (here the incongruities are of the international beer market, which is not exactly the same everywhere – locally significant classificatory distinctions may require more careful 'fieldwork', see O'Hanlon 1993:81). The review of 'Paradise' starts as a second-person narrative description of a visit to the Museum of Mankind in London. The addressee 'You', I presume, could be Clifford's 6-year-old son, who accompanies him, or it could also be the reader, for whom the significance of the various incongruous commodities of a PNG pig festival are explained. We are like a child before the critic's explication. The focus is on the 'strangeness of everyday things' (Clifford 1997:154). A third photograph in the chapter, of Kulka Kon looking 'authentic', has Clifford on two occasions wondering what he would look like dressed in a Hawaiian shirt, as a taxi driver, a Christian – Clifford likes to play dress-ups with the natives (1997:183, 187). There is yet another reference to the past of anthro-monography as one of the 'natives' looks covertly at the camera in a staged shot, just as Clifford has already pointed out with regard to Malinowski's photograph of a kula presentation in *Argonauts* (1988:21, 1990). Clifford's review of this exhibition explores a wide range of themes: PNG design; art which includes beer advertisements, of a particular PNG style; reports on exhibition catalogue cover controversies (who chose to crop Clifford's cover? who controls the text?); inclusions and exclusions; debt and obligation; echoes of the past and experimental innovations. It was also a relief to get to this Museum of Mankind exhibit after a gruelling visit, with son trailing behind, poor kid, to the Guinness Book of World Records Trocadero show at Piccadilly (we do not get the younger Clifford's views on either show). But we also do not know if there is any sense in which Clifford feels drawn into the obligations and debt alliance with the Wahgi people which he discusses in the context of O'Hanlon's collecting (Clifford 1997:170). Although their presence seems to be ever more elided in the abstracting processes of exhibition and then in exhibition review, the Wahgi were the ones who enabled O'Hanlon to put together the exhibition and they consciously involved him in ongoing obligations, which Clifford details. Being able to fill a book – at least a chapter – with images and discussion of the exhibit must, in these terms, indebt Clifford to the Wahgi too, yet we do not find out how such 'relations of collecting', all 'exchanged and appropriated in continued local/global circuits' (1997:171), obligate him, nor how his routes-review returns anything to the Wahgi themselves. Pointing out one's complicity in these relations of collecting and appropriation does not begin to undo them.

We have long known that what appeals to Clifford is the incongruous and the hybrid. He wants to 'quibble' with the terms used by those who would suggest that souveniring the incongruous and celebrating the syncretic initiates a new round of intellectual imperialism (Clifford 1997:180, citing Shaw and Stewart's use of 'hegemony'). I sit up to take notice when he also paraphrases Marx when discussing the ways that people from PNG 'make their own history, though not in conditions of their own choosing' (Clifford 1997:161; the quote, to acknowledge it at last, is from the opening of the '18th Brumaire' and can be found in Marx 1968:96) and he celebrates the hybrid in the face of those who would think it 'axiomatic' that culture is diminished 'in direct proportion to the increase of Coke and Christianity' (1997:161). Though it is not simply these two scourges of humanity that should be marked, surely it is necessary to rethink easy incongruity-hunting since the conditions of making history are now everywhere the context of an international capitalism that, as Clifford notes again, thrives on just such hybridity and cultural differences.[17] For me, it is not quite enough to suggest that the notion of some sort of 'anthropological hegemony' conjures up 'disempowered intellectuals – privileged no doubt, but hardly in a position to enforce their definitions' (Clifford 1997:182). In a review of a definition-setting exhibition in London or in an anthropological text that circulates the world via bookshop, conference and course guide, this is blatant mystification. It is not the case that, since 'the Trobrianders are free to read Malinowski's accounts of their culture as parodies' as Clifford claims in *Predicament*, this somehow unravels any of the authority or privilege of either ethnographer or critic. Neither James Bosu nor the Trobrianders publish their diaries for global circulation via Harvard University Press, nor do they curate exhibitions in the old imperial capital.[18]

There is more that could be said on the incongruous bits and pieces Clifford collects, especially so in the context of his museum studies. I would also want to question why trinket collection has taken the place of more systematic analyses? His text is a phantasmagoric, but ultimately limited, cabinet of curiosities, relics and snippets. Indeed, considerations of Clifford's much favoured collecting tropes, collage and pastiche, often seem to sidestep the political. Just as travel, according to hooks and Kaplan, is of use to the well-placed and comfortable, might it also be so that collage has certain ideological effects? Collage everywhere.[19]

In a post-Clifford anthropological universe everything is in danger of becoming collage. Even Malinowski was a surrealist in Clifford's estimation. Wrenching details of Trobriand trade behaviour out of their context and identifying these with canoe magic and myth, then comparing kula valuables with the English crown jewels, is an example of 'the surrealist moment in ethnography' where the 'possibility of comparison exists in unmediated tension with sheer incongruity' (Clifford 1988:146). Surrealist procedures 'are always present in ethnography' for Clifford, although Leiris' *L'Afrique fantôme* is the only pure example (Clifford 1988:146). The ethnographic surrealist attitude has other Trobriand avatars however; one Clifford singles out as prime illustration is Leach and Kildea's film *Trobriand Cricket*, where a gentleman's game brought by missionaries at the time of Malinowski – indeed he refers to it in *Coral Gardens* (Malinowski 1935:211–13) – is turned into 'ludic warfare' by the Trobrianders with the inventive cultural skill of a Picasso (Clifford 1988:148).[20]

Writing in *Routes* of *The Predicament of Culture*, Clifford describes the use of collage 'as a way of making space for heterogeneity, for historical and political, not simply aesthetic juxtaposition' (1997:3). Yet the question is how useful are even 'historical and political' juxtapositions without thinking politically about what to do with them? And what does this mean in anthropology?[21] Is such collage meant to represent the world more adequately? If so, what distinguishes this from the political and historical, and somewhat random sampling techniques, I can achieve with dextrous use of my remote control while watching the CNN and BBC satellite news feeds? Remote control? Not much control, say some. Another kind of politics awaits.

*   *   *

What we can take from Clifford is his examination of how the polyphonic heteroglossia of Malinowski's experience in the Trobriands was rendered into text as a coherent, worked up, sifted and arranged, coordinated and orchestrated narrative. Whether Elsie had a greater or lesser hand in this,[22] whether Conrad was the deity hovering behind the project, and whether the *Diary* and the letters reveal some more primordial truth is not the point. What is revealed is the process of making narrative out of events. Editing, arranging, conjuring. The travel metaphor here does the trick, in large part, for Malinowski. It also does so for Clifford, indeed, organising not just one text, but increasingly his entire oeuvre. This has implications for understanding travel, and tourism, since travel stories – whether told after the trip, or pre-packaged in the brochure as a promise, or narrated by the guide as a product – are the stuff of contemporary travel economics. So, it is important to ask why travel theory emerges when it does, why Clifford in the 1990s, etc., and rather than suggesting that Malinowski and Clifford are the same just because both write travel diaries, I think it is useful to point to the structural conditions of their travelling production. Such a reading would begin with the importance of the 1914–18 imperialist war for the practice of long-term fieldwork and the political conditions that have now forced a rethinking of fieldwork. In between these moments, the emergence of anti-colonial movements and non-aligned states, which, among other things, developed a shared suspicion of anthropologists. The 'fieldwork' discussion may seem to have been interrupted, but it was not displaced by the success, and failure, of the anti-colonial movements, of the Soviet experiment, and the ongoing permutations of the Chinese revolution and its subsequent adventures with Naxalites in India, Khmer Rouge in Cambodia, Shining Path and Tupac Amaru in South America, et cetera.[23] Comrade Malinowski's postmodernism aside,[24] the difference between advocates of fieldwork now and then seem not so great when considered in terms of the necessity of 'safe passage' and the 'pax Europaea' (Stagl 1996:262). Both Malinowski and Clifford (sensibly) seek out that safe site.[25] It cannot be a simple coincidence that aligns the range of interests, concepts, modes of analysis ('ethnographic' audience research for example) and criteria of relevance of travelling theory with processes of transnational restructuring. And though it is not yet clear that Malinowski's analysis of the kula really does line up so conveniently with the coordinates of post-First World War social and political dynamics,[26] to begin to analyse travel politically with these possibilities in mind might entail an opening for critical anthropology, compared to Clifford's complacent yet grand breadth of vision (when such a vision only looks at and tells stories about itself, something more is required which can come to grips with the interrelations of meaning and the production and consumption dynamics of travel).

In the end, what is there to carry away from Clifford's travel stories? I would not say I have no problems with travel – much as it might seem very worldly, and even at times humble, to gloss anthropology as travel, such a characterisation does not satisfy. This is not because anthropology should be defended as something better than travel (I recall a certain American anthropologist at one seminar holding up his passport stamped with an Indonesian 'Research Visa' to prove that he was different from a tourist – at which someone quipped, 'Where did you get it, CIA?'). Can anthropology become something better than it has been? The task of confronting, understanding and intervening in the violence and exploitation that so often (past and present) accompanies human movement requires much more than elaborate brochures. The paradigm offered by the travel guide, with scenic views, staged authenticity (however sustaining) and carved souvenirs is insufficient for a writing that would respond to the troubles and tribulations of the various movements we witness. Human dwelling together has often also meant moving past each other without comprehension, or worse, as Malinowski did also notice (but often failed to discuss), with violent and deadly repercussions. Without a critical perspective grounded in a practical politics dedicated to changing such troubles, and transforming the conditions of inequality, exploitation and oppression from which they arise, anthropology (multi-site or bounded), travel (alternative or mainstream) and 'the history of ethnography' (orthodox or Cliffordian) remains only so much sightseeing. How long can we keep on saying 'Je haïs les voyages et les explorations'.

# 2
# Fort Ross Mystifications

This second chapter of Part 1 continues the focus upon Malinowski and Clifford, but attends more closely to Clifford's politics and, specifically, his uses of Marx in the context of the essay 'Fort Ross Meditation' which ends his book: *Routes: Travel and Translation in the Late Twentieth Century*.[1] The questions to be asked concerning this essay, which seems to offer a model of reconstructed 'ethnographic' and historical, research, have to do with context, motivation, intentions and uses. How significant is it that Clifford takes up a study of Russian colonial presence in 'America' at this time? How important is the study of Pacific trading empires of the past in today's context? How does this intervention into heritage-site memorialism, eco-tourism and cultural history mesh with contemporary agendas and geo-political investments? How significant are the sea-otter pelts he caresses? Does the metaphoric invocation of the fault lines of San Andreas say more about Clifford's Californian view of the world than he intends? And what does the contemporary fascination with the travelling histories of commodities signify when Marxist analysis is trivialised and twisted into misrecognition by West Coast professors rejecting pessimism but applauding uncertainty in the place where analysis might be preferred? It is not my intention to answer all these questions, but to raise them as a framework for critical evaluation of what Clifford is trying to do.

\*   \*   \*

Given a propensity for drawing upon signifying conjunctions and traffic in theory on Clifford's part, I also want to point to certain connections. Not between Leenhardt and Malinowski – though Clifford reports that 'In the same year that Malinowski published *Argonauts* ... Leenhardt met and impressed Marcel Mauss' (1982: 106) – nor between Malinowski and Marx – though the textual self-fashioning of *Argonauts* and *Capital* might be added to the sad fact that usually only the first chapter of either book is read these days. Instead, I want to conjure a meeting between Malinowski and Clifford (another kind of dress-up). Both recognised that power determines fieldwork location. Malinowski as an Austrian passport holder in Australia during the war was packed off to the South Seas. Not 'interned' as the myth says, notes Young, but nevertheless restricted (Malinowski 1967:xiii; Young 1984:24), he knows he was there by the grace of white Australia policy advocate and deporter of Kanaks, Governor Attlee Hunt, who supported Malinowski's research on the recommendation of Baldwin Spencer because of 'its potential value for native administration' (Mulvaney and Calaby 1985:322, 453n). Having made the point that colonial power underwrote anthropological fieldwork in the past, Clifford himself crosses the Mexican border and goes to Chiapas, just before the Zapatista uprising and the signing of NAFTA (North American Free Trade Agreement). In the chapter 'Fort Ross Meditation' he extends his research into heritage tourism sites and Pacific trade at the time of the developing US interest in the region via APEC (Asia Pacific Economic Co-operation forum). It would be a lesson we have learnt from Clifford that no research is without its institutional contexts.[2] In these cases – Malinowski and Clifford – the geo-political circumstances seem overdetermining.

Stocking reports that at the time when Malinowski arrived on Mailu for his first stint of fieldwork 'an Australian expeditionary force was already occupying German New Guinea' (1991:62). His introductory village visit was with a police escort (1991:38). The prerequisite of colonial protection for the anthropological mission was recognised well before Clifford set off for Mexico. Stocking quotes Rivers' suggestion that the optimal time for ethnographic work was ten to thirty years:

> ... after a people had been brought under the 'mollifying influences of the official and the missionary' – long enough to ensure the 'friendly reception and peaceful surroundings' that were 'essential to such work' but not long enough to have allowed any serious impairment of native culture.
>
> (in Stocking 1991:10)

The Trobriand Islands had been visited by missionaries since the late 1890s at least, and it is possible that still earlier explorers and traders had visited syphilis and other diseases on the island.[3] Clifford's close attention to the political underpinnings of anthropological research would have been honed through his studies of Leenhardt, noting that the mining industry, forced labour, wage slavery, conscription and brutal repression were the lot of the New Caledonian 'Canaques' (Clifford 1982:34–5, 45–6, 92).[4] A similar list may be gleaned from Malinowski's writings. In early articles for the International Africa Institute, Malinowski mentions forced labour, conscription, coercion, enticement and hangings. In one remarkable passage he notes how the ignorance of a European who might (is the example wholly fiction?) unintentionally violate native custom, may set in train events which, after retaliation, trial, hanging, blood debt, revenge and then punitive expedition, might bring 'whole native tribes to grief'. Malinowski suggests he could quote numerous cases from the South Seas, but confines himself only to mentioning the history of 'black birding' in Melanesia (1930:411). In a language perhaps not preferred today, Malinowski comes remarkably close to certain contemporary concerns when he says 'the functionalist anthropologist ... studies the white savage side by side with the coloured, the world-wide scheme of European penetration and colonial economics' (1930:419). A multi-site ethnography which would have to confront the violence of slavery and exploitation is not far away here ('black birding' was a form of slave trade practised in Australia and the Pacific until the beginning of the twentieth century), though it must be noted that, at the same time, Malinowski was attempting to mobilise anthropology for 'the task of assisting colonial control' (1930:408) and even to address the problem of 'what might be termed black bolshevism' (1929a:28–32) and to find ways to encourage men of different cultures to be 'satisfied with work' (1929a:35).

How is it possible to ignore the political implications of the field? Perhaps a part-answer is that anthropologists writing texts 'after the fact' (Geertz 1995) fashion themselves after literary models and so in the process some of the immediacy of context recedes. As Clifford points out, Malinowski writes wanting to be the Conrad of anthropology but his 'most direct literary model was certainly James Frazer' (1988:96). Clifford himself is heavily influenced by the ethnographic diary style of Leiris, although we might argue that his 'most direct literary model' is Malinowski's *Diary*, with polyglot exchanged for trinketisation. 'Imagine yourself set down ...': Clifford self-consciously sets down too, not only in *Routes* looking 'out' to the Pacific, but also travelling in *Predicament*, with Leiris' trip and the autobiographical essay 'postcards', in *Person and Myth* tracing Leenhardt's to and fro to the South Seas, and throughout his work with plenty of references to books like *Moby Dick* and *Between the Devil and the Deep Blue Sea*. Maybe not too much more of theoretical interest can be made of Malinowski's *Diary*, but there is ample evidence in Clifford's essay 'On Ethnographic Self-fashioning' that Malinowski's polyglossaria is the key (Clifford 1988:97). A close affinity in the narrative devices which render the chaos and flux of the world as text in both Malinowski and Clifford can be discerned. What necessitates rectifications of confusion through ordered writing might be common to all social science, but it has been Clifford who has pointed this out in Malinowski, and practised it most publicly in his own textual experiments. As I suggested in Chapter 1, further parallels might begin to consider why the work of a certain author catches on at a particular place and time: why Malinowski in the 1920s? Why Clifford in the 1990s? Why travelling theory now? Should a critique of anthropology explore the role of ideology in reinforcing the 'New World Order' in an era of escalating chaotic conflict by pointing to the vicissitudes of new world ordering, and the textual strategies that might be recruited to facilitate this?

In emphasising that the travel metaphor organises Malinowski's anthropology as it does Clifford's work, I am not suggesting there are no differences between the two, nor would I want to suggest that postmodernists are secret functionalists (but uncertain ones), or that nothing important is contained in the reflexivity and self-questioning Clifford displays. The point is what to do with this? More diary entries would serve little purpose. What matters today is the capacity of scholarship to understand the current complexities of the human (global) condition, and, as Gayatri Spivak adds, 'tamper with it' (1995a:10; see below). An area where I think the Malinowski–Clifford concurrence becomes important has to do with the politics of multi-site ethnography. For Clifford this takes the contemporary form of diasporic research projects and – I argue – flirtation with trans/global-isation as the ideology of transnational corporate enterprise. Clifford writes, early in the Fort Ross chapter, that 'today these transpacific and hemispheric involvements make renewed sense. They prefigure something ...' (1997:303). Here he means that the eastward movement of Russian fur traders towards California, collecting merchandise to exchange for tea in China, makes 'renewed sense'. What does it 'prefigure'? The movement to and fro across the Pacific is diasporic: 'As contemporary California fills with Pacific and Asian immigrants ... and as the state's southern border becomes ever more porous' (1997:303). Clifford will return to this scene again and again: discussing the trade in sea-otter pelts he is reminded of the 'overwhelming Chinese demand for exotic goods' in past centuries that returns today and 'Asia feels nearby again. Now Japanese are buying up prime properties along the Sonoma coast.' Why this attention to property? He immediately adds: 'Chinese exports disrupt the US balance of trade. The otter pelt lies limp in my hands' (1997:321). Again, no more than ten pages on:

> Fort Ross. The West Coast of the United States ... is being bought up by investors from Japan and Hong Kong. Is the US American empire in decline? Or perhaps in metamorphosis? It's unclear. We are not yet able to recognise these wavering contradictions as the beginning of an end.... Currently the changes look more like realignments, recenterings. 'Transnational capitalism' is the inheritor of Euro-American imperial dynamics.... Anglo California is being displaced by the Pacific and Latin America. People, capital, commodities, driven by global political-economic forces, do not stop at national borders. Will 'English Only' movements, immigration restrictions, xenophobic terror attacks, and back to basics initiatives be able to stem the tide? Can a rusting 'American' assimilation/exclusion machine be repaired?
>
> (1997:330)

Three times Clifford notes that Asians are buying real estate in America. Again: 'Asian economic power is an inescapable reality, whether centred in Japan, Korea, Indonesia or – most powerfully perhaps – in diasporic and mainland China' (1997:331). Of course, he does not intend to sound alarmist, and the irony of his questions at the end of the above quotation show that he is not on the side of those who would renovate the exclusion machine. His work on Fort Ross is part of an attempt to 'dislodge a dominant' and foster a more inclusive heritage history, 'for a United States with roots and routes in the Asia Pacific' (1997:303). This would have the site show not only the Russian presence of the middle 1800s, but would also acknowledge the impact of this presence on local peoples (and environment), and would understand the lives of the Aleuts, Siberians and Koniags, who came with the Russians to Fort Ross. This reconfigured heritage would note the creoles and the interrelations between these groups, including their effects – Clifford recognises the number of local women attached to the Fort and counts the mixed-race children (1997:332), and makes valid criticisms such as pointing to how there is no narrative which tells of forced recruitment or hostage-taking and that 'accounts of relations at the fort with the local Indians stress intermarriage, but do not mention epidemics' (1997:339).[5] Clifford suggests a 'flow of history' approach to the Fort Ross heritage park project, yet wonders who will write the new narratives when (if?) resources become available to replace the outmoded ones. Clifford's own chapter begins the task, but, we must ask, with what effects? Does focusing on the Chinese desire for sea-otter pelts not tend to obscure these local impacts and excuse the constitutive interests of Western traders in Chinese spice, porcelain and tea?

\*   \*   \*

Discussing a 'Northern Pacific zone of trade and exploration' linking California, Moscow, China and so on (Clifford 1997:341) is perhaps only possible in the years after the decline of the Soviet experiment. Today, Clifford says the Soviet Union, which he sees as a continuation of the Russian Empire, 'is in disarray' (1997:330[!]). Some may find it difficult to accept this continuist history, but the frame for this perspective is based on old fears. As a schoolboy Clifford was fascinated with maps which showed the line of demarcation running through the Aleutians. He admits a memory which appears determining, his family's apartment in New York City held a basement fall-out shelter:

> We formed vague images of Russian missiles crossing the Bering Strait ... then there would be sirens, perhaps some kind of roar.... I grew up in the everyday fear of this implosion and the real possibility that I and everyone else I knew might not survive. The fear, a fact of life for more than three decades, has receded. I, my family, and my friends will probably live into the next century.
>
> (1997:344)

The extent to which some sort of apocalyptic threat has evaporated is of course open to debate, as the US sets out to become the police force of the entire world, but Clifford is, he says, 'living and thinking inside a triumphant Western history' (1997:343) and so perhaps we can understand, if not excuse, such pathologies. We all live with this threat, only some are more responsible than others. On the horizon of realignments and recentering of economic relations in the Asia-Pacific zone, the extant inequalities of firepower suggest new dangers and anxieties.

But the scholarly context of all this is a post-apocalypse anxiety about the future and the role of research and cultural production in the face of a kind of pessimism about the world, and one that is disabling and/or complicit in a (neo)colonial anthropology. Clifford would point out what is wrong – too many Japanese buying up America, heritage sites that do not tell about the extermination of local peoples – but his wistful reflections can offer nothing to change these circumstances. Here is a difference with Malinowski who had the will to grasp the *realpolitik* nettle and set up the Africa Institute with Rockefeller money so as to fund a practical anthropology. Well, something had to be done. But neither man feels comfortable with their predicament, and neither can find a path through. Travellers stranded again.

*   *   *

I would like to ask a slightly different set of questions in the context of contemporary anthropological criticism as practised by Clifford. The first and perhaps most difficult to ask of travel is: what sort of solidarity politics can emerge from this? But also: what sort of politics operates in Clifford's text? Where in the various spectrums of Left and Right (admittedly these can be overly reifying constructions today) does Clifford's work lie? I think it is symptomatic that it takes 180 pages in *The Predicament of Culture* before there is even a hint that Louis Aragon had taken up revolutionary politics. Leiris' politics seem to have been elided by the literary appreciation Clifford provides. Except for a brief reference to *Les Temps Modernes* (Clifford 1982:197), and a few other asides, Leiris is more readily rendered as the diarist and documentarist of the everyday mundane. With a nod to towards the influence of Aimé Césaire and anticolonial struggle in Vietnam and Madagascar,[6] very quickly Clifford has Leiris packed off to study with Mauss after just the one brief outrage: he is reported hanging out of a window denouncing France at a surrealist meeting before he settles down into a 'more concrete application of his subversive literary talents' (Clifford 1988:122). Leiris himself has made much more of his own oppositional political interests and his mobilisation against colonialism (in Price and Jamin 1988). How is it that we get mostly only literary 'subversives' in Clifford's rendering? Reading Clifford on Bataille you might never imagine that large sections of his work were dedicated to a critical engagement with communism.[7]

What we have in place of a politics of anthropology is fascination with spicy little details and wondrous incongruity in preference to analysis. No solidarity politics can be successfully built on such a basis. It can be contended that this belongs to a sustained (somewhat absent-minded) anti-Marxism on Clifford's part – here bad Marxism manifests in its negative form. Clifford's understanding of economic production is drawn from a sketchy version of Marxism found not in Marx but in anthropological consumption texts (especially Miller 1987, 1994, 1995), and admittedly brilliant but quite idiosyncratic forms of Marxist ethnography (Taussig 1980, 1987). He says he has taken 'a complex sense of local/global commodity systems' (Clifford 1997:346) from Miller, but his reference to Marx on commodities, page 72 of a 1961 text, is forgotten in the bibliography of *Routes*, making it difficult to tell what is from where (the quote, discussed below, is actually from *Capital* 1867/1967 – it could be that this symptomatic second omission, added to the unacknowledged paraphrase of Marx on history earlier in the book, is as significant as, say, noticing that one Trobriander is surreptitiously looking at the camera in *Argonauts*). The important point is that Clifford belongs to the group of academics who seem ready to reject systematic theorising for fear of a 'relapse' into some kind of secret Stalinism, Leninism, homogenisation or bounded thinking – allowing a red-baiting scare to equate a legitimate critique of homogenising categories with rejection of any kind of serious analysis at all. It is too often the case that Marxism is glossed as some sort of orthodox monolithic concrete categorical bogey, and this is especially dubious when the actual references and alleged details are omitted. In pursuit of what I would identify as a secret anti-bolshevism then, in the Preface to *Routes* Clifford presents himself as 'unlike Marx', favouring 'no revolution or dialectical negation of the negation' but 'democracy and social justice' (1997:10–11). In this project Clifford claims he also will not aspire to have the final word or present an overview, and his travel is about paths, not maps.[8] His 'situated analysis is more contingent, inherently partial' (1997:11), and this means that 'unlike Marx' there will be 'no cure for the troubles of cultural politics' (1997:12–13) only travel and translation. Uncertainty, wandering and being lost are elevated as method.[9]

In *Routes*, the politics of a 'lucid uncertainty' (1997:13) is the preferred response to the predicament of this world, and Clifford maintains a certain consistency with this theme over all his work. In the

*Predicament* book, he posits a 'condition of uncertainty' from which he is writing (1988:95). Within this framework – confidently asserted – the dissolution of 'natural' languages and of those constructs and fictions which contained and domesticated heteroglossia, syncretism, parody and transience makes it 'increasingly difficult to attach human identity and meaning to a coherent "culture" or "language" '(1988:95). Some people will get suspicious when citizen-ideologues of the singularly dominant world power tell us there is no culture, and imply that the global extension of Coca-Cola and Christianity (1997:161) entails no remarkable threat.

All this matters at the point where Clifford offers a political diagnostic (of sorts) for the fate of the planet. In our responses to the politics of travel in a world rife with political and racialist inequalities, for sure we do not need further parochialisms and anachronisms (Clifford 1982:197). In the domain of writing about cultural production, the 'ethnographic' motive must be further questioned, far beyond the postmodern epistemic doubts of the *Writing Culture* debate (Clifford and Marcus 1986) and its prolific progeny. 'Elegiac regret' is not enough. The institutional context of ethnographic description must surely always be considered in political terms. A critique of ethnography would also take up the practices of anthropology teaching and dissemination of its product – through the global apparatus of publishing, conference circuit, booksales, libraries, citations, etc., and within which Clifford himself is a star commodity. Similarly, the increasing integration of ethnographic and anthropological expertise – be it fully trained PhDs or degree-holding candidates – into business, consultancy, policy formation, travel and national heritage work, etc., must be evaluated politically.

\* \* \*

In his introduction to *Routes*, Clifford announces that he is interested in exploring movement across borders and boundaries inflected by the 'connected global forces' of 'continuing legacies of empire, the effects of unprecedented world wars, and the global consequences of industrial capitalism's disruptive, restructuring activity' (1997:6–7). It is not clear if he includes the 'Cold War' here as an unprecedented example, but certainly the significance of restructuring in the wake of that long conflict leaves its mark on Clifford's path. His Fort Ross meditation begins with him looking out to the Pacific from California and realising that, for the Russians who arrived there in the early 1800s, looking 'out' would have been looking 'back'. Significantly, he also realises that among all the arrivals since then, there are none who 'remember a time on the coast before strangers arrived' (1997:302). Indigenous populations seem continually to strive to appear from underneath the myriad travellers in Clifford's text, as the focus is instead on the west-to-east extension of Russia's 'great Asian encounter' and the development of its trading links with China, and the luxury goods which 'fuelled' the transformation of the Pacific (1997:303). The focus of this part of Clifford's work is the exchange requirements of those with a love of 'spices, porcelain and especially tea', who then 'unleashed destructive scrambles' to find sandalwood, sea cucumber and sea-otter pelts to trade in Canton. Was it the Chinese, then, who brought destruction upon the indigenous peoples and animals of West Coast America? He equates this destruction with the crashing together of the planetary plates which meet at San Andreas. Who is at fault?

*   *   *

Clifford offers many juxtapositions, but wants to draw no conclusions and offer no overview. This attitude has been seen before, even in more confident versions. Spivak, gently, firmly criticising Derrida's discussion of Marx makes the 11th thesis point by quoting *Capital* where Marx writes: 'the scientific analysis of the composition [*zersetzung*] of the air left the atmosphere itself unaltered in its physical configuration' (1867/1967:167) and she clarifies for a Derrida who 'goofs a bit' on Marx: 'Knowing the signification changes nothing. One must tamper with the force that establishes it', and again, 'simply to see the relations of production clearly is no big deal' (Spivak 1995a:10).[10]

Clifford can be seen sometimes goofing off too. What is it, for example, for Clifford to point out that certain persons, usually 'scientists' (Freud for example, [Clifford 1997:279]) can travel the world collecting culture? At what point does his enthusiasm for museums become something more than the cheap fascination of difference that elsewhere he wants to avoid? Clifford collects (Strathern [1991] would rather not, but I think it's a sleight of words). In the interests of a political evaluation, it is worth considering Clifford's notion of commodities in the light of his collecting practice. The citation of Marx – the one that is dated 1961 but is not in the bibliography – is, like so much else in the text, picked up as a bright shiny object and chucked into the nest. A crow's Marxism (nesting Marx). And by abstracting this bauble from the whole, Clifford loses his way:

> Marx called the commodity 'a mysterious thing, simply because in it the social character of men's labour appears to them as an objective character stamped upon the product of that labour; because the relation of the producers to the sum total of their own labour is presented to them as a social relation, existing not between themselves, but between the products of their labour' (Marx 1961:72).
>
> (Clifford 1997:322)

So far so good, this much discussed text from *Capital* (Marx 1867/1967:72) is a clear opening definition from the first chapter of a book which works by abstraction, starting with the commodity form (the often-read fetishism chapter) but continually working outwards in demonstration of the larger whole.[11] *Capital*, though it also is conjured every which way, is a text organised on the principle of explanation with a purpose, and not as if the commodity were the prior moment in the real. I would contend that to focus on commodity fetishism without recognising or waiting for the contextualisation of commodities that happens throughout the rest of the book, and the subsequent volumes, is to risk an error.

No surprise that this happens in the Fort Ross chapter. Clifford follows his unsourced citation with a revealing sentence recalling Marx as he strokes 'the luxurious, dead otter skin' (1997:322) – and with a rather less than Marxist point, he writes of the past:

> Seen as commodities, sea-otter skins and bales of tea exist as relations of equivalence independent from the work of Aleut hunters or Chinese coolies. The skins are valuable because they can be exchanged in Canton. Tea is worth producing in quantity because strangers will pay with rare luxury items. Exchange value, as Marx recognised, determines production.
>
> (1997:322)

This is where things go off track. Yes the hunter would not hunt in large quantities 'without the material compulsion of the market and the labour discipline it required' (1997:322), but this does not mean that the story can be stopped at 'Exchange value determines production.'[12] Surely anthropological examples, which Clifford must know, should warn against hasty evaluation here. For example, Malinowski's discussions of the kula would demand a more careful reading of economic causation in context, or even Malinowski's comments on the pearl trade and the difficulty of convincing 'the niggers to swim' (Malinowski in 1915, his testimony to the commission on South Pacific trade [Stocking 1991:46, but see also Malinowski 1935:19–20]) would have indicated some problems with any too-easy formula. Marx himself often pointed out the need, especially at the moment of transition, to coerce the 'workers' to sell their labour, to produce.[13] To begin and end with exchange value misses the entire point of the hidden social relations and exploitations that are entailed in the commodity form.[14] The 'abstract relation' and 'mystery' that Clifford's traders do not see is not exchange value, but the creative capacity of labour which has been appropriated by others. A half paragraph further along in *Capital* we can read of 'a definite social relation between men, that assumes, in their eyes, the fantastic form of a relation between things' (Marx 1867/1967:72), and:

> Since the producers do not come into social contact with each other until they exchange their products, the specific social character of each producer's labour does not show itself except in the act of exchange.
> (Marx 1867/1967:73)

In Marx's analysis the products of labour are social things with a dual quality, at once perceptible and imperceptible to the senses (he uses the analogy of light entering the optic nerve – we see something, but not all that is going on in the phenomenon that makes sight possible).[15] The task then, is – and Marx is prescriptive here – to understand how this mysterious – even, by analogy, religious – operation works. The trick that conjures relations between things out of the social relations of productive human beings must be confronted. Exchange value is the appearance, what Marx exhorts us to see is the social, that is the 'secret' – that 'the determination of the magnitude of value by labour-time is therefore the secret, hidden under the apparent fluctuations in the relative values of commodities' (Marx 1867/1967:75).[16] And as knowing this does not yet alter how it works, one must tamper ...

Instead, Clifford will 'struggle to keep commodities mysterious' and not reduce, as he says Marx wished to, the fantastic equivalence to 'a true measure of equivalence in social labour' (1997:323). Here we can appreciate his good intentions as Clifford is concerned that 'capitalist markets expand, virtually unopposed, throughout the planet' and the gap between the rich and poor grows (1997:322), but as he wants to find an ethical Marx rather than understand the labour theory of value it is obviously necessary to ask what this displacement into ethics can achieve. The problem is that it is not equivalences, but Capital which moves here. Clifford has left the Capital out of Marx! The secret is the creation of surplus value through labour-power as commodity,[17] which then allows the appropriation of the creative value of labour by the owner of the means of production, hence accumulation of capital – because of the general equivalent of money, as a kind of facilitating arbiter of exchange value. It is through accumulation that the capitalist can then deal in goods, luxurious furs, tea and the like, so that there will be the extension of this plunder to the most 'remote' reaches of the planet, including Fort Ross: 'Russian America was coastal extractive, not a settler, colony' (Clifford 1997:304).

In Marx's discussion of the 'illegal' opium trade there is reason to question Clifford's formula in the vicinity of the very examples he uses in the Fort Ross chapter – trade in Chinese tea. Admittedly here the trade is from India to China, but no matter. After the Chinese suspension of the East India Company's trade in tea in middle 1800s, and the so-called 'Opium wars' in which the 'civilisation-mongering' English found ways to profit from this 'illegal' opium trade they had encouraged themselves (Marx *New York Daily Tribune* 25 September 1858), Marx notes that should the Chinese legalise the opium trade and tolerate cultivation of the poppy in China, the secret monopoly of the English and their Calcutta-based smuggler-partners would be smashed. It is clear that the extent to which 'exchange value ... determines production', as Clifford would have it, is only a small part of the story and some important factors are ignored. If it were not for the might of the British imperial power, and the 'protection' it is able to afford the 'smugglers', as well as its prosecution of the opium wars, the Chinese government might well have then begun to produce opium in China, thus destroying the East Indian Company's dubious profiteering, production in India shifting to China and at lower values of exchange. Thus the collapse of the level of profit to be reaped from this trade as it is maintained by the dealings of mercantile and imperial power is envisaged (at the same time that Marx comes out in favour of legalising class A drugs). What is important, however, is that the use of power on the part of the English imperialists should not be ignored when making an analysis of exchange, or of Pacific trading empires, then or now. By stopping at the level of exchanged commodities, Clifford doesn't follow through with the political project of Marxism. The furs he strokes are definitely soft. Clifford has the block of Chinese tea in his hand as well (alas we do not get his views on legalisation).

There are perspectives on this we can adopt from other parts of Clifford's work, however, that assist in reading Marx. This is especially so for his understanding of a text's rhetorical fabulations and authority claims. The importance of Marx's mode of address, the narrative construction put together after his years of research, and the implied readership, should be considered as Clifford strokes the fur and sniffs at the tea. Just as Malinowski, and I guess Clifford, had a certain idea of what the narrativisation of the material was meant to achieve, so did Marx. Perhaps his ambitions were a little loftier, but for all the right reasons. The key point, as Spivak tells it, is that 'Marx exhorts the worker, his implied reader, to grasp the gap between "experience" and "the social" ' (1993:119).[18] What Spivak, and before her Marx, wants to keep in mind is that under industrial capitalism, workers do not exchange their labour for its value, or, in what I would call the 'trick' of capitalist play, they [we] work twice as much (and more) as would be needed to reproduce their [our] value. It is this surplus that moneybags appropriates, and which is the basis of accumulation, and also of the possible future abundant society of communism. If this point is not grasped, the political force of Marx's endeavour is left to one side. If it is taken up, it becomes possible to begin to see where interventions against this exploitation might be made, differentiations among the various modes of appropriation discerned, and tactical, more or less militant, challenges to the rule of the robber barons, and civilisation-mongers, mounted. Marx was, though scholars may tend to forget this, a revolutionary.

This would seem to invoke rather a different scenario for research and writing than that which Clifford constructs in his discussion of otter pelts and Chinese tea. Contexts matter. In a scenario which is one with which anthropologists in particular have perhaps reason to concern themselves, since it is very often the horizon of their work, past and present, the matter of tea exchanged for fur, and the circulation of luxury goods at the time of Fort Ross and the Russian settlement, might better be thought of in terms of superexploitation, and the operation of absolute surplus labour extraction, as distinct from relative surplus labour (the distinction between two means of extracting more surplus value can be recalled here – lengthening the working day, and improving the rate of production). This would require a deeper reading of Clifford's comment that the Russian explorers recruited Koniag and Aleut hunters by the 'familiar early-colonial combination of carrot and stick: mutually beneficial trade, alternating with naked terror' (1997:305). It is not without relevance to the Fort Ross scenario that, as Spivak notes, superexploitation more often than not extends to feminised labour – today to the sweatshops in every corner of the globe.[19] Even the historical example of the operation of superexploitation in the fur trade might usefully occupy anthropologists in a re-evaluation of their notions of exchange (and this could be immense fun for pomo trinket collectors since we could make all sorts of jokes about otters, and other furry critters, like beavers – given the historical significance of the beaver in the anthropology of Louis Henry Morgan and in the work of Charles Darwin).[20] Caution over the distinction between mercantile capitalism and industrial capitalism is also important if one is to talk about Marx and production. As well as 'acknowledging consumption' (Miller 1995), it might be plausible still to consider accumulation, the circulation of capital, competition between different capitals and the processes of restructuring, expansion, crisis and restructuring that all follow from the labour theory of value. Leaving the matter at 'exchange determines production' means that analysis is abandoned at the wayside. There are different kinds of capital to be distinguished before leaping from Fort Ross traders to commodities in the late twentieth century, and there are similarities to be specified. If the logic of capitalism does not operate in mercantile trade exactly as it does in advanced industrial capital, just as it is not the same in the forced extraction of surplus value in slavery, or in the so-called 'pre-capitalist formations', then there is scope for anthropologists to explain why. The key, though, is that trick which separates the owner of the means of production from the producer, and the pretence that the exchange of 'a fair day's work for a fair day's pay' is some sort of good deal.

In a book that wants to come to terms with travel today, and where much of this travel occurs across the demarcation line that is the international division of labour, it is important to do more than collect souvenirs, celebrate (new?) narrative modes of writing, and champion hybridity and complexity. The processes of capitalist exploitation may be presented abstractly, and it may be less than simple to name, but there is no reason not to make the attempt to understand it. Indeed, for an historian of anthropology, it is all the more important. Fort Ross is one of the sites upon which the history of capitalist trickery is marked. And here it does matter to ask why Clifford would be, at this time, engaged in a project which shows that the US is 'historically constituted from Asia as well as Europe ... in the shifting borderlands of the Americas, connected to the Island Pacific, to the Alaska/Siberia crossroads' (1997:331). This rewriting of Fort Ross may well 'offer resources for thinking historically in the present emergency' (1997:332), but in a scene where contrasting and non-commensurate perspectives prevail in place of analysis, some will see the 'present emergency' as too many 'Japanese buying real estate', while some will see it as a chance to make better heritage museums, and all along capital will forge further exploitative trade regimes under APEC, NAFTA and other travelling formations. Sure, when it comes to documenting that history it might be useful to see the narrative reconstruction as a pedagogic one, but can we learn to recognise the trick, and tamper with the tricksters more effectively?

All this only serves to show the trinketisation of Marx in Clifford's souveniring travel theory. What remains, however, is the possibility to extend the 'lucid uncertainty' with reasoned theoretical work. Clifford plus Marx, travel plus a political project: this might even begin to work if it was reconfigured under the sign of transition, the dynamics of movement, displacement, transformation and change. Transition could encompass travel, Fort Ross, museum collecting and the transformatory project.[21] Though he does not have such a plan in mind, at one point Clifford suggests further exploration of the revolutionary, destructive and productive, 'as Marx understood', character of Capitalism in a way that moves towards transition theory:

> As Marx understood, capitalism is revolutionary, destructive *and* productive. And it does not usher in a unified, 'bourgeois', or 'Western' sociocultural order as it spreads. It has proved to be flexible, working through as well as against regional differences, partially accommodating to local cultures and political regimes, grafting its symbols and practices onto whatever non-Western forms transculturate its logic.
>
> (1997:331)

This could be the subsumption thesis, recognisable in Marx's *Grundrisse* and in the later parts of *Capital*. An interest in 'transculturation' in this register, even if it were to be called 'hybridity', could line up with other useful work that Clifford does at least read carefully (Gilroy and Brah on diaspora, etc.). This could then form the basis for continuing to try to work out just what is going on in the contemporary conjuncture, with its uneven global socio-economic and population flows and the destructive–constructive complex of capitalism. The problem is that, even if Clifford was not limited to descriptive trinketisation in his collecting practice, it is very difficult to imagine how he might want to respond to the complexity of the world. Reading his varied statements on culture, trade, power and so on it becomes possible to wonder what would be needed to provoke an attempt to intervene? What set of circumstances would be necessary to provoke even a preliminary essay on what is to be done? Meekly anguished fascination at the phantasmagoric vista before him seems to be all we will ever be offered. Since *Routes* addresses travelling commodities, it matters to get Marx at least a little right.[22]

Would travelling theory reconfigured as transition be useful for thinking through the most 'particularly violent examples' of travel: slavery, exploitation, imperialism, flight capital, et cetera? Might it even be possible to comprehend the ways book writing is co-opted into the service of this formation – how the meanings of a text transit from context to context? The display of souvenirs, trinkets, cultural examples wrenched from context, and a mix of celebration and quietism in the face of capitalist restructuring, would suggest that, in Clifford's hands, it cannot. Is it possible to use 'travel' as a way to unpack the tricks of capitalist exploitation without lapsing into a simplistic orthodox-isation of Marx, a mantra of the new and a celebration of (the anxious, reflective) self? Further work on the notion of transition might be opened up here. The work required for another kind of politics of anthropology and travel would not be easy of course. But I believe it can be found in reconfiguring Clifford's version of diaspora as an agenda for more than multi-site ethnography.

What multi-site research should be directed towards is a political comprehension and political practice within the current conjuncture. Instead, both Clifford and Malinowski offer awe, frustrated travel tales and stalled research projects. Compare their statements about the future, which to me indicate an anxiety and uncertainty that itself needs analysis. Established and comfortable in 1930, Malinowski complained about a science which had 'made us into robots' in 'an enormous mechanism', which 'pushes us with a relentless persistence and terrible acceleration'. The world for Malinowski was changing 'uncannily' and everything was transformed with an 'ever-increasing speed in communication' and 'endless opportunities in cheap and mean forms of enjoyment; leisure to do a thousand irrelevant things' so that we are 'kept down intellectually by journalism; moving and feeling to the rhythm of jazz; united by a world-wide net of broadcasting ... an infinitely elastic nervous system ...' (1930:405). This pessimistic, anti-progress (anti-jazz?) routine – reminiscent of more recent laments at the speeding up of life; the proliferation of travel; the Internet; the 'ever increasing speed of communications' – suggests that today we have not understood very much more than the anti-Bolshevik Malinowski.[23] And with a little irony too, wanting anthropology to be to colonialism what physics was to engineering, Malinowski already noted that in the South Sea Islands he was hard pressed to reconstruct 'stone age' life because he was: 'pursued by the products of the Standard Oil Company, weekly editions, cotton goods, cheap detective stories, and the internal combustion engine in the ubiquitous motor launch' (1930:406).

Clifford's pessimism in the face of the world follows a similar trajectory, though he wants to refuse it, to deny the ubiquity of a 'contemporary capitalism' which 'works flexibly, unevenly' through 'flows of immigrants, media, technology, and commodities' (1997:9). So that in such a context his essays are 'written under the sign of ambivalence, a permanently fraught hope':

> It is impossible to think of transnational possibilities without recognising the violent disruptions that attend 'modernisation', with its expanding markets, armies, technologies, and media. Whatever improvements or alternatives may emerge do so against this grim backdrop. Unlike Marx, who saw that the possible good of socialism depended historically on the necessary evil of capitalism, I see no future resolution of the tension – no revolution or dialectical negation of the negation.
>
> (1997:10)

He does, however, derive hope 'from unexpected news' – 'for example, accounts of the pope's visits to New Guinea and Africa.... What historical changes have brought John Paul II, of all people, to preach the value of indigenous culture?' (1997:342). This Pope also came out demanding a nicer version of capitalism, one that wasn't so brutal. Clifford, devotee of the sky-god religion, continues to derive revealingly:

> Something like hope.... Not prophecy or a revolutionary vision.... But is it not blind, even perverse, to speak of hope in the face of so many

devastating facts: relentless environmental degradation, neo-colonialism, overpopulation, a growing gap between privileged and desperate people virtually everywhere? The question is inescapable, crushing. Yet pessimism gets one nowhere and frequently lapses into cynicism. It must be possible to reject pessimism along with its opposites – the celebratory, ameliorist visions of progress through development, techno-science, the internet … .

(1997:342–3)[24]

Claiming that Gramsci 'named a problem, not a solution, with his formula "Pessimism of the intellect, optimism of the will" ', Clifford asks why is hope 'always on the side of the nonintellectual "will"?' (1997:343). If he wants to shift the formula to accommodate this reversal, he must end up naïve and paralysed: (an uncertain) optimist of the intellect, but a pessimist in regard to activity. This amounts to thinking (hoping) the world will be nice, but being too depressed to do anything to achieve this. Against development, technology, advanced communications and … this is worse than pessimism, for an abdication from human life, pastoralism and the consciousness of sea-otters – a return to the swamp of religion and mystery seems Clifford's ideal. The extreme passivity of touristic violence. Surely we deserve better than this from California.

With Clifford the horizon seems to offer a grinning paralysis (more conventional than surrealism), and the lack of confidence in any sort of transformatory project reflects a more general cultural and political exhaustion. Clifford can ask (or list) 'urgent' questions 'at a time of rampant neoliberalism' (1997:322), but cannot answer; he is able only to revel in his phantasmagoric trinketisations:

What is corn for a Mayan Indian? A fax machine for Subcommandante Marcos? What is a sea-otter skin to an eco-tourist? A VCR and acrylic paint in the hands of Australian Aboriginal artists? A rum bottle in a Santeria altar? A Bob Marley recording in Hawaii? A Rambo T-shirt in Lebanon? A pack of cigarettes and a beer can left at the Vietnam War Memorial? A car used by Californian Indians to return to their reservation for a festival?

(1997:323)

Without capacity to order the (text of) the world, humanity must abandon itself to 'uncertainty'. This is an abdication that plays into the hands of the right (and fears that the Russians/Japanese are coming), and though at one point Clifford did offer a Nietzschean decolonisation project, no longer does analysis even seek to plot the paths, let alone propose a minimal political programme. Uncertainty reigns – at best narrated by a happy consciousness that marvels at the conflagration.

# Part 2
# derrida@marx.archive

# 3
# Fever

Three quotes as talismans of this writing.

> All distances in time and space are shrinking. We now reach
> overnight, by plane, places which formerly took weeks and
> months of travel. We now receive instant information, by
> radio, of events formerly learned about only years later, if at
> all.... Everything gets lumped together· into uniform dis-
> tancelessness. How?
>
> (Heidegger 1971:166)

> ... electronic mail today, even more than the fax, is on the
> way to transforming the entire public and private space
> of humanity ... at an unprecedented rhythm, in quasi-
> instantaneous fashion.
>
> (Derrida 1995/1996:17)

> ... with the development of transport facilities not only is
> the velocity of movement in space accelerated and thereby
> the geographic distance shortened in terms of time ...
>
> (Marx 1893/1974:253–4)

I think it is important to take seriously the assertion that things are
speeding up and not to deny its importance. Yet it is also quite easy
to find statements delivered at such speed that thought and cliché
clash in hyperbolic overdrive. A quick and dangerous slippage has
become all the rage for those who talk of changes in productive
technologies without analysis, so that we receive discussions strewn
with such metaphors of the apocalypse as acceleration, hurricane,
cyclone, the tumultuous crescendo of speeding capital. In the past
the realm of production used to bring us together, while circulation
atomised opportunities for class organisation; so, today, do mediatised telematic societies offer a chance to extend cooperative
self-activity? Must radical political efficacy rely only upon the proximity of really existing factory and workplace cells, as opposed to,

for example, shared experience not necessarily of immediately co-terminous space? Given an abundance of resources for organising, why despair in the face of speed?

//speed.metaphor

Marx and Derrida via Heidegger and Freud. Part 2 of this book responds to a particular moment in time that was not just an anniversary. Not just an occasion. It concerns rather a possible different way of marking time. More than 150 years ago in France Marx published a book called *The Poverty of Philosophy* (Marx 1847). Although this work has always been eclipsed by another text written at the end of that year,[1] I argue that it is worth consulting and is as much deserving of reprint as the *Manifesto of the Communist Party*. The latter enjoyed a publishing industry reprint frenzy in 1997 – with at least eight new editions that I was able to collect that year, and no doubt many more the next. This at a time when both texts could be accessed via the world wide web at <http://csf.Colorado.EDU/psn/marx/Admin>) or picked up at bargain basement prices in certain musty second-hand stores – I, fetish-wise, cherish (and trinketise) the Progress Press copy of *Poverty* I picked up in Gould's bookshop in Newtown, Australia.

One of the points Derrida makes in *Archive Fever: A Freudian Impression*, has to do with how an 'archive ought to be idiomatic' (Derrida 1995/1996:90). Certainly Marx's *Poverty of Philosophy* is replete with idiosyncrasies; it is an almost contemptuous critique of Proudhon, with early formulations of some of Marx's most brilliant insights into political economy. The idioms Derrida has in mind though are not only idiosyncratic, but pertain to language, context, time, meaning and translation. It is worth considering, then, just what kind of idiom is there when we read Marx today. What kind of Marx comes to us today through the prism of time?[2]

The first worry I have with discussions of Derrida and Marx has to do with the inevitable practical and political question that must be kept in mind throughout. This concerns the political value of reading Marx, Derrida, theory in general; it concerns the speed, and expertise, with which we read, the ways in which we claim authority to have read, and the implications of this reading for how we live in the world ... . (These are not easy or uncomplicated issues, and they are not to be rushed – obviously reading is also in the world, political and practical. The question is how? What sort of politics, what kinds of practice, what speed of reading?) It worries me that reading slowly would also of course be no guarantee, but I am concerned that the speed at which we often read is too fast, and my worry is that the times in which we find ourselves reading are not understood. Amidst this worry and concern, I'd suggest that the whole metaphorics of speed has infected our understanding to the point of paralysis, and that political practice takes time. This has important implications. Nearly everyone seems to accept with no problem the acceleration of capital which today reaches such a degree that the instantaneous is privileged as never before. Capitalism has speeded up and now moves so fast, it is often said, that all is a blur (financial transfers by electronic optic, hyper-cyber-giga acceleration, etc.) – I think at least some of these rates need to be disaggregated. There are many examples and, even in a critical tone, it is not uncommon to find gee-whizz declarations of the hyper-intensity of capital flows that seem only to lead to stasis and quietism. On the *Speed* journal link to the Feed website it is possible to read:

> Surveying the turbulent, early-industrial landscape of England in the 1830s, Edward Bulwer-Lytton wrote: 'Every age may be called an age of transition – the passage from one state to another never ceases. But in our age the transition is visible.' It's a remark that would go *without saying* [my italic] in today's society, where the sheer velocity of technological change has become a slogan and a sales-pitch, echoing through the furthest reaches of the media sphere. Open up your daily paper's business section or flip through any of the bubbly entertainment rags, and you'll read about paradigms being shattered, old forms giving way to the new, 'interactive multimedia' ushering its sluggish, page-bound ancestors to the ash-heap of historical irrelevance. (<http://www.speed.com/**>)

I want to read speed, time and the poverty of philosophy in relation to Derrida's *Archive Fever* in what may seem initially to be only a convenient correspondence, but which will become more important. Looking for correspondences, I have drawn my quotes in part from Marx archived (in English = idiomatic translation?) on the worldwide web. It is now possible to read, search and download more than enough Marx text to keep anyone busy. The 'Marx and Engels Internet Archive' (MEIA), maintained on a server in Colorado (<http://csf.Colorado.EDU/psn/marx/Admin>) begins with a sentence I want to misread. I want to misread this sentence carefully, since to do so raises all the issues that concern me in an attempt to read Derrida's books – *Specters of Marx, Archive Fever* and *The Politics of Friendship*. The Marx and Engels web introduction begins: 'The M/E Internet Archive is continually expanding, as one work after another is brought on-line. While quite comprehensive as is, it's not complete.' This expanding, unfinished archive then...

Should we be concerned that we can 'search' Marx electronically? What does it mean to do so? I have to begin with this archive, because, if you have been reading Derrida for some time you will know that a very predictable beginning by now is to consider the question of beginnings. And so many of Derrida's texts follow this pattern (see Spivak, introduction to Derrida 1967/1976). What if we began by reading Marx on the web? Or Freud for that matter, or Derrida? None of these examples will do justice, but theory does not just sit on the shelf, it arrives.

//derrida.freud

As if to mark the moment, Derrida begins *Archive Fever* with an avoidance of conventional times. 'Let us not begin at the beginning, nor even at the archive' (1995/1996:1). In a lecture delivered in London at the conference 'Memory: the Question of Archives', Derrida entices 'us' to begin with a meditation on the word. To begin, before time, with a word.

*Archive Fever* deserves attention for several reasons, but its tone is such that, I think at least, we should already beware of how it – how Derrida – suggests we read, not just this word, but what reading the word means in general. Derrida will, towards the end of this book, tell us that 'nothing is less reliable today than the word "archive"' (1995/1996:90), but as yet this has to be demonstrated. In the (not) beginning, the word 'archive' suggests, among other things, order, and so command, and this might already warn us that we are in the realms of power, and unreliability. It may be well to remember that this is where the power of a certain metaphysical thinking operates, positing the real and the lived, conserving and memorialising power. Derrida notes a certain archiving distinction is at the heart of this order when he says the archive 'takes place at the place of the originary and structural breakdown of memory' (1995/1996:11). (It does matter who controls and orders the archive. If every reading is transformational, archives are not repositories nor as 'conservative' as they pretend).

Time will be bound up here with memory, the time of memory and its technologies: for 'there is no archive ... without a technique of repetition' (1995/1996:11). Archive fever will be the problem of wanting to repeat the origin, to return (1995/1996:90). This return privileges the origin and makes the technical apparatus of that return (the apparatus of the archive) secondary. Derrida says this is the fever of psychoanalysis. What is analysed like a symptom here is a double structure, a contagious pattern – one that is first of all laid out in Freud's book on that very old (and archived) resource called 'Moses'. Derrida is less interested in Moses than in Freud's comments on the value of his own archiving, and there will be reasons to think this is Derrida speaking through Freud – he later comments on the 'dramatic twist' of Freud speaking of himself through speaking of a colleague (1995/1996:89).[3] At the moment of the analysis of Moses, Freud asks the question of the value of his own writings, and he gives the answer, according to Derrida, that one 'can only justify the apparently useless expenditure of paper, ink, and typographic printing, in other words the laborious investment in the archive' by putting forward a novelty, a discovery (1995/1996:12).

Freud's discovery, in the Moses text, is that of the destructive impulse. 'Was it worth it?', might have been Freud's and Derrida's question, and it is a question I want eventually to put to Derrida's work on Marx. It might have been Derrida's question, and ventriloquy plays havoc with the analysis here because, although it is not, it could be ('Perhaps', if we follow the hesitations and affiliations of *The Politics of Friendship*, it is). Instead, Derrida's text revolves – returns to – questions of the technical apparatus that occupied him in his early essay 'Freud and the Scene of Writing' (1967/1978). Based on the fact that 'Freud did not have at his disposition the resources provided today by archival machines of which one could hardly have dreamed in the first quarter of this century' (1995/1996:14), Derrida will ask if these new machines will change anything: 'What is at issue here is nothing less than the future' (1995/1996:14) and he adds 'if there is such a thing' – this future will be very important when it's time to look at *Specters of Marx*.

In an innocent way accepting the homogeneous context (of method) in which a question such as this can be asked, Derrida would investigate the various technical apparatuses of psychoanalysis – 'for perception, for printing, for recording, for topic distribution of places of inscription, of ciphering, of repression, of displacement, of condensation' (Derrida 1995/1996:15). So often we are left with a promise that an investigation would show something, perhaps, but there is not time, and it's not surprising that he does not actually advance the inquiry beyond asking. Nevertheless, we are well used to seeing questions concerning technology these days, in Derrida's words:

> Is the psychic apparatus *better represented* or is it *affected differently* by all the technical mechanisms for archivization and for reproduction, for prosthesis of so-called live memory, for simulacrums of living things which already are, and will increasingly be, more refined, complicated, powerful than the 'mystic writing pad' (microcomputing, electronization, computerisation, etc?)
>
> (1995/1996:15)

What the mischievous questioning Derrida then offers is to dream of a cyber-Freud. He should have such visions. How about a webbed-up, Internet-surfing, micro-chip probing, psycho-cybernetical, Oedipolaroid, electra-callibrational, pentium-envying, hyper-Freud? Derrida's fantasy question also possibly hides a lament for a place as Freud's analysand – perhaps he wants to post-date his communication and set up an appointment to examine his own nocturnal visions:

> One can *dream* or speculate about the geo-techno-logical shocks which would have made the landscape of the psychoanalytic archive *unrecognisable* for the past century if ... Freud, his contemporaries, collaborators and immediate disciples, instead of writing thousands of letters by hand, had had access to MCI or AT&T telephonic credit cards, portable tape-recorders, computers, printers, faxes, televisions, teleconferences, and *above all E-mail.*
>
> (1995/1996:16, my emphasis)

Above all, email. Derrida's dream privileges the new personal communications format on the basis of a view of technology that to me seems to take on a messianic tone. Could it be that that Derrida is mesmerised by the novelty of email – as if we would not 'recognise' its use in psychoanalysis? Today, to cite just the most tabloid of examples, analysts in Manhattan have their dictated notes telephoned through to VDU operators in places like Bangalore, India, to be typed up and transferred back to Manhattan the next day.

Would this night-time archiving really be so unrecognisable? Whatever the case, Derrida's enthusiasm for new technology is clear: 'electronic mail today, even more than the fax, is on the way to transforming the entire public and private space of humanity' (1995/1996:17).

What is Derrida saying here? Transforming the *entire* space of humanity? Surely, not in its entirety? – a slippage here into the globalising Eurocentrism he so often guards against – as in his critique of Lévi-Strauss, discussed below (see Chapter 4).[4] So often the fetish for new technological 'product' in the shopping malls of Paris, New York, Tokyo, etc., is extended to the *entire* planet. Declarations of a transformation of the entirety of human space seem a little hasty, the sort of thing to be expected from the propagandists of AT&T, not from staid old philosophy. And again: even more than the fax? The transferability of office memos across geography – from identical offices in London to Cairo, from Sydney to Santa Cruz. Is the fax so old hat? Why does Derrida make so much of the process of electronic archiving effected by new technologies that inaugurate a distancing effect? He suggests that these technologies move Freud's works 'away from us at great speed, in a continually accelerated fashion' (1995/1996:18), and he compares our relation to them as akin to that of archaeologists, or biblical philologists, or medieval copyists (Moses and the archive again). He does not want to denigrate philology, but this 'should not close our eyes to the unlimited upheaval underway in archival technology' (1995/1996:18). Why, I want to ask, is this unlimited, and what are the implications of saying so?

Derrida also asks if the received protocols of reading, interpretation and classification 'must' be applied to the, supposedly unified, 'corpus' of Freudian psychoanalysis (1995/1996:36). There are interesting moves afoot here, not only with regard to the unity of the corpse – the integrity of the dead, we could say – but also of the protocols of reading that will be applied to the archive in the future. Derrida says this is a question of the future 'to come', one we will 'only know in times to come' (1995/1996:36). He refers, in this paragraph, to his book on Marx, and to a 'spectral messianicity' (which is not messianic – he does not invoke the ghost of Benjamin which haunts here), and there can be no doubt that the question of protocols of readings 'to come' are important in relation to both Marx and Freud.

What are the themes signalled here and how do they fit the current conjuncture? I think all this has to do with a new astonishment at time and technology, not that these aren't old topics for the now elderly Derrida (he has often written that 'time is violence').[5] Never alone in worrying about time, recently he shows certain symptoms of being less subtle than he previously so often was. Increasingly thinking about death, as Freud did at the end (these are not just jokes: *Of Gerontology*), Derrida refers to 'upheavals' in the 'economy of speed' of psychoanalysis. In the course of raising questions about the techniques of investigation and interpretation in the face of technological transformation (and it is still necessary to raise questions about psychoanalysis as cure, as normalisation), upheavals in the 'progress of representation' in psychoanalysis become pertinent. No longer just the children's toy of the magic writing slate upon which the trace of what is written remains beneath the surface even when erased, but today, tape-recorders, video, electronic telecoms. The economy of speed concerns 'all that is invested in the representational models of the psychic apparatus for perception' (Derrida 1995/1996:15).

Are the techniques of Freudian analysis out of date as Derrida's questioning might imply? Indeed, the 'laws' or rules of the consultation, of free association and the absence of 'technological' recording devices in the consultation rooms seem to ensure this is so. What then of other disciplines that have embraced at least some of these devices – the video camera in anthropology or cultural studies, the electronic retrieval systems in history, or vice versa? I wonder at this, since email – and Derrida writes: *'above all* email' – is nothing much more than the electronic delivery of letters and so does not seem so different to Freud's scrivening practice, if on a grandly different scale (questions of scale are different from questions of speed). Some postal history should be remembered – there used to be a half dozen deliveries of mail each day in major metropolises like London: back and forth, first mail to invite someone for morning tea, second to postpone to lunch, third to rearrange for the afternoon, and fourth to cancel and agree to meet later at the club – admittedly all this only for the upper-class urban elite, but it is a pattern replicated on the larger scale of those who are electronically wired today. Some may say even that email is a step back from the immediacy of the phone – and all of Derrida's work on phonologism would echo here.... Certainly the hype of email has its political critics, none more so than those writing about the parts of the Third World less adequately webbed up than elsewhere,[6] and where it is also sometimes a two-hour walk to the nearest phone (see Scott McQuire's [1997b] essay on the 'Uncanny Home' on differential rates of internet access, privileging the US, UK, Australia and Canada, and also see activist group discussion of First World demands for information vis-à-vis time constraints and access costs to phone-lines etc., on the autonomous Marxism discussion list aut-op-sy <http://jefferson.village.Virginia.EDU/~spoons/>). The point is that there are still significant delays in the relays that exchange meanings here (much of the circuitry remains copper, for example from a mine like that of Bougainville in the Pacific, rather than optic fibre).[7] Of course, the advent of broadband video-exchange, in 'real time', will both displace the text of email, and move a step past the telephonic into immediacy of audio-visual linkages across space for the well-resourced elites. Sure, this may be good news for archivists vis-à-vis Freud, communicating face-to-face across time and space, but sorry, Freud cannot accept the call. Being dead, as we will see, he cannot answer except through Derrida's control of the archive, through what Derrida can show that he has already said. Derrida knows this, and says 'Freud can only acquiesce' (1995/1996:41).

But what line is he on? Since when does an 'unprecedented rhythm' (1995/1996:17) factor here as a change in the instrumental possibility of production in a way that was not already discussed in the earliest texts of Marxism (do I mean those by Marx)? And since when does technological change in itself lead to political transfor-mation? Heidegger's essay on technology, which could be deployed against the hype of time and space, might be recalled here too.[8] And remembering Avital Ronell's great book on Heidegger and the call of national socialism (Ronell 1989), and Heidegger's work during the war as a postal censor, recalling Derrida's book *The Postcard*, it is easy to suggest there is something uncanny in these particular lettered correspondences. However, the point about email vis-à-vis the phone is that you can leave replying till later, it is not as immediate as it seems. Let us continue to ponder this one, leaving it in the in-tray.

What then for the social sciences in a time of telematic advance? What then for Marx and the Internet? The accelerated circulation of struggles, or more of the same? Everything changes, or nothing at all – should the 11th thesis be emailed to Derrida, or did he already receive this from Marx and leave it unread? On the phone and the Internet in politics we would also need to take account of the 'engaged' tone. Of a tone of 'engagement' adopted by Derrida. Also call-waiting, the answer machine, the conference call, ring back, dialler identification, taps, surveillance, bugs, the state and the press and … all this heard over the frequency of the names Marconi, Edison, Bell and Gates – corporate names now, not persons.

\* \* \*

On engagement, we might look at the series of images of people, mostly Derrida, collected at the end of a dual-texted commentary on Derrida by Bennington and Derrida himself (indeterminate authorship rules). The last images of the book are explicitly related to a kind of politics: a photograph simply captioned 'On his return from Prague after his arrest' – 'his', when of course there were several others arrested at the time, and is this the only arrest of an 'internationalist' intellectual? It is almost a compulsory pose (cf. Sartre, Foucault, Mick Jagger). Another photograph is from the film *Ghost Dance* and quotes: 'I believe on the contrary that the future belongs to ghosts, and that the modern image technology, cinema, telecommunications, etc, are only increasing the power of ghosts.' (Is this a regret for literature, or for Proust before Telecom?)[9] A third image pictures the press conference at UNESCO on the publication of *Pour Nelson Mandela*, with Derrida quoted saying 'The postscript is for the future…. I wanted to talk about the future of Nelson Mandela.' The second last photograph shows Derrida speaking at the podium at the Mutualité in 1989 demanding voting rights for immigrants in local elections – 'The combat against xenophobia and racism *also* goes via this right to vote. So long as it is not gained, injustice will reign, democracy will be limited to that extent, and the riposte to racism will remain abstract and impotent' (Bennington and Derrida 1991/1993). The last photo is of Derrida with a drawing of himself. There will be cause to consider just what is arrested here, just what is meant by the future or by democracy, just why a vote matters so much and what sort of anti-racist riposte this might be. The point, however, is to mark the importance of a political Derrida of the 1980s and the future. It would be too hasty to limit Derrida's 'politics' to these brief snapshots, but they are symptomatic (of possibly many things, the constraints of the time perhaps).

## //speed.reading.quotes

It is time to consider the three emblematic quotations that I have used to organise my reading. These are difficult quotes to read, not just because of the idiom, nor of the content, but of the time, and how time affects idiom, content, meaning and reading. The ways we read have to do with archive management as well. There are many archivists, and the ordering and command – a whole series of shalts and shalt nots – proliferate. Avoiding reading because it is difficult should be no excuse (but I think this is sometimes one of the biggest problems – and I wonder if the electronic search of the archive feeds the controls that operate this fear). Rather than a long exegesis, I want to just quickly read three avoidances and three quick quotations on technology. The set revolves around the names Derrida, Marx and Heidegger.

*Avoidance 1*. Although there would be many Marxists, and others, who would be quick to find excuses for not reading Heidegger's difficult work – and for that matter, for not reading Bataille, Negri, Derrida, etc., or even for not reading Marx – there are times when attention to the hard and the difficult are necessary. Other excuses for not reading Heidegger include the now all-too-easy accusation that he was never not a National Socialist,[10] that he is an obscure and all-too-difficult philosopher, and so not pertinent to politics (this is obviously a stupid excuse) or that Georg Lukács called him bourgeois (this is a rather more well-read form of the same stupidity – Lukács also described Nietzsche as 'witty').

*Avoidance 2*. Avoidances of Derrida seem more prominent, and yet at the same time more beleaguered, as there are a good many readers who have been reading Derrida for some time, and some of those who would want to avoid reading Derrida would do so because a sometime shibboleth-monster called Postmodernism has captured intellectual ground that was, more or less, that of the Left. The abundance of reading of Derrida, however, has not stopped these readers from also avoiding much of what Derrida has been saying, so that they can be accused of misreading, or better, of mistranslating, Derrida[11] – though I want to insist that it is necessary to be very cautious with such assertions. For my money, the best example of a misreading of Derrida is argued out between Scott McQuire and David Holmes in an exchange of articles in the Australian magazine *Arena* (see McQuire 1990 – inevitably one reads past the other, and I am far more sympathetic to the close, less hasty, reading by McQuire in this case. Holmes' vituperative reply to McQuire's criticisms made his target look magnanimous). There will be occasion to refer to this debate again below.

*Avoidance 3*. Missing Marx also has a long orthodoxy. It has become more than commonplace and boring to quote the passage in Marx where he claims not to be a Marxist himself. Chapter and verse on the deviations and distortions of the orthodoxy may be cited. I will spare you the details, but you can imagine a swathe of debate over economism, vulgar materialism, ultra-leftism, ultra-rightist tendencies, tendencies in themselves, absence of tendencies, opportunist social democratic, counter-revolutionary, sectarian, pseudo- and crypto-positionings, Trotskyite socialism of all stripes, tenured Marxists and weekend raconteurs. And yep, me too.

The three quotes (expanded a little from those in the preamble): Jacques Derrida, in *Archive Fever* (the first part examined earlier):

> ... electronic mail today, even more than the fax, is on the way to transforming the entire public and private space of humanity, and first of all the limit between the private, the secret (private or public), and the public or phenomenal ... at an unprecedented rhythm, in quasi-instantaneous fashion, this instrumental possibility of production, of printing, of conservation, and of destruction of the archive must inevitably be accompanied by juridical and thus political transformation.
>
> (1995/1996:17)

A rather long time ago, Martin Heidegger wrote:

> All distances in time and space are shrinking. We now reach overnight, by plane, places which formerly took weeks and months of travel. We now receive instant information, by radio, of events formerly learned about only years later, if at all.... Distant sites of the most ancient cultures are shown on film as if they stood this very moment amidst today's street traffic. Moreover, the film attests to what it shows by presenting also the camera and its operators at work. The peak of this abolition of every possible remoteness is reached by television, which will soon pervade and dominate the whole machinery of communication.... What is happening here when, as a result of the abolition of great distances, everything is equally far and equally near? ... Everything gets lumped together into uniform distancelessness. How?
>
> (1971:166)

Karl Marx, in the second volume of *Capital* wrote:

> ... with the development of transport facilities not only is the velocity of movement in space accelerated and thereby the geographic distance shortened in terms of time. Not only is there a development of the mass of communications facilities so that for instance many vessels sail simultaneously for the same port, or several trains travel simultaneously on different railways between the same two points, but freight vessels may clear on consecutive days of the same week from Liverpool

or New York, or goods trains may start at different hours of the same day from Manchester to London.... The development tends in the direction of the already existing market, that is to say, towards the greater centres of production ... these particularly great traffic facilities and the resultant acceleration of the capital turnover (since it is conditional on the time of circulation) give rise to quicker concentration of both the centres of production and the markets.

(1893/1974:253–4)

I am not interested in those who would offer only ways of not reading the archive at a time when an 'open' reading would be most required. Nothing is new in this – the primers, the prefaces, the 'Marx dictionary', the authorised translations, the signed seal of Derrida's name, the long introductions, the Psychoanalysis Dictionary, *Heidegger for Beginners*, the Marx excerpts, the seven-point programme, the Magi's singular pronouncement, the summary (dismissive) quote – the 'rumour' of Marxism, the rumour of Freud, the rumour of the hidden king – all these have operated as ordering and controlling codes for the archive and the future, and in just the way Derrida says archives work, his books will also operate according to these rules. Indeed, though perhaps not in exactly the same ways every time, deconstruction falls prey to its own critique (Derrida 1967/1976:24), and especially in the hands of quick readers (like me? How do we negotiate the subtleties of Derrida's control? How do we reconcile Derrida's critique of the archive dream of a total record, with the supplement that insists on misreading and an idiomacy that works as limit?). So how do we read these scenes in an open way? As with any code, there is no way to avoid ordering Marx about, or Derrida, or Freud, or Heidegger, but there are certainly ways of closing down readings that can and should be avoided. What readings of Marx are needed now? Paradoxically, of course, the Marx electronic archive will both fix and open interpretations, order and reorder. This is not new either I guess, nothing that the Progress Press had not achieved (they who in 1991 were pulping books and using the collected works to fuel the furnace heating their building). What is it about email and electronic communications that makes Derrida think everything has changed so much – and doesn't the idea of instantaneous electronic transfer already presuppose the homogeneous space of time, and a separation between the inscribed archive and the lived, that Derrida seems to have so often critiqued? Here is the problem of writing and extension, of communicability – and, I will want to add, of political practice – as Derrida promises an 'inevitable ... political transformation', something new appears. I am left with technology determination and concern about reading as a technology – if there will be many readings generated by the archive, what sort of nostalgia for an originary reading would it be to mourn the ways Marx – or Derrida, or Heidegger – can be read now?

//derrida.text

Misreadings of Derrida have been particularly prevalent around these issues and much of the bad reputation that 'deconstruction' has among Marxists and others has been due to what I would insist on calling misreading. Untimely readings perhaps, though I can imagine no time when the right-wing literary apolitical appropriation of deconstruction could be justified. Some clarifications can hope to move towards a more (bad Marxist) open reading. As a 'conservative' mechanics fixes and orders meanings, Derrida will have spoken through the archive already of course. I want to defend a Derrida, both against the right-wing apolitical ('right-wing' and 'apolitical' go together as votes for the status quo) appropriations, and against the reluctance of some Marxists to engage with his ideas. The defence will not go by way of saying that Derrida's inconsistency will be an illustration of his coherence – as if the to and fro of 'falling prey' were sufficient alibi, nor will it be to critique the notion of the idealism of a constant and singular identity, held under the proper name, and trade-mark, *Derrida*™. The metaphors chosen for his discourse could be read – indeed should be read – symptomatically, and this is a lesson already well taught and it is worthwhile to ask what the metaphors reveal, where they move, how they pass and what other possibilities they either exclude or provoke. But this would not be reason for any damning critique, especially since Derrida is quite careful with metaphor – or quite excessive, elaborate, expressive, extreme.... Instead, perhaps, time and movement, political mobilisation and uses – the protocols of reading philosophy in a political context – would be the criteria to choose here and now.

In an exchange initiated with the text 'Signature, Event, Context' in 1977, followed by 'Limited Inc, a b c ...' (in the journal *Glyph*, collected in Derrida 1988), Derrida is at pains to correct some misconceptions that arose out of his discussion of the text and writing in the general sense. He does this in a tone that is at once pedagogically mischievous, and at the same time grounded in phenomenological styles of questioning. In a section entitled 'Writing and Tele-communication' Derrida raises the question of context: 'To say that writing extends the field and the powers of locutory or gestural communication presupposes, does it not, a sort of homogenous space of communication?' (1988:3). There is an 'empirical boundary of space and time' for the voice and for gesture, which writing can extend. By its different means, writing extends the scope of the space of communication – at least in the 'currently accepted sense', in what Derrida calls '*the*' system of interpretation, something like the 'commonsense' interpretation. In this homogeneous space and time, even where extended:

> … the meaning or contents of the semantic message would thus be transmitted, communicated, by different means, by more powerful technical mediations, over a far greater distance, but still within a medium that remains fundamentally continuous…. Any alteration would therefore be accidental. (1988:3)

What is at stake here is nothing so easy as might be glossed as Derrida saying 'there is nothing outside the text', or that 'all meaning is undecidable'. This is simplification and error. Derrida is pointing out that the 'representational character of written communication' has been a constant motif which includes an 'economic reduction' – writing 'as picture, reproduction, imitation of its content' and a 'homogenous and mechanical' aspect (1988:5). With writing, as Derrida discusses in relation to Condillac, there is an absent addressee, and representation which 'supplements' this absence, and so extends presence. A key point is that writing supplants presence. Here writing is an example of communication which 'circulates' a 'representation as ideal content (meaning)' (1988:6; but in Alan Bass's earlier translation the verb is 'vehiculates' not circulates [Derrida 1972/1982], which suggests carriage more readily). Derrida explains that as a written sign is set down with the addressee absent, this absence is only a kind of delayed absence, and so a 'distant presence' idealised in representation (1988:7). Here is the homogeneous time and space of extended communication which depends upon the repeatability of the writing (Derrida replaces repeat with iterable from *itara*, 'other' in Sanskrit [of course an alternative etymology gives *iter* as Latin for 'journey']). The point is, however, that this is also the condition of all meaning, communication, transmission, not just written communication in the strict sense – 'a certain self-identity of this [any] element (mark, sign etc) [of spoken language] is required to permit its recognition and repetition' (Derrida 1988:10). The entire edifice of alterity, difference, deference, writing in the general sense and so on, is bound up here. Derrida opens – through reading Husserl, but against Husserl (there would need to be another text devoted to unravelling this affiliation, but see Gasché 1994) – a series of political questions in philosophy that have had significant impacts in many fields.

Derrida does not say there is no truth – a common misapprehension. In *Positions*, he had said: 'In no case is it a question of a discourse against truth or against science. (This is impossible and absurd, as is every heated accusation on the subject)' (1981:105n). In clarification, he writes:

> I have never 'put such concepts as truth, reference, and the stability of interpretive contexts radically into question' if 'putting radically into question' means contesting that there *are* and that there *should be* truth, reference, and stable contexts of interpretation. I have – but this is something entirely different – posed questions that I hope are radical concerning the possibility of these things, of these values, of these norms, of this stability.
>
> (1988:150)

This does not 'destroy or contradict' truth, reference or context, but seeks to submit questions of truth, reference and context to 'the norms' that require 'one to prove, to demonstrate, to proceed correctly, to conform to the rules of language and to a great number of other social, ethical, political-institutional rules, etc.' (1988:150–1). What this does is raise the question of whether it would be OK to consider the context in which Derrida makes his comments – radical ones – as being that of a particular political milieu and trajectory in France, that of a particular reception of philosophy, of psychoanalysis and of Marxisms, and so on? To do this it will be necessary to consider Derrida's times of communication, and conveniently this is something about which he has offered ample evidence in interviews over the years (see below, and Chapter 5).

Is Derrida consistent when he talks of email and communications? Some years ago he said that in all communications that move from one to the other, the reference will invoke 'the tone of the other that is there but as having been there and before yet coming' – the presence is always already there and surely then also with email, although, as Derrida says, 'there is no certainty that man [sic] is the exchange of these telephone lines or the terminal of this endless computer' (1984:27):

> And if the despatches always refer to other despatches without decidable destination, the destination remaining to come, then isn't this completely angelic structure, that of the Johannine apocalypse, isn't it also the structure of every scene of writing as well? ... wouldn't the apocalyptic be a transcendental condition of all discourse, of all experience even, of every mark, of every trace? (1984:27)

Today, now, email transforms everything so that we 'can only dream or speculate' (Derrida 1995/1996:16) what a psychoanalysis equipped in the past with telematics would have looked like. Today, doesn't this imply, we must be in the presence of instant Freud? A Freud that was always already there when email arrived. What then for Marx? (Deutsche Telecom have an advertisement that shows Marx carved in stone, speaking on a mobile 'handy'-phone – the caption refers to the then-recent reunification of East and West Germany: 'which company catapulted an entire country from the stone age to the twentieth century?' Subtle, huh?).

## //derrida.marx.metaphors

Derrida on Marx. There are examples and they can be multiplied. When multiplying examples there can never be a point where the idiom of each can be generalised into a law or a proof – and Derrida often points out that there is not time to demonstrate conclusively. Yet, there are these examples to be taken into consideration: at the beginning of his career in America Derrida had made a point of marking his solidarity with anti-Vietnam war protesters in the US during a talk at an International Philosophy Colloquium in 1968 (Derrida 1972/1982). What is more interesting however is his specific relation to organised Marxist politics, and I want to get on to read this 'political Derrida' and specifically *Specters of Marx*. How does reading Marx – even if one reads the archive in an ordered and controlled way, and as he will say, 'so very late' – correspond to the party question, to that of the explicitly Political programme, and to Justice and to Democracy (to use the words that Derrida favours – I would lean towards redistributive justice and 'towards new democracy' if I were to use them at all).[12] It is convenient that there is a great deal in the chronicle of Derrida's interviews and occasional writings to discuss on these accounts. The first catalogue of comments can be grouped around the theme of justice. (Themes will necessarily interweave.)

In a footnote to *Archive Fever*, Derrida writes that his book on Marx, *Specters*, is an attempt to 'situate justice' as a 'resistance to forgetting', in relation to the law it exceeds and requires, and to memory (1995/1996:76n). Much earlier, in the essay 'Force of Law', Derrida sets out – he is again doing this arrival scene routine – 'to show why and how what is now called Deconstruction, while seeming not to "address" the problem of justice, has done nothing but address it, if only obliquely' (1992:10). In this essay, Derrida wants to demonstrate that this oblique is necessary and that 'one cannot speak directly about justice' without immediately betraying justice (1992:10). Alongside this I would want to recall another 'necessary' side-step – Derrida says it elsewhere – and it is a side-step, an 'oblique' that may suggest both the symptom and cure. Derrida says that he was reticent to speak among students and colleagues in that famous educational institute in Paris. It would be worth examining the displacements inaugurated in that place (if there were more time, perhaps, we could think of what Derrida says of educational institutions, and the power of institutions in general, in 'Mochloss'; Derrida 1987/1992), this silencing, this censure of the archive at a founding place of sorts.

It is possible that the ways of asking about politics pursued here are themselves countered already by Derrida's comments – to explicitly demand 'what is to be done?' with this is to miss the oblique, to circumvent the productive politics of oblique intervention that would be the preserve of the 'falls prey' public intellectual. To fall too quickly into sectarian evaluation without considering this possibility would not be open reading, and would not acknowledge the possibilities of complexity and strategy that could attend Derrida's own relation to the archive of political struggles. Already the demand excludes other possible readings....

Yet the task of questioning theory from the perspective of the somewhat naïve but necessary question 'what is to be done?' can never be finished, certainly not in this time of reaction and fragmentation. It would be an error to allow the question to be posed only in front of a fixed horizon. The timing of this question is also important: what is to be done and in what time is it to be done?

(Here the false horizon of Western triumphalism imagines that the time of socialism is over, except for a few recalcitrant Cubans, a billion Chinese and a few others – thus we hear of some very hasty readings.) We should ask about the timeliness of a reading. There are many questions. How useful is Derrida's protocol of reading Marx in *Specters* and elsewhere? Does it organise? Over what frame? Does it draw more people into an anti-capitalist politics? When? How is it open? For how long? What apprenticeship, if any, must be served (quite an exclusive one, it seems)? Does it further the kind of justice that is required? Now? Here? Surely justice must be that which tends towards a redistribution of the products of labour in a way that is equitable to all – glossed as 'to each according to their needs'? How long shall we wait for this (before realising again it must be taken)? To elaborate the detail on this gloss would be the task of an anti-capitalist politics, and this of course will also take time, and will not necessarily be prior to the revolutionary seizure of power, printing presses and philosophy. Nor will it be complete even then. There is only justice in that which opens the possibility of living to its fullest potential on the horizon of all lives. To each according to their possibilities, from each according to the effort to extend possibilities (how else might newness continue to enter the world for us?). Is this the justice that Derrida will name as 'to come' as he dreams of his talking cure? It must still be possible to evaluate a text against criteria of this sort, and alongside the question of what is to be done (with a text of this sort, with texts, with the archive and electronic mail).

The question can be broad – who is Derrida speaking to when he writes about Marx? About, near, almost … not quite? Spectres of Marx. What are the effects of this text (especially as taken up by activists?). This has consequences with regard to uses of the archive that are readily available as never before. Instead of a politics in the old and mundane sense – which surely should never be left innocent, which today, as much as ever, includes so many omissions, so many exclusions – Derrida's work inaugurates a new round of spiralling commentary, and 'scattered speculations' (Spivak 1985: 73–93). There is reason to applaud work which could release a whole host of studies of the metaphor in Marx, for example of the table which dances to market, of cold Marx in London dreaming of just how much time it takes to make a warm winter coat, or hungry Marx scheming for soup (he includes a soup recipe in *Capital*). These metaphorics are all very interesting, and perhaps have led a few people to read, maybe even return to read, Marx, but is this a contribution to international justice? Is this the best contribution? How useful is this contribution to those who find themselves already in the midst of struggles, and where metaphors do count in ways that have drastic socioeconomic and political consequences (everything from state-sponsored, government-authorised, media-circulated labelling of the 'underclass', 'terrorists', 'welfare cheats', 'drug-fiends', the indolent unemployed, etc., to the equally institutionalised descriptions and prescriptions of sociology, anthropology, psychology and disciplines as diverse as politics and philosophy through to physics and geology; above all cultural studies)?

If Derrida is to make a gesture towards the importance of a debt to Marx, and even to suggest that one should take up reading Marx, what does this mean for already engaged political groups? Is this a gesture that welcomes new recruits? Or is this an invitation to consider anew, from a refreshingly philosophical perspective; to reflect and deconstruct, the categories of politics, of justice, of engagement, and even of reading, in a debt to Marx? Is it a gesture to read Marx? Welcome to the archive, haven't we been here before?

Derrida's gesture is timely. He knows it, and says in an interview: 'today, when in France any reference to Marx has become forbidden, impossible, immediately catalogued, I have a real desire to speak about Marx, to teach Marx – and I will if I can'. He continues, reflecting upon the past and earlier texts which avoided Marx: 'at that time, though, I must have thought I could or should not. It perhaps would have been better if I had been able to devote to Marx a great study.... But who knows?' (Derrida and Sprinkler 1993:201). Later Derrida claims 'There is much more allegiance in avoidance than in explicit problematisation' (1993:208) – it is quite likely he means here both the debt to and avoidance of Heidegger by Althusser and other French intellectuals, and his own oblique debt-silence on Marx. In response to Sprinkler's interrogation Derrida later asserts: 'what allows you to say that a discourse like mine teaches Marx less than some other discourse that cites Marx at each page while neutralising, paralysing, doing nothing with him?' Said not to 'justify' himself, he claims that 'someone who knows how to read' his discourse will find that 'Marx is always there'. 'Marx is always immediately or virtually taken into account' (Derrida and Sprinkler 1993:218). It would be still interesting to examine this 'virtual Marx' alongside the medical pharmacological metaphors in this text (another beloved Derridean thematic) – the contagion, the paralysis, the deaths (discussed as spectres and forgotten Marx – a work of mourning here). And the cure or prescription. Derrida's ambition is 'greater than [that of] many Marxists' – he wants 'to call for a new reading of Marx' (Derrida and Sprinkler 1993:219).

But did Derrida avoid Marx, always attend to Marx, or just read too quickly? He gave a seminar on ideology and Marxism in 1976. There are many promises to engage, asides, footnotes and allusions. He will follow whoever can 'produce a new reading of Marx' that would 'understand modern economics and geopolitics' – he would 'subscribe to it with open arms' and 'with no reservations' – indeed, it is 'not certain' that he isn't already doing it himself (Derrida and Sprinkler 1993:220). Derrida is the Marxist of our times, although in his need for a new reading of Marx, 'everything must be revamped' (1993:229).

# 4
## Spectres

A new Marx? Revamped? Back from the dead? Let's cut to the chase – there are some problems relating to what I am sorely tempted to call 'the a-political tone recently adopted by Derrida'.[1] The full title is *Specters of Marx: The State of the Debt, the Work of Mourning and the New International*. The problems appear at the very moment when Derrida has (finally) (re)turned to Marx. Derrida does call it a return, and though he had promised it long ago, Gayatri Spivak has rightly quipped: 'when was ever the time to have left off reading Marx?' (1996). Derrida has anticipated, and writes: 'And if one interprets the gesture we are risking here as a belated-rallying-to-Marxism, then one would have to have misunderstood quite badly' (1993/1994:88). I want to read this 'gesture' and indeed I do think we 'have to' misunderstand in just this 'bad' way, to insist upon this misunderstanding so as to draw out consequences and politics, to insist upon a bad Marxism that will become clearer. It will also be possible to later show that even gesturing to a belated rallying Marxism is unlikely in Derrida's case.

What is the problem? Derrida proposes the foundation of a New International. I will want to argue that this call, which is an explicit call for an Internationalist 'politics', abruptly empties and simplifies where previous confrontations – say with the conservative Claude Lévi-Strauss, for example at the very moment when that author claims to be most anti-ethnocentric, or with hasty readings and denunciations, say, of Heidegger – called forth more. This recent Derrida however, if I were to call out some names, is a Social Democratic Derrida; Opportunist Derrida; Liberal, Universalist, Bourgeois Derrida. Of course, this is not about getting into a sectarian slagging match, but I do want to mark the possibility of reading a political practice into some of Derrida's early 'internationalist' work that now seems to resolve itself into only a new elite International. Where previously an inspiring critique could be found in Derrida's detailed readings, the concern of the newly proposed International with justice seems more rarefied and inaccessible – indeed, it could be open only to a cabal of well-trained and credentialled (frequent-flyer, internet-connected) experts in law. An anti-class, anti-proletarian, anti-party International might do for the shorthand critique of what Derrida proposes in *Specters of Marx*. Then, a book or two later, in *Archive Fever* the extension is to an International connected via the worldwide web.

In *Specters of Marx*, evoking ghosts of 1848 (the year of the publication, if not the writing, of the *Manifesto*), Derrida announces a new International that would be:

> ... without status, without title, and without name, barely public even if it is not clandestine, without contract, 'out of joint', without co-ordination, without party, without country ... without common belonging to a class. The name of new International is given here to what calls to the friendship of an alliance without institution among those who, even if they no longer believe in the Socialist-Marxist International, in the dictatorship of the proletariat ... [or in the] ... union of the proletarians of all lands, continue to be inspired by *at least one* [my emphasis] of the spirits of Marx or Marxism ... even if this alliance no longer takes the form of the party or of a workers' international, but rather of a kind of counter-conjuration, in the (theoretical and practical) critique of the state of international law, the concepts of State and nation, and so forth: in order to renew this critique, and especially to radicalise it.
>
> (Derrida 1993/1994:85–6)

The important words here are the alliance with just one of the spirits of Marxism (minimal programme), and this International's dismissal of the party, the class, the workers, the proletariat and of their 'union' in all lands (and thus, in all lands this will be 'barely public' – and we should remember that the 'entire public and private space of humanity' is to be transformed by email). In favour of an international critique of law and concepts, of the state 'and so forth', which would no doubt be worthy and worthwhile, but surely in favour too of a massive restriction of the scope and possibility of Marxism so much so that its internationalism becomes almost unrecognisable. Indeed, an avoidance of using, in this context, the c-word for the International (socialist, he says, not communist) – is it too hasty to read this as symptomatic of a non-Marxism, of a reduction sliding rapidly into renunciation of those who might still remain organised in the party-worker-communist forms? There is much in the way of rampant anti-Marxism and anti-Leninism about today, and surely Derrida would not want to further contribute to this. Yet, the Marx Derrida deals with seems to offer less even than the electronic archive. An International that gives up on institutionalising at the very moment of its constitution seems inadequate in the face of a recognition that justice must exceed its examples.

Why this particular International, from Derrida, at this time? Derrida elaborates on ten points, ten important points, which we will read soon, where he is telescoping telegraphically, his analysis of the contemporary state of Capital. Immediately after this introduction of the International, a moment after, he complains – and who should not find it worthy of complaint, indeed, why only now, after so many books he should find cause to mouth these words? – that the world is made up of 'innumerable singular sites of suffering' such that 'no degree of progress allows one to ignore that never before, in absolute figures, never have so many men, women and children been subjugated, starved, or exterminated on the earth' (Derrida 1993/1994:65 – with a parenthetical remembrance, in order to leave aside with regret, also the unavoidable question of what is becoming of so-called animal life; we will soon read another aside which similarly side-steps, in this case by way of 'not to mention the third world' [see ch. 3, note 6, this volume]. What is achieved by this oblique dismissive gesture with regard to reading, debts and time?). For Derrida here, progress, no degree of it, will ever allow him to ignore the innumerable and singular sites of suffering he sees under these ten signs. Although in relative terms, the percentage of peoples subjugated, starved or exterminated under the slavery, plantation and bonded labour period of colonialism might cause a revaluation of these figures, there is no doubt that the situation is dire. The world is fucked up. Conditions of despair; prospects appear slim. And this despite a good many previous ten-point programmes (indeed, these programmes of whatever number are markers of orthodoxy in various stripes). Yet, as Eugene Holland has pointed out, Derrida's ' "tableau" of current day catastrophes … owes little or nothing to Marxian analysis' (1997:manuscript). We are the heirs of Marx, and Holland points out that Derrida accepts this 'whether we like it or not' (1997, quoting Derrida: 'And whether we like it or not, whatever consciousness we have of it, we cannot not be its heirs' [1993/1994:91]). And what is inherited here is an unfulfilled 'messianic promise' which 'rushed headlong towards an ontological content' (1993/1994:91 – the double gesture of praise and condemnation will appear yet again). What is owed then by the heirs might be a question for some archival research, but urgency impinges here – the state of the debt is huge – does it matter that Derrida's debt to Marxism is settled only with the ghosted shadow of Marx? We have been taught, by Derrida among others, to be wary of those who enter into debt deals and the exchange of gifts – a gift is never a gift, but a counter-gift (see Part 4, on Bataille, in this volume).

But what are Derrida's ten buzzwords? Already thinking telematically, perhaps of email, he writes: 'If one were permitted to name these plagues of the "new world order" in a ten-word telegram, one might perhaps choose the following words' (1993/1994:81). Is he writing to Freud or to Marx? And why send a telegram to these voracious readers? Telecommunications today allows much vaster texts to be transmitted over the wires. Why truncate? Nevertheless, the words are: Unemployment, Homelessness, Economic War, Free Market, Foreign Debt, Arms Trade, Nuclear Weapons, Inter-ethnic Wars, Drug Cartels, International Law. Actually Derrida elaborates a paragraph on each of these, so it is more than a mere telegram, but not much. Was he pressed for time perhaps? We will read this correspondence more closely still.

We should ask what work is to be done by these ten words that are telescoped here as the analysis of contemporary capitalism in so few pages.

Surely the point is clear that this is not going to do the trick, that this proposed International, however new, is not enough. A critique, even a very accessible (ten-word) analysis, is inadequate to pose a challenge at this time. Does this mean nothing can be done? Ah, but asking what is to be done may be going too fast here (that way lies 'bad' Marxism, or what Derrida characterises as the 'fatalistic idealism or abstract and dogmatic eschatology' [1993/1994:87] of previously existing Marxisms). It is important to slow down, to resist the tendency to read too quickly, to comment too fast, to chatter. The thing is, though, how should we deal with speed and technology? Must we side with Derrida in a kind of educated despair and go running off to Freud for help? (Derrida pauses to email Freud; for that matter he also wants to chat with Marx's ghost, still waiting to talk with the dead, and so speak with the class inflections of Hamlet.)

What is in the in-tray? Still those ten words from *Specters of Marx*. Derrida's point is also, insightfully, that changes in the way we archive things changes the things – or rather, the translation is 'what is no longer archived in the same way is no longer lived in the same way' (Derrida 1995/1996:18). For me, this recalls the scene in *Of Grammatology* where an older (younger) Derrida discusses the violence of naming, where Lévi-Strauss is complicit in a transgression that reveals the secrets of the Nambikwara, and that these secrets, though the anthropologist does not notice and Derrida must point it out, reveal that the Nambikwara already have a kind of writing (in the general sense) since they can erase the proper name. What does this scene say of Derrida's proclamation of a new International that keeps, as a sort of secret, only one Marx among many, and fails, except as displacement, to mention previous Internationals – as many as four contend, perhaps more, and who could forget the Situationist International? – while naming, or archiving, the analysis and struggle against capitalism in too-swift decimal code?

What follows is a commentary[2] on the ten-word telegram.

## UNEMPLOYMENT

Under this sign Derrida wants to rename labour and production, as well as saying that 'unemployment' perhaps deserves another name today. For him 'tele-work' in the deregulated context of 'new market, new technologies, new world-wide competitiveness' is something that 'perturbs both the methods of traditional calculation and the conceptual opposition between work and non-work, activity, employment, and their contrary' (1993/1994:81). What methods of traditional calculation were these if not, for at least one Marx, the calculations of the labour theory of value, and of 'unpaid time', necessary labour time, surplus, etc. As Antonio Negri among others has shown, the labour theory of value was elaborated alongside concepts such as real and formal subsumption (Negri 1991; see also Marx 1858/1973) which happen to come in very handy for thinking about the relations between work and non-work, and the recruitment of social relations and non-work time increasingly to the imperatives of the commodity economy (be this the recruitment of existing pre-capitalist-transition social forms to labour – say, the employment of local chiefs by colonial administrations, formal subsumption – or the generation, increasingly evident, of social forms exclusive to capitalist societies, say, yuppie households, real subsumption). Similarly, the analysis of prostitution, housework, the home and women's labour as unpaid contribution to capitalist production in the work of Leopoldina Fortunati deserves close attention. (She writes:

> Under the pressure of the feminist struggles and those of other
> non-directly waged groups, some sections of the male left were forced
> to realise and acknowledge that non-directly waged work not only
> existed but also that the struggles against it were at least as relevant as
> those of the directly waged working class. [Fortunati 1981/1995:95])

In all this the notion of 'unemployment' has long been more complicated, and already in Marx, than conventional usages might presume. There would be scope to rethink the position of the 'reserve
army of labour' in the context of telematic skills (not just the curious
stories of *wunderkind* youth hacking into corporate systems and
gaining prestige programmer jobs for their efforts, but also the transferability of keyboard skills from Nintendo to check-out register, etc. –
all this in the context of the social factory argument of Negri and
autonomous Marxism, and complicated by its differential refraction
across different parts of the planetary work machine).[3] The trouble is
that for Derrida unemployment is 'like suffering' only it 'suffers still
more' in being social inactivity whose 'habits, models and language
are lost' – a situation which calls for 'another politics'. What other
politics, however, would this be? The unemployed will not be the
ones best placed to organise within Derrida's International. The other
politics Derrida offers is a concern which laments the suffering of the
reserve army, a kind of moralism, which could not be called Marxist
at all. For the record, the role of the 'new technologies' Derrida names
was already calculated in Marx in the context of time, especially
where he writes of 'the creation of a large quantity of disposable time
apart from necessary labour time' (Marx 1858/1973:708). The analysis which looks at the extent to which 'general social knowledge'
becomes a 'direct force of production', and the degree to which 'the
conditions of the process of social life itself have come under the control of the general intellect' (Marx 1858/1973:706) also indicates how
'free time for a few' is also the theft of free time from the many, making it evident that 'the mass of workers must themselves appropriate
their surplus labour' (Marx 1858/1973:708).

## HOMELESSNESS

A 'new experience of frontiers and identity' is heralded by the racist
expulsions and immigration laws of fortress Europe. I would hope that

Derrida does not here propose new monographs on the social construction of the frontier or the video-graphic invention of identity. It is enough that identity politics already has its internal police and boundary patrols. In France, even movie stars take up the political struggle of those 'without papers' (see the work of the organisation '*sans-papiers*', but also remember Bennington's photo of Derrida calling for 'the vote' at the Mutualité in 1989)[4] – an extension of this politics would work for the abolition of all immigration controls and not only by means of the parliamentary experiment and the right to vote – if capital can move freely, why should not labour also insist? There has never been a better time for the call to open all borders, introducing a rather more libratory 'new experience'.[5] It might be worth considering the archive of the political frontier here in the most public operation of the law – the police – and especially the immigration cops. Are 'identity' and 'the frontier' political for more than one reason? It might be suggested that Derrida engages with a kind of mental policing of bounded language that is endemic in western metaphysics and more. On the Police – and there will be reason to go back to this crime scene again and again – Derrida says there are police and police: this is something like the double cop show of the police with truncheons and the police in our heads. Derrida knows there are police who are 'brutally and rather physically repressive', but these police are never purely physical, and there 'are more sophisticated police that are more "cultural" or "spiritual" ... every institution designed to enforce the law is a police' (1988:135). Here Derrida would even say the Academy is a police (much Althusserian ISA [ideological state apparatuses] here). Derrida does not want to say that the police as such 'are "politically" suspect' or that 'the very project of attempting to fix the contexts of utterances' would be (1988:135). (Why not?) Though the hint is there in this clarification, and he points out that the police are 'never neutral either, never apolitical'. Derrida asserts that there 'is no society without police' and reserves only the possibility of a dream (send for Freud) where one could imagine 'forms of police that would be more sublime, more refined and less vulgar' (1988:135).[6]

## ECONOMIC WAR

It would not be too hard to proclaim a return to analysis of an interstate system that can be described in terms not far removed from those provided by Lenin, Luxemburg, Bukharin in so many texts, generally called 'imperialism'. With 'the ruthless war among countries of the European Community', between them and 'the Eastern European countries' and of course between 'Europe and the United States, and between Europe, the United States, and Japan' (Derrida 1993/1994:81), is it any surprise that squabbles for opportunities to profit amongst these blocs have knock-on and knock-down effects in other theatres? The point, predictably enough, would not be to reproduce the 'highest stage of capitalism' thesis mimeographically, but to look to the continuities between these moments, interrupted perhaps by the New Deal, the Marshall Plan, the Cold War and the 1960s, so as to recognise the logic of capital and its crisis, the competition between imperialist powers within a system of broad agreement – that is, that there is no alternative to the market – and the destabilisation and danger that the current conjuncture provides. Amidst this, to be enamoured with the 'newness' of the new world order is akin to being fascinated with the blurring speed of information technology, and doing nothing about it. Is it that imperial rivalry has intensified, or rather that the density of information has disrupted perspectives on very common processes – so that the change is not so much in time, but in depth? This topic inevitably leads on to the next two categories, but I cannot see how complaints about the 'inconsistent and unequal application of international law' (Derrida) would offer any constraint upon imperialism.

## FREE MARKET

Derrida writes here of 'The inability to master the contradictions in the concepts, norms, and reality of free market.' Capitalist states protect their own workers from cheap labour 'which often has no comparable protection' (1993/1994:81). The question he asks here is 'How is one to save one's own interests in the global market while claiming to protect one's "social advantages" and so forth?' (1993/1994:81–2). First and foremost the imperative to expand is the context:

> The need of a constantly expanding market for its products chases the bourgeoisie over the entire surface of the globe. It must nestle everywhere, settle everywhere, establish connections everywhere.
>
> (Marx and Engels 1948/1952 *The Manifesto of the Communist Party*; quoted from <http://csf.Colorado.EDU/psn/marx/Admin>)

But more complicated than this, the expansion must be continually reconfigured and renewed, and is renewed through the brutal self-cannibalising tendencies analysed in Lenin's *Imperialism* and other such texts. This can be found in *Capital* too. The theory of crisis, in the classical Marxist sense, would allow an understanding of the imperative of the 'global market' as an attempt to circumvent the crisis of declining rate of profit through a new round of transformation of the means of production. The competitiveness and destructive creativity (the mergers, sell-offs, buy-outs and dismantlings) that this entails are only the outward signs of crisis. In the centres of capital the process is ruthless – it amounts to the trashing of an old mode of production and its institutional forms (and in the West we have seen, for example, the university well and truly trashed in terms of its old collegiate mode, made anew into a factory of commercial application, selling overseas education to Third World elites, at ever increasing cost and with scholarship transformed into an entertainment forum with conference stages graced by jet-set intellectual superstars). From the detritus of this trashed mode of production in the 'advanced' sectors – any still viable component parts are transferred overseas – there arise new attempts, via technological innovation, to institute forms of working, of production and of manufacture that can renew profitability, capture and deploy considerably greater proportions of surplus value, and, through dextrous and/or brutal reconfigurations of market relations, return advantage to those capitalists with foresight and vision enough to exploit the opportunities within the crisis.

This directly impinges on the speed question, and on how Marx shows, in *The Poverty of Philosophy* how time really does equal money. Despite increased circulation, the process of capital accumulation and expansion still operates. We would still need to evaluate the analysis of capital Marx provides, but we certainly do not want to forget it. While he notes that the 'improvement of the means of communication and transportation cuts down absolutely the wandering period of the commodities', so that goods circulate from workplace to market, and profits return to the capitalist more quickly, this 'does not eliminate the relative difference in the time of circulation of different commodity-capitals arising from peregrinations, nor that of different portions of the same commodity-capital which migrate to different markets' (1893/1974:252). Marx's example is simple, but clear – improved sailing vessels and steamships, for instance, shorten travelling time for both near and distant ports. He also recognises that 'a railway which leads from a place of production to an inland centre of population may relatively or absolutely lengthen the distance to a nearer inland point not connected by rail, as compared to one that is geographically remote' (Marx 1893/1974:253). Today, this train example would still apply in some regions, as would this matter also with regard to access to aviation, and even to the telephone, not to mention internet and satellite televisual services. Marx notes that absolute velocity need not necessarily increase because of the frequency of improved transport or communication, but that by spreading the return of invested capital over several successive periods of time, 'the total time of circulation and hence also the turnover [of capital] are abridged' (1893/1974:254). What is important for Marx is the recognition that because of this facilitation, capital accumulates in fewer and fewer hands as circulation gives 'rise to quicker concentration of both the centres of production and the markets' (1893/1974:254). The improvement of the means of communication and transportation in turn makes it imperative 'to work for ever more remote markets, in a word – for the world market' (1893/1974:255). In other terms, improved communications and transportation allow capital to extend its uneven development across the globe. This never happens without the participation of a large amount of living labour power, in the form of skilled technicians, manufacturers, management, worker support staff (doing housework etc.) and so on, who are also part of the facilitation and communication process, if in an alienated way (this would include professors of philosophy extolling the virtues of email). The various characteristics of this expansion are what remain to be analysed. Indeed, this hardly differs from the research programme already set out for the membership of the first Workers' International over 150 years ago.

In that work Marx and Engels formulated a paragraph that can be read in many contexts, but deserves certain emphasis here:

> The bourgeoisie, by the rapid improvement of all the instruments of production, *by the immensely facilitated means of communications,* draws all, even the most barbarian nations into civilisation. The cheap prices of its commodities are the heavy artillery with which it batters down all Chinese walls, with which it forces the barbarians' intensely obstinate hatred of foreigners to capitulate. It compels all nations, on pain of extinction, to adopt the bourgeois mode of production; it compels them to introduce what it calls civilisation into their midst, i.e., to

become bourgeois themselves. In a word, it creates a world after its own image.

(Marx and Engels 1848/1952: 47, my emphasis)

Interestingly, the 'immensely facilitated' means of communication of the English translation might also be rendered more strongly when translated as 'infinite release' – the *'unendlich erleichterten'* (Marx and Engels 1848/1970: 47) suggests also the release of a never-ending opening of communications that already anticipates the continually developing communications environment characteristic of the information order today. The idiom of translation has its effects.

In these broad circumstances, worrying about 'social protection' for the workers in the cheap labour sites to which manufacturing moves, does not in itself disrupt the liberalism that 'cares' about the 'Third World' while primarily protecting 'one's' own 'social advantages' and 'interests in the global market' (Derrida 1993/1994:81). Social protection for all is a transitional demand, it easily becomes an 'historic compromise' if left only there. Pointing out that the interests of capital are to reduce the necessary costs of production is not new, but this does not mean that the struggle should be only to increase those costs with 'protection'. It is worth remembering Marx's critique of the limits of trade union demands to improve conditions and wages as being insufficiently revolutionary. Old Beardo at his best; in the essay on 'Wages, Prices and Profit' of 1865, a speech delivered just two years before the publication of volume 1 of *Capital*, Marx calls upon workers and trade unions to do more than lobby for higher wages, to demand as well the abolition of the exploitative system:

> ... the working class ought not to exaggerate to themselves the ultimate working of these everyday struggles [for higher wages etc.]. They ought not to forget that they are fighting with effects, but not with the causes of those effects; they are retarding the downward movement, but not changing its direction ... [and let there be no mistake of Marx's words, he writes in English] ... they ought to inscribe on their banner the revolutionary watchword: 'Abolition of the wages system!'
>
> (Marx 1898/1950:404)

If, through the workings of Derrida's new International, some 'comparable social protection' were extended from Europe and generalised to the Third World, would this mean liberation or accommodation? Labour time would still be thieved.

## THIRD WORLD DEBT

The aggravation of the foreign debt and other commercial mechanisms is starving or driving to despair a large portion of humanity.
(Derrida 1993/1994:82)

Derrida's comment on foreign debt also suffers a similar limit, and
emotion. Clearly starvation and despair are (IMF/World Bank-
induced) horrors for that 'large portion of humanity' subject to
debt, but a resolution that would enable debtor nations to participate (again) in an extended market does not seem much different
than the contradictory 'discourse of democratisation' Derrida also
mentions. Of course we should be against the debt, but beyond can-
celling the debts, go further, the entire debt system must be abolished. Wiping the slate (or mystic writing pad) clean does not of
itself do anything but inaugurate a new round of repayments. The
debt crisis is not just the aggravation that some countries – in the
'Third World', the 'banana republic' economies, etc. – are in debt,
and massive unpayable debt at that. Derrida's anti-debt call is a
mode of reckoning that accepts the system that creates debts, and
condemns those with debt economies, which is to say, those, more
often than not, whose comprador elites sold whole populations into
the cycle of increasing poverty and if they were lucky (!) wage slavery. This isolates such countries according to the very logic of the
debt, and its inverse, credit (also, no doubt, aggravating). Isolating
and dividing, this logic still accepts the system of colonial plunder,
the extension of credits to re-finance the corporations that operate
this plunder, and the slave–profiteer, exploiter–exploited dualisms,
which are perhaps the most successful exports of European economic science. Those who call for debt cancellation ask too little.

## ARMS TRADE

The arms trade can be shown as intricately implicated in the global
economic calculation. What is interesting in Derrida's paragraph is
recognition of the role of 'the cutting edge of tele-technological
sophistication', which is 'inscribed in the normal regulation of scientific research' (1993/1994:82). The opening of research 'normalisation' to questions of the morality or politics of arms trafficking and so
on is worthwhile, but could be more succinctly, and more provoca-
tively put in the question 'Is Your University an Arm of the State?' as

one sloganeer did some years ago. Why is it an 'unimaginable revolution' (1993/1994:82) that would suspend or cut back (or, imagine it, end) the arms trade? It is not fear of unemployment that forces Western democracies into the mad science of telematic death rays et cetera. The socialisation of labour to which Derrida refers already calculates the unemployed time of workers, as well as that allocated in the secret labs for weapons research, manufacture and deals. That the arms trade is equated by Derrida with drug deals is merely moralistic and does not necessarily qualify (too strict a requirement? Derrida is claiming a 'spirit' and paying a debt isn't he?) as a Marxist point.

## NUCLEAR WEAPONS

Conjuring with the bomb has often been a vehicle for liberalism. A slippage continually evident in the words of those who, like Derrida, worry about the general danger of nuclear proliferation being 'out of control' to those who would impose sanctions and interventions on places like North Korea under some red-baiting scare-mongering while ignoring the role of the US as the one country that has actually dropped the bomb on really existing people, and never, to this day, made any apology. Derrida suggests that 'the spread ("dissemination") of nuclear weapons ... is no longer even controllable, as was the case for a long time, by statist structures' (1993/1994:82). I do not know that dissemination here affiliates Derrida's work with proliferation – though it certainly does proliferate, but it is very evident to me, at least, that it was precisely these statist structures that were the impetus for the massive accumulation of nuclear arsenals in the first place. Shorn of control, these structures initiated the 'spread' beyond all possible ad hoc or covert possibilities. Without an organised state-sponsored nuclear industry there would be nothing like the scale of planetary threat that we live with, constantly, today. In this, the nuclear capability of North Korea, India, Pakistan or even that media-villain Saddam Hussein,[7] is relatively insignificant compared to the currently primed and armed warheads of the US, NATO and CIS (Commonwealth of Independent States). What will Derrida suggest as a mechanism of 'control' today – his International? The UN? (We will see a pro-UN stance below).

## INTER-ETHNIC WARS

From the bomb to the culture-bomb, and tales of blood and nation. Referring to inter-ethnic conflict Derrida asks if the notion of community – he means ethnic community – is not 'made more outdated than ever … by tele-technological dis-location' (1993/ 1994:82). The 'process of dislocation' has accelerated and 'spread in an unheard-of fashion' (unheard of = uncanny?) such that what is new is that dislocation is now 'acceleration itself, beyond the norms of speed that have until now informed human culture' (1993/1994:82). Although this unheard-of speeding culture of dislocation was always there in the originary moment of stabilisation – of ethnicity, of community – as 'all national rootedness, for example, is rooted first of all in the memory and anxiety of a displaced or displaceable population' (1993/1994:83). Here the confusion is one of whether displacement is always the condition of sedentarisation and stability – as an always present threat of dissolution – and whether, because of tele-technological dislocation, acceleration and unheard-of speeds, a new condition, beyond the norm of community, makes dislocation not only 'what gives the movement its start' (1993/1994:83), but its condition. Can we have it both ways? Does it not seem rather that dislocation has always been mediated by tele-technological flows and the violences and appropriations, thefts, pain, remain the same? I have in mind displacements and ethnicities born of slavery, of labour migration, of colonial and imperialist empire building. And also of the mediation of technology in the writing lesson among the Nambikwara, where the use of writing to appropriate goods is the cause of disbanding a community (is this Lévi-Strauss's, as well as Derrida's, primal scene?). In these calculations, the violence is unheard-of only because of an operation of an archiving censor, which according to an ethnocentric code, edits contexts to suit remembrances. What is new, for Derrida, is only the acceleration, but if the norms could be shown to circulate still at these greater velocities, would that be accelerated culture? Paul Gilroy's discussions in *The Black Atlantic: Modernity and Double Consciousness* (1993) would demonstrate that the tele-technological is not the condition of the 'outdating' of community, and indeed can increasingly be the condition of its maintenance.[8] The point here being that there is not a totalising logic or a singular velocity to this technology and its impact on the ways people organise, however much Derrida's chosen words proclaim the transformation of the '*entire* public and private space of *humanity*' and 'the norms of speed that have informed *human culture*' (my emphasis). (Was the arrival of syphilis among the Nambikwara a slower viral decimation than that promised by email?)

## DRUG CARTELS

Thomas Pynchon has a group of men running down the lanes of Aspen in full riot gear chanting 'War on drugs, war on drugs' in one of his novels (*Vineland* 1990). This slapstick moment would be sufficient criticism if it were not that the spectral existence of these cartels is of more importance, and less, than Derrida allows. He singles out narcotics and the Mafia, but narco-traffic is no more than a flourishing form of capitalist trade, and why does the spectral character of the Mafioso scare him more than the legal variants known as cartels – for example the Oppenheimer/RTZ nexus in mining, or Murdoch in the media? Such cartels and their spectrality might make it relevant to retrieve a distinction that is glossed over in the telegraphing action of *Specters* – in 'Force of Law', Derrida noted that the state would not fear crimes of a certain restricted code:

> ... what the state fears ... is not so much crime or *brigandage*, even on the grand scale of the Mafia or heavy drug traffic, as long as they transgress the law with an eye towards particular benefits, however important they may be. The state is afraid of fundamental, founding violence, that is, violence able to justify, to legitimate.

This fear is the fear of the revolutionary violence that would overthrow the state, through the general strike, as Derrida discusses with regard to Benjamin and Germany in 1921 – 'all revolutionary discourses ... justify the recourse to violence by alleging the founding, in progress or to come [this phrase again], of a new law' (1992:35).

The drug cartels follow the same logic as all expansive capitalism, calculating profit and loss et cetera. A numbers game. On the calculation of profits – although some parts of volume 2 of *Capital* may be deemed unhelpful and even obsolete by some for an analysis of today's capital (even Engels points out that Marx's sums were often wrong – he 'did not get the knack of handling figures' [Engels in Marx 1893/1974:287]), it is still the case that we should not be too quick to mistake development of scale or tempo as transition or change.

Are there still no clear reasons why we cannot plan redistribution at system-wide equitable levels that assure prosperity and quality for all? The 'new law' founded on a violence that was sufficient to overturn the cartels would quite likely still need to utilise spreadsheets to do away with the alienating and conflictual necessity of continuous competition over the 'size and distribution of the fruits of surplus labour' (Resnick and Wolff 1995:210) – and why couldn't optimal productive power be made to obey the directives of a well thought out plan? Not just a planned economy schemed up in empty halls of power, but a system-wide participatory redistribution by all for all (including free quality drugs 'perhaps'). Of course, from here this demands something more than the usual social movements, education programmes, street protests, party mobilisations and international solidarities – but this 'more' should not be impossible, merely necessary, possibly violent (and time-consuming?), but adequate.

The need for redistribution can still be understood by working through Marx's old categories. The falling rate of profit is a consequence of a simple mechanism that remains comprehensible even in the heightened media environment of the present. Capitalists still drive towards raising productivity levels. First of all by trying to undercut their competitors, capture a greater slice of the market, and so increase their income from sales. Here is the scenario that can be glossed as 'shopping as civil war', where the search for the cheapest price by shoppers (workers) means that the capitalist with the lowest overheads (and hence who pays workers the worst rates) gains market dominance. Oftentimes productivity increases arrive by means of technological innovation and transformation – where new technologies and machineries are deployed per worker, but since the source of profit is by means of the exploitation of the (surplus) labour of the workers themselves, the obvious way in which this proceeds is by paying workers far less in wages than the value that is produced through their labour. The capitalist must attempt to get more surplus relative to costs so as to increase 'productivity'. This refers back to the problematic discussed under the earlier point 'Free Market'. In the expansion that is entailed in technologically driven productivity increases, the base of investment relative to exploitable labour (that which can be appropriated as surplus over costs) necessarily is relatively less. Profits are measured as the rate of surplus extracted relative to total investment in equipment, raw materials and labour, and as the enterprise necessarily expands, the rate tends to fall. The rounds of restructuring and reconversion of boom and bust counteract this tendency only to a degree; the general rule applies – though perhaps not ever in the cold light of the 'last instance' – which as Althusser points out, never comes. Nevertheless, it is still possible to examine the specificities of this tendency and to cite empirical examples where productivity and profit levels do not expand fast enough to maintain continued rounds of investment and so recession and contraction emerge in the form, first of all, of increased taxation, state subsidies to flagging industries, cuts to spending (for example the end of the welfare state) and, second (though perhaps this first and second ordering is fictitious), in the allocation of credit mechanisms, which permit centralisation, consolidation and avoidance of the immediate and impending constraints upon profitability. What is crucial in all of this is the time of circulation, the time of expansion, reinvestment and reconversion, and the time of credit, boom, merger, take-over and bust. It is exactly the times of circulation that Marx examined in *Capital* that are so relevant for an analysis today. The struggle is still about time and it is quite clear: we want to liberate time from wage slavery. The bosses want to extend surplus labour time. This conflict consumes the world.

## INTERNATIONAL LAW

'Despite a fortunate perfectibility, despite an undeniable progress' – Derrida has some generous things to say about international law 'above all, above all' (1993/1994:83), and sees the limit only in an allegiance to 'certain European philosophical concepts' and a 'universalism' dominated by 'particular nation states'. Here 'techno-economic and military power' already ensures certain decisions, and commits the international bodies – the United Nations for example – to play the role of enforcer. The 'incoherence, discontinuity, inequality of States before the law, and the hegemony of certain states' is not enough, for Derrida, to 'disqualify' international institutions. He says 'Justice demands, on the contrary, that one pay tribute to certain of those who are working within them in the direction of the perfectibility and emancipation of institutions that must never be renounced' (1993/1994:84). But is it enough to 'remain vigilantly on guard against the manipulations or appropriations' to which such good works can be subjected? There are already too many in the UN who have 'radicalised' the notion of the state and law as Derrida's new International will do. However dedicated and well-intentioned the efforts of 'certain of those' who have made 'undeniable progress' (but let me be so crass as to deny it) working within the frameworks of international law, talk of paying tribute and of permanent organisations, which 'can never be renounced', makes Derrida an apologist for a series of bodies – the Bretton Woods organisations, the IMF, World Bank, etc. – that it would be very difficult to defend from the point of view of those receiving international attention in the form of structural adjustments, UN 'peace-keeping' enforcement and the international debt system (not just the debts, the whole debtor system). Immediately after providing these alibis Derrida turns to propose his new International. There is much that could be said about the temporal disjunctions that would need to be considered in the workings of such international bodies, in the role of their legislations in regulating, often brutally, the 'free' time of international marketeering, and, no less, in the relation of such a tele-technological international to what Marx called the 'general intellect', as deployed as a means of social co-ordination (see earlier under 'Unemployment'). Among all that is proposed, and conjured with, in Derrida's Spectrology, perhaps most untimely of all, is the suggestion that a defence of the UN, IMF/World Bank, et cetera, operates in the name of some 'spirit' (apparition, not to be believed, illusion, ghostbusters needed) of Marxism.

# 5
# Struggles

//derrida.in.moscow/stalinism/the-party-question

It matters. What is it that allows a telegraphed, programmatic analysis in a book on Marx in a way that Marx is not necessary for the analysis? It may be useful in this regard to explore the archival traces of Derrida's relation to Marx and the programme.

In an 'occasional piece' written on return from a brief ten-day trip, Derrida talks about travel stories and sketches his own 'phantom narrative' – a ghost here – that reads Benjamin and Gide alongside his visit to Moscow. Amidst this discussion, he also reflects upon the party:

> ... to specify a 'background': I shall soon have to describe in what respect, even though I have never been either a Marxist or a communist, stricto senso, even though, in my youthful admiration for Gide, I read at fifteen (1945) his *Back from the USSR*, which left no doubt as to the tragic failure of the Soviet Revolution and today still seems to me a remarkable, solid and lucid work and even though, later, in Paris in the 1950s and 1960s, I had to resist – and it was not easy – a terrifying politico-theoretical intimidation of the Stalinist or neo-Stalinist type in my most immediate personal and intellectual environment, this never kept me from ...
>
> (Derrida 1993:211)

Let me interrupt here to note, before we see what Derrida is leading us to, and how he categorises it, the list of a 'never'-Marxist, who already at 15 years of age had confirmed that the revolution was a tragic failure, and who personally (at college, in his classes) had to resist an intimidation by Stalinists. The overdetermination here seems excessive, but still, despite this, Derrida has kept, I resume the citation, a 'romantic relation with the Soviet Union', which, we hear, takes a musical and lyrical form:

> I am always bowled over when I hear the *Internationale*, I tremble with emotion and then I always want to 'go out on the streets' [these are Derrida's quotation marks, and they would indicate a feint] to fight against the reaction.

> (Derrida 1993: 211)

Here we have Derrida as a squaddie.[1] The repetition – from 1990 – of a familiar narrative of anti-Stalinist, anti-party 'struggle' can be found here in the not-'Marxist' who sings the 'Internationale' and wants to fight.

Michael Ryan began his book *Marxism and Deconstruction* by saying that 'Millions have been killed because they were Marxists; no one will be obliged to die because s/he is a deconstructionist' (1982:1). This may or may not be accurate, not because the first clause is false – it is all too horribly true[2] – but because perhaps some may be obliged to die through neglect because of the second clause also. Despite the oblique, Derrida has said he is not a Marxist or a communist in the strict sense – though Ryan reported that Derrida had said he was a communist during one of the GREPH seminars of 1976 (on Gramsci) (1982:xiv). The strict sense of being a communist suggests a host of problems for bad Marxism; to do with discipline, the party, commitment to a certain practice, a shared level of theoretical and principled agreement, a theoretical and practical obligation to collective will – to those things it would seem Derrida would call dogma or doctrine and would separate and forget: dictatorship of the proletariat, class struggle, dialectical and materialist method. Today, in the face of the ten catastrophes and more, the question of organisation, the need for (party) discipline (even in the party of the new type), the need for, at least, coordination of struggles.... All this suggests that at some point a strict discipline must be considered. (This does not mean that Derrida must be first up against the wall, but rather that the question must be discussed.)

What has Derrida said explicitly on his relation to the party? I am not particularly interested in whether or not Derrida signed a membership form – the issue is about what is useful in the struggle against capital. For certain, close reading and a vigilant watching over metaphor, meaning and context can be learnt from no better teacher than Derrida. But a 'practical politics of the open end', as I think Spivak called it, seems to be beyond this version – Capital is far more serious, now more than ever, for us to forget that the struggle must actually be fought (grimly, but let us not always frown). Metaphors need to be fashioned into the keys to unlock the armoury – I just hope we can remember to smile like Derrida does in the Bennington photographs.

Derrida's affiliation to the party question might be considered a non-issue in evaluating his commentary on Marx (there is more to political engagement than reading groups and paper sales), yet there is considerable commentary on Derrida's relation to party politics that must be considered, which sheds a certain light on his current internationalism and in some respects is of interest with regard to the history of the party question in France. In an interview with one of the editors of a conference volume, and *festschrift* of sorts, to Louis Althusser, Derrida provides reminiscences on his early career and the political scene surrounding Althusser and company in the 1950s and 1960s. Derrida's friendship with Althusser is demonstrated – Derrida gave a funeral oration, also included in the book – and this friendship was always very good, 'affectionate even (it has always remained so, even through some later shockwaves)' (Derrida and Sprinkler 1993:185). From the beginning Althusser was instrumental in Derrida's intellectual career, he was his teacher at the École Normale Supérieure from 1952.

Derrida's work for his first *agrégation* paper was for Althusser and the topic was time – the problem of genesis in Husserl. Althusser sent it to Foucault to get his opinion, saying it was too difficult, too dangerous, to grade. Foucault said it was either a fail or an A+. Of such origins legends are made.... Later, Althusser invited Derrida to give courses at the École, and supported his promotion to his own old position as *caîman* (director of study), and the two were colleagues for 20 years. Derrida began teaching a course on Heidegger at the time when Althusser began the seminars that were to give rise to *For Marx* and *Reading Capital*, and although Derrida's relations with Balibar, Rancière and other students who took both classes were good, he 'felt quite ill-at-ease' and 'marginalised' when Althusser's seminar 'captivated all the attention of those students' (Derrida and Sprinkler 1993:187).

Derrida did attend one or two sessions of Althusser's seminar, but his attitude is clear in this excerpt from the interview:

> However, from the philosophical point of view, I felt as if I were in an embarrassing situation. The whole problematic seemed to me necessary,

no doubt, within the Marxist field, which was also a political field, marked in particular by the relation with the Party of which I was not a member and which was slowly moving away from Stalinism (and which, while I was a student there, moreover, dominated in a very tyrannical manner). Yet at the same time I found that problematic – I wouldn't say naive or lacking in culture, far from that – but too insensitive to critical, transcendental, and ontological questions which then seemed to me necessary.

(Derrida and Sprinkler 1993:187)

It is worth noting in passing, the rhythm of this passage ('the text of the interview was left largely as it was spoken, Derrida mostly in French, Sprinkler almost exclusively in English' preamble): the *fort/da* of this text moves from the 'however' of embarrassment to recognition of the necessity, marked by the limit of being 'within' a political context, that Derrida did not share, perhaps because it was only now moving away from Stalinism, and which had been tyrannical for Derrida as a student, yet 'at the same time' the problematic was not quite uncultured, but was insensitive. Some might take this as a vacillation that tends towards a red-scare. But Derrida continues in this way without noting the danger.

He suggests that he was paralysed before them because he did not want his questions 'to be taken as crude and self-serving criticisms connected with the Right or Left – in particular with the communist party'. Although he says 'their discourse seemed to me to give way to a theoreticism or a new fangled scientism' he knew that such questioning could be used as an accusation and used 'in quite summary fashion' by the party against Althusser, who was conducting a struggle against 'a terrifying dogmatism or philosophical stereotypism within the Party'. This language of terror and use of phrases like 'in summary fashion' suggests a certain tone, one of executions, to which Derrida would be 'the last to subscribe'. Indeed, within the 'limits of its context' the struggle seemed quite necessary (Derrida and Sprinkler 1993:188). He even calls his paralysis 'a political gesture' – he 'did not want to raise questions that would have appeared anti-Marxist' (Derrida and Sprinkler 1993:192), and claims, no doubt with good reason, that in the milieu of the time any objection at all would be taken as anti-communism. (Although Althusser's struggle within the party did not stumble in the same ways.)

Derrida is repeatedly interested in the dynamics of a double movement that has many ramifications, and not always ones he can escape himself. When he writes: 'We all have an idiosyncratic way of working, reading, not reading, of reading without reading, not reading while reading, to avoid without avoiding, to deny' (Derrida and Sprinkler 1993:190), he introduces another theme that has preoccupied his own commentaries on others – for example Lévi-Strauss's to and fro, give and take, tribute to Mauss and more.

In April 1989 Derrida reflects upon the period of the 1960s and says: 'I did read Marx, you know... . I did not read him enough. One never reads enough Marx' (Derrida and Sprinkler 1993:195). He reads many Marxes: 'I told myself "OK, Marx's text is heterogeneous like all texts" ' (Derrida and Sprinkler 1993:195) and reads against the Althusserian bifurcated early and late Marx and points out that to break in two homogenises on both sides (how does this relate to the taking of sides discussed in *Given Time*?). The assertion is that the Althusserian division of Marx homogenises as a 'ruse of dialectics' – against this, Sprinkler objects that Althusser is noting that the problematic changes, rather than suggesting that Marx ceases to be humanist at the point of the break. Derrida seems to stereotype dialectics and the tone of the interview becomes tense: Derrida replies that the 'staging' of the break between scientific and humanist Marx was very strong in Althusser, and that the later Marx, in this conception a 'scientific' one, was somehow uncontaminated by the humanist problematic (Derrida and Sprinkler 1993:196). Here Derrida hangs on tightly to the divide he sees in Althusser's Marxes – reifying in a way that is not quite convincing.[3]

Derrida then castigates those who were sleeping, or pretending to sleep, at the time when the Stalinist 'degeneration of the Party' in France was under way (Derrida and Sprinkler 1993:198) – this is not only the party in France but later the 'failure' of 'Communist Parties in general' (1993:209). In the face of this he admits that his silence, born of not wanting 'political objections' to be 'confused with conservative reticence', was not the only option, and that others 'found a clear way to take that risk which I didn't take'. That those who did find a way to speak out did so in 'a code' that Derrida did not want to be associated with was 'the deepest reason' for his silence, rather than shyness or intimidation. Indeed, some of his current silences or abstentions, he says, could be similarly explained in that the code of expected expression lacks 'rigour' and is 'laden with unacceptable presuppositions' (Derrida and Sprinkler 1993:198). But if this is the case, how is it that the ten-point code can be offered in *Specters*? How rigorous, how laden with presuppositions, is this code?

It is important not to make too great a gap appear between Althusser and Derrida where one does not exist. On time, Derrida writes alongside Althusser's 'entire and necessary' critique of Hegelian notions of history and 'aims at showing that there is not one single history, a general history, but rather histories *different* in their type, rhythm, mode of inscription – intervallic, differentiated histories'. In a key turn of phrase, Derrida says 'I have always subscribed to this' (Derrida 1981:58). There must then be several times, and so several speeds of Capital are on the cards. The point is that these may be missed by too rapid readers.

We could also read Marx on time. It is clear from *The Poverty of Philosophy*, and from the later works, that time is, for Marx, a social relationship and is to be understood as the intertwining of three different temporalities, that of production, that of circulation and that of reproduction. These are perhaps not all the temporalities that are relevant – for example there may be that of the movement from formal to real subsumption, and we might add the different rhythms of resistance, of critical commentary, of organisation of the class struggle, all of which might complicate the above. Yet, it is obvious that in Marx's text there are differing temporalities that impinge upon the calculations of capitalist production, and time is central to its working. Importantly the rhythms of these circuits are not always the same. First and foremost it is value that is the time of socially necessary labour, and it is clear that this is not a simple calculation. More recently (relatively), the work of Fortunati (1981/1995) mentioned earlier has demonstrated the determination of socially necessary labour, the role of domestic labour and sexual reproductive work – in several senses – is not calculated explicitly, indeed, this is the criteria of its hidden character under patriarchal capitalism. Similarly, the abstract calculation of circulation time in the paperwork of moneybags may not correspond to the practicalities and specificities of circulation and distribution, but must work in averages and means. Also, the antagonistic relations between capital and labour throw variously speeding spanners into the most carefully calculated plans, to a greater and lesser extent in the differing domains of production, in the circulation phase and in reproduction (where shopping is civil war). Similarly, the subsumption thesis could be rethought in a context where centre and periphery no longer work geographically or temporally in the same ways. The subsumption of inner-city relations may also be formal or real in the financial centre that is optic fibre inner London etc. (but this would be another research task – see Thrift's informative and pithy attack on the newness of the electronic city and those 'driven by a desire to fix on metaphors of modern life like speed, circulation and travel, which were already tired before they were recycled last time around' [Thrift 1996:1466]).

Derrida has said that he was paralysed, embarrassed and silenced. But this can also be considered in another way, and is presented sometimes quite differently. Some 20 years before the above characterisations, Derrida would think that there was 'no theoretical or political benefit' to be derived from engagement or articulation of problems where dogmatism, confusion or opportunism were to take advantage of the absence of rigour and lucidity. He silences himself because he takes seriously 'the difficulty, and also the heterogeneity, of the Marxist text [and] the decisive importance of its historical stakes' (Derrida 1981:62). It would not do to complain that this reticence to speak is a kind of camouflage – it is indeed an honesty to be admired. What matters, however, is an evaluation of the text that is eventually articulated and the context of that overcoming (is it *aufhebung*?) of paralysis. In the 1971 interview Derrida says he has never formulated any 'reticence' about dialectical materialism, and that a (rigorous) theoretical elaboration remains 'still to come' (Derrida 1981:62). It is now a matter of record that when it came, dialectical materialism, characterised almost as a totalitarian Diamat©, was to be dropped.

Revamping ruthlessly, Derrida's excavation of concepts also leads him to drop (any simple notion of) class. In the Sprinkler interview of 1990 he says: 'The concept of class struggle and identification of a class are much more problematic than the Althusserians thought at the time. Thus any sentence in which "social class" appeared was problematic for me' (Derrida and Sprinkler 1993:204). This means he could not engage in discussion with those who used such terms. There is a troublesome contradiction here, that sends any contemporary discussion of Marx back to the past of the nineteenth, or 'at least ... the first half of the twentieth century'. He suggests that the end of the decade (Mai '68 and all that) obliged the Althusserians to 'complicate their discourse', but there is no evidence that Derrida did likewise with regard to this snapshot of Marxism in the 1960s. We are left waiting to find out when Derrida is to debate his own more complicated analysis of class. He remains contradictory where he claims a 'modern' difference for the context of his own view: he says:

I believe in the gross existence of social classes, but the modernity of industrial societies (not to mention the third world [but why not?])

cannot be approached, analysed, taken into account within a political strategy, starting off from a concept whose links are so loose.

(Derrida and Sprinkler 1993:204)

But he still believes that the analysis of conflicts in social forces, at which the concept of class struggle was aimed, is 'still absolutely indispensable' (Derrida and Sprinkler 1993:204). What is it that allows this silencing of the Third World and class politics inside Derrida's text, and the promotion of First World modernity? And this alongside an acknowledgement of class, but outside political strategy? It amounts to class struggle without class, or class analysis without struggle. It is not clear which is indispensable, now or in the past. And what horizon of time is crossed here, where an old conflict with Althusser retains salience for the 'International' today? What debts are deferred?

Extending from this modernity are some significant claims for the role of 'theory' and the character of 'new' communications: Derrida writes of contemporary capitalist society in a way that seems again to homogenise and simplify – and lead to paralysis – at the very time that he wants to warn against these things: 'A developed capitalist society is characterised by the fact that the worlds of education, research and information (universities and research institutes) directly or indirectly irrigate the social fabric' (Derrida and Sprinkler 1993:230). In this context (should we refer to centralisation, or rather to the process of subsumption as discussed by Negri?), the role of ideas becomes 'more and more' important, more central and more marked by 'new' forms of communication:

> … what is called theoretical discourse … is more directly in contact with the decision-making instances – it is both more permeable and more penetrating. It communicates along new, more diversified, more overdetermined trajectories with the 'general' discourse of society, with 'public opinion', with the discourse of politicians, with the military discourse, with the juridical discourse.
>
> (Derrida and Sprinkler 1993:230)

But the International Jury Derrida conjures into being will be only the global end of a system of codification, regulation and normalisation that extends throughout contemporary capitalist societies. The constitution of social subjects in law occurs in line with a mode of production managed by the state and the social sciences which requires 'communities' within society, within the state, constituted via market forces, enforcements, educative disciplines etc., all arranged to bring individuals into a universal form/mode of production. Recuperation of social antagonisms occurs here (via 'theoretical' disciplines of cultural studies, philosophy, law, education, etc.) to align all production not via mediating institutions, but via institutionally managed divisions, separation and differences. These divisions were once only institutionalised, but are now so fully generalised throughout society that the enclosures are smooth and there seems to be no outside. As Hardt and Negri write in their book *The Labour of Dionysius*: 'Social space has not been emptied of these disciplinary institutions, but completely filled with the modalities of control' (1994:260). How is the International anything but the absolute extension of such a modality? The warning Derrida offers is that we should not 'underestimate what is happening in places where this discourse appears too complicated or sophisticated'. But he then asserts that, really (?), this discourse – and so our chance to follow it, to not simplify, to 'renew', is limited because 'it is indeed less decipherable, more confined, more "private" than before on account of the mass-mediatisation that homogenises, and thus simplifies and censors, more and more' (Derrida and Sprinkler 1993:230). The pattern recurs over and again – a back and forth that produces a verbose paralysis, and analysis that simplifies as it complicates, complicates and simplifies. It would be an error to dismiss this only as a bourgeois and wordy dialectics with nothing to say, but there is a certain force in the critique which archives in a closing way. All too quickly into a white static dead end.

## //derrida.future-to-come

… there is not yet any democracy worthy of this name. (Derrida 1992:46)

The 'still to come' becomes an important refrain – we come across it also in terms of Europe (in *The Other Heading*), Democracy, Justice (in *Specters of Marx*), and in the text of *Archive Fever*. What is this future time that is always deferred? Derrida says of the archive:

It is a question of the future, the question of the future itself, the question of a response, of a promise and of a responsibility for tomorrow … if we want to know what it will have meant, we will know only in times to come … later on or perhaps never.

(Derrida 1995/1996:36)

Responsibility and promise are important words for the thinking of justice, no-one could doubt this.

With regard to reading protocol at least as pertains to the homogeneity of Marx, Derrida's strategy is as expected: 'I do not believe that one can speak, even from a Marxist point of view, of a homogenous Marxist text' (1981:75). This is a telegraphed repetition of an earlier point that raises issues of responsibility, response and, at least an allusion to, political activity: 'we cannot consider Marx's, or Engel's or Lenin's texts as completely finished elaborations that are simply to be "applied" to the current situation' (Derrida 1981:63). Not inconsistently with Marxism, he proclaims reading as transformational. Although he has not yet found any – any? – 'protocols of reading' that satisfy him (1981:63). On aufhebung, Derrida notes that 'there is always *Aufhebung*' (Derrida 1981:94), by which he seems to mean nothing less complicated or vague as that every repetition – even a reading – is already transformational. The archivist always sorts the stacks, but is this revolutionary every time?

What theoretical and political resources are required that would be adequate not only to understand the contemporary character of capitalism – its speeds, its flows, its disguises and its delays – but also adequate to a practical and organised militancy against this capital? The partyless International is under-theorised, but this does not mean that it is impossible to research these topics, to develop and further the sets of ideas that release and circulate struggles in ways that do more than any single-word single-issue spot-protests might do. Those who provided revolutionary organisational theory in the past were operating in a somewhat differently weighted informational zone, but this does not mean that Lenin, for example, was wrong to advise the party that it must use the most advanced media tools at its disposal to debate, agitate and propagandise – hence *Iskra* and *Pravda*. Surely it is necessary to do more than produce inky old tabloids; or more than, say, Gilroy or Clifford with their lists of what is interesting in the cross-border flows and alliances of modernity (Clifford 1997; Gilroy 1993; see Hutnyk 2000c). From these beginnings it is possible to move to relate various contemporary struggles both politically and theoretically, to pursue internationalist work that is more than just publishing (or charity), and to promote a wild creativity that might, just might, inevitably realise the sense and reason of communist futures (which would, of course, not necessarily be the same as rule by communists).[4] Let us not be duped into thinking that we cannot analyse and act upon the manifestations, however fleeting, of contemporary appropriation and its forms – just-in-time delivery, service and information economies, flight-capital, hyper-crisis and super slump.

The flash world of speed-hype creates just enough smoke to disguise the expanding immiseration of the cul de sacs of development. If anything increases or intensifies it is the 'increasing exploitation of the peripheral proletariat in relation to that of the center' (Deleuze and Guattari 1972/1983:231). Large parts of Africa, South America, Asia, exist where previously development meant industrialisation. Today it means attaching local elite capital to multinational mobile capital and ensuring open markets for investment, generous tax concessions, labour deregulation, state subsidies and other privileges for capital in conjunction with the loss of local livelihoods. In this conjuncture, the impoverishment of life under neo-colonialism is exacerbated by a superexploitation described as speed so as to ignore its effects. The colonised parts of the world – nearly everywhere now, including the inner urban metropoles – are denied web access and existence in the texts of cultural analysis except as exotic or erotic image sites at the end of jet streams or video documentary cameras. In the context of superexploitation, financial hyper-transactions, structural adjustment, DFI (direct foreign investment), spiralling loan repayments and proliferating export processing zones, an analysis mesmerised by speed ends up saying that nothing can be done. At the most basic limit this even denies the option of simply growing more food, let alone suggesting any project of redistribution. Too many of those writing about development these days offer small-scale solutions like the wind-up radio, while the other half offer development as a mode of ensuring Western market dominance, in say grain, and increasingly in manufacture – any serious level of redistribution does not figure in either set of calculations.[5]

Where the realm of production used to bring us together while circulation atomised opportunities for class organisation, perhaps today's mediatised telematic societies offer a chance to extend co-operative self-activity. At one level it is the Derridean critique of the privileging of the authenticity or originality of presence (Derrida 1967/1976:137–8) that would provide some impetus for thinking that new forms of organising and alliance are possible across telematic zones. Why must radical political efficacy rely only upon the proximity of really existing factory and workplace cells, as opposed to, for example, shared experience not necessarily of immediately co-terminous space? This does not mean that the old styles of face-to-face branch and cell meetings, class solidarity, study groups, militant protest and action are out of order, but that these are not the only ways to go. Indeed, it is also a sectarian cul de sac to insist on incompatibility here in telematic times. Given these new transformatory resources for electronic organising, why not see the advent of speed as reason to rejoice?

Derrida is not exactly pessimistic, but it seems that he would rather talk to the dead than with us. For my money I wish that it had been Deleuze who had written his book on Marx before he died – the extravagance of the title promised so much more – *The Greatness of Marx* – and the engagement promised to be more profound (both Fredric Jameson and Eugene Holland demonstrated how we could expect that a book on Marx by Deleuze would be based upon a more systematic and long-term engagement with Marxist concerns [Perth conference, December, 1996]).[6] Derrida instead writes on Shakespeare and keeps Marx among the dead; inscribing himself into a heritage of philosophers, detached from any other more 'Marxist' practicalities, as the medium in a seance with old father figures. But what is Derrida doing alienating Marx? He refers to ghosts and to television, but ignores the possibility of a faulty reception (not that we will insist on the Habermaniacal ideal of communicative competence, but there are avoidances and misreading here). This ghosting image of M, of D behind M, of D and M on the couch of F – enamoured with homo-erotic jokes about P and S, with D beaming out on the international networks ...

The presentation of versions of Marxism impacts upon the reception of other Marxists also, other strategies, other histories.

In *The Politics of Friendship* Jacques Derrida takes up the suggestion that, of all the ghosts who might be invoked, Mao Zedong represents a 'new stage' or 'rupture' with classical 'political' criteria by introducing a 'mutation' in the concepts of 'the enemy' and 'the partisan' (Derrida 1994/1997:141–2). This belongs to a 'decisive' 'technics' or a 'tele-technology' glossed as 'the speed and expanse of transmission, mobilisation and motorisation'. On the one hand, following the historian Carl Schmitt's 'impressive' and 'valuable insights', Derrida cites this as a 'remarkable sign of the times', and on the other hand, it has the consequence of inaugurating a new form of guerrilla war – the examples are Mao, Ho Chi Minh, Fidel Castro, and 'the war for independence in Algeria, the Cypriot war, and so forth'. These new forms produce, by 'speed of motorisation, and ... tele-technical automation', a 'break' with an autochthonous mode of being a partisan. Against Schmitt, Derrida points out that already any former mode of partisan was also, whatever its speed, a response to a form of tele-technology (Derrida 1994/1997:142) and that what can be said of the modern partisan 'driven by technical and industrial progress' could also 'have been said of the most "classical" combatants'. Yet he does seem to accept a distinction, a break, that can be discerned as 'one of the numerous advantages' of Schmitt's 'precise and differential analysis'. The 'essential factor in the mutation' of the concepts of enemy and partisan is no simple matter of 'dating and periodisation', but clearly Derrida wants to underline the role of technologies in the political, and in doing so tends towards a determination by speed. This then immediately leads him, with Schmitt,[7] to 'the edge' of an 'abyss', but he refuses to 'take advantage of this pretext for pathetic eloquence over the bottomless depths of chaos which is ours today' (Derrida 1994/1997:143).

Mao's mobilisation and a paralysing, ordering, archiving silence should be remembered here, at that very point where Derrida finds himself at the edge of an abyss refusing any 'pathetic eloquence'. Why speak so much of Marx and so much less of Mao if Mao's 'partisan rupture' is so important, even as a critique of Schmitt? In the *Politics of Friendship*, where Derrida talks of the technological speed break of the new partisan, instead of knowing who the enemy is, and other certainties, he seems to accept that 'today' cannot be understood. He is content to make an aside about being 'ready to listen to this screaming chaos of the "voiceless"' (Derrida 1994/1997:143). Voiceless because of an uncertainty, chaos because to 'talk politics' one must swallow 'all the assurances of "clear cut distinctions"' and so, I guess like Mao, know who is 'the enemy' at any given time. Derrida is reluctant to do this, and instead of – as might have been expected – making some comment on Mao's essay 'On Contradiction', which at the very least applies some dialectical sophistication to the 'assurances', offers rather a further extended aside devoted to computer espionage, bugs, spy networks, cryptography, cybercrime and the 'hopeless debate' in the US about communications technology and privacy (Derrida 1994/1997:144). These matters, and the structural effects of 'technological mutation', should not be ignored, but it is revealing that Derrida, voiceless in the face of chaos, and verbosely unassured, does 'decide' to forgo any detailed discussion of contemporary capitalism, or of the form of organisation required in the face of its telematics, or of any resistance relevant to the times, and 'so forth'. Instead, only ten words and a bracketed worry that the Chinese revolutionary struggle against invasion from Japan was a 'fratricidal' one, between brothers 'of the same race' who became enemies (Derrida 1994/1997:148).[8] Yes, of course it is interesting to consider issues of 'fraternity' in 'civil' war, and to criticise Schmitt for not speaking of sisters (Derrida's kinship system is equally boysy), but isn't this familiarisation a domestication of the sharp conflict of politics? The *Politics of Friendship* misses an opportunity here by transmuting a struggle against imperialism into a sibling rivalry. It is symptomatic of the level at which uncertainty forces a decision to abstain from politics (again note that it was Derrida who said that undecideability forces a decision. Uncertainty is not the same as undecideability, but the conservative nature of the decision not to take up the struggle is clearly not 'partisan'). How is it that Derrida can say, in the face of the 'screaming chaos of the voiceless', to hear of which 'one has only to lend an ear to any news item', about anywhere, that there is 'nothing new here'? This nothing – the 'shouting hunger and suffering' of Rwanda, ex-Yugoslavia, Iran, Israel, Palestine, Cambodia, Ireland, Tahiti, Bangladesh … 'will always have been', and occurs 'despite the leap of technological mutation' (Derrida 1994/1997:143–4). Yet Derrida's email is new. Again it is in the 'instant' when a 'new stage has opened up', that a 'modern technics' removes the distinction between private and public through the work of the 'police qua spy network' – the Clipper Chip, bugging devices, 'cybercrime', etc. – and this 'ruins in advance and from within the possibility of the political'. Surely here, where the 'entire' space of humanity will be transformed a yet more radical Marxism (called Maoism) is required?

## //productivity.ingenuity

Pessimism/cynicism – self-doubt and cringe of the Western project manifests as an abstention from politics and a romantic valorisation of *'tribalismo'* in the face of a rampant (capitalist) system which has reached, it seems, uncontrollability before which nothing can be done but withdraw. Fascination with speed – sitting grinning like a monkey at the zoo – or with technology, leads to a descriptive wonder that may sometimes look elegant but offers only a deferral of despair. Dreaming of speed, or even of Capital somehow escaping its ties to labour (via automation, cybertronics, etc.), ignores the ways in which it is labour that actually moves production, not capital. Autonomy arguments apply here; but to celebrate speed or capital flight is to think paralysis – the abdication of class struggle. Other possible analyses of Fast Cap could proceed in a more adventurous tone, – the struggle is grim/not so grim et cetera.

To be *for* production. Derrida questions this, but it is clear that there remains some sense in insisting that production comes at least logically prior to consumption. Even in a service economy something must be produced in order to be consumed. Shouldn't the criticism of productivism be that production should not be valorised in all forms, since production for profit is based upon appropriation and exploitation. It matters most of all that we ask who profits from production. This does not mean being against production, but against production of a particular – albeit pervasive – type. The danger is perhaps that this concern with the pervasive capitalist character of the direction and social relations of production today leads to a comprehensive loss of confidence in human productive ingenuity and the capacity of our collective efforts to transform, improve and enhance our lives. This loss of confidence may be understood as the slippage from the specificities of capitalist violence into a general anxiety, taking the form first of a particular critique of what is a growing global realisation – born primarily out of Marxist critique – that the effects of production for profit are detrimental, but extending in panic to a denunciation of everything. Perhaps at one level this qualifies the critique of everything as necessary, but criticism (self-criticism) need not be to the exclusion of our capacity to imagine creative and exuberant forms of anti-capitalism in which we build our own lives. Auto-poïesis, self-fashioning, ecstatic paranoia, call it what you will – the foundation of a critique of capitalist production has to be an analysis that proposes a rampantly creative productive capacity in its place, and destroys the old repressive modes of domination and control that restrain us.

The extent to which both the Marxist threat to capitalist productive hype, embodied in the Russian and Chinese revolutions, and in the anti-colonial struggles worldwide, provoked a loss of 'faith' in productive power should not be underestimated. The point, however, is not to throw away the capacity of human ingenuity under the withering and corrosive impact of years of red-scare revisionism over these struggles, but instead to throw out those who would appropriate the benefits of this ingenuity for some rather than all.

Instead of an international clique of deconstructing jurists and a list of ten code-words telegraphed to Marx, organised resistance around a series of struggles on an internationalist register could be considered. Abject paralysis, however verbose, in the face of capital and telematics, and a nostalgia for the pastoral face-to-face of community or old school vanguard might instead be reconfigured through recognition of new sites of contestation alongside older, not yet exhausted ones. There would have to be more than ten words to signal this recoding, based upon actually existing struggles and potential zones of engagement. Where Derrida mentions unemployment and homelessness, we might point to the struggles around the Job Seekers' Allowance in Britain (see *Aufheben* 4 for an excellent and informed discussion of this in relation to squatters, hunt saboteurs and the various campaign coalitions against the Criminal Justice and Public Order Act of 1994: <http://jefferson.village. Virginia.EDU/~spoons/aut_html/auf4cjball.htm>); where Derrida mentions economic war or the global market, the campaigns against Maastricht and the European Union (Contra the Capital of Europe, Madrid Summit Alternative Declaration), or against ASEAN and APEC (Manila Peoples' Forum, for example: <http://www. geocities.com/~cpp-ndf/intl3.htm>). The various campaigns against neoliberalism encompassing a politics that is anti-debt and anti-SAP (structural adjustment programme) also. The proliferation of the arms trade and nuclear weapons would suggest examination of the various campaigns against militarism, for example in Europe and in Australia, if not almost everywhere to some degree, and of course in various political stripes. The issue of so-called inter-ethnic wars demands attention to movements against chauvinism such as the coalition against the Bharatiya Janata Party in India, which brings together differing communist and progressive elements in principled, sometimes more, sometimes less, alliance; and the issues of drug cartels and international law might suggest attention to the anti-heroin trade campaigns in Ireland, community struggles in the inner city which do not buy into the 'war-on-drugs' scaremongering of bureaucrats; or movements in several nations to regulate police powers and covert insurgency, usually backed by Reaganite Contra-style cloak-and-dagger support, such as the people's movements in Latin America or defence campaigns against police violence in the UK (for example see <http://www.injustice film.co.uk>). To this I would add attempts to recruit and organise R&D workers of all levels to political action that addresses the institutional role of research in technology development and expansion; mobilisations among professional and intellectual associations to reject co-option to good news consultancies and provision of alibis for transnational corporations; struggles against casualisation, wages for housework and against immigration and asylum law. Cultural work to foster alliances between anti-racists and anti-imperialists for cooperative struggle. And many more. What this requires is some effort to read at several speeds, working out the contemporary dynamics of class decomposition and recomposition, the relation of 'ethnicities' to political alliances, the practicalities of agitation and revolution adequate and necessary in the face of current restructurings, the tricks of subsumption and co-option. It is not necessary to cower in the confusion that comes from celebration of speed, nor only to revel in the dilettante semantic flamboyance of fashionable pessimism (which may be entertaining, and gets a few stage laughs, but ...). All this may proceed with party and organisational structures to greater or lesser extent debated and disciplined in each case, but always more organised than Derrida's proposed anti-party, anti-located, undeclared pomo-International. (I am starting to slide into rant mode here, so should temper this with less typing ...)

# Part 3
# Tales from the Raj

# 6
# On Empire

This section focuses upon Michael Hardt and Tony Negri's blockbuster *Empire* (2000), taking them to task for a variety of minor sectarianisms and self-promotional pretension. However, the major criticism I make has to do with their take on imperialism, and specifically their evaluation of the East India Company in the context of the British Raj. This seemingly incidental (but brutal) historical moment turns out to show all that is wrong with Hardt and Negri's contention that the advent of Empire inaugurates something new in the project of capitalism. It pertains to the very conception of the operation of the capitalist world system and the relation of the state and government, as executive committee of the bourgeoisie, to capital and capitalists. The debate revolves around not only what Gayatri Spivak shows is the necessary conceit of the 'Asiatic Mode of Production' – a term not often used by Marx – but also around what activism means in the context of transition. Marx and Marxism is a practical politics after all. This erasure of the political lesson of the Raj is then, in Chapter 8, to be found as a symptomatic problem with cultural studies in other (related?) fields or work, specifically in Subaltern Studies and the scattered comments of Homi Bhabha on hybridity. A glance at Spivak's notion of learning to learn from below proves that the reliance of Hardt and Negri upon her good name is perfunctory (name dropping), and her work is shown to have more to offer to a bad Marxism than cultural theory has yet to acknowledge.

What is Empire? What is not? Where is it? Where is it not? The most general back and forth questions to begin. We could start by asking if there is now anything outside the Empire of capital? Hardt and Negri declare their initial task as 'to grasp the constitution of the order being formed today' (2000:3). It is undoubtedly helpful to see an increased arsenal of concepts available for the difficult task of naming the conjuncture at which contemporary capitalism currently sits, but a deft handling of concepts requires careful contextualisation and consideration. Notions of difference, hybridity, travel, subsumption, dialectic, multitude and rights are all, in various ways, sanctified and talismanic terms. There will be reason to examine the tricks more closely. It is also very good news to find these concepts discussed in a 'postmodernist' text that does not pretend that the political heroes of the working class are never-to-be-mentioned ghosts. Stalin, Lenin, Luxemburg, Mao and Ho Chi Minh are cited on occasion – names airbrushed out of scholarship far too often are at least given recognition here. A kind of camouflage-oriented air-brushing wafted for many years throughout the Western academy as demonic and un-American activities were reified and simplified, and the notion of Marxism, and the future of Communism, became a congealed orthodoxy. This misrepresentation is hard to dislodge, it is welcome news that at least some attempt to rework the terms has arrived.

With these initial commendations then, two levels of largely critical reflection are offered to animate readings of the big bumper book of *Empire*: the heritage of Marxism misrepresented and deformed, and a barrage of concepts and their uses or abuses. I affirm again that this book is welcome. It releases discussions that should and must be had. However, the fuse starts to burn, the theatre lights dim, someone shouts action. ...

The hinge moment in the drama of Marx's own big book, *Capital*, is when he asks us to leave the marketplace and look behind the factory gates. This is a rhetorical flourish that appears to drive the text. The dictates of his chosen mode of presentation required Marx to begin with the commodity, only for this abstracted item to be further contextualised in the market, and the market in production and so on. This staging occurs because the book *Capital* was designed to provide the working class with analytical tools useful for struggles against capitalism. In a similar way Hardt and Negri claim such a dramatic momentum, and I believe their analysis also abstracts, but does so in order to present a critical and useful set of concepts for intervention – from the start I'm tempted to think that the notion of Empire is not an empirical reality simply 'found' first of all, but the name of an enemy, and one that is constituted, or rather co-constituted, through questioning and against which there shall be struggle. Empire is the name given to that system in which 'nearly all of humanity is to some degree absorbed within or subordinated to the networks of capitalist exploitation' (Hardt and Negri 2000:43). Intentionally located within a certain tradition of analysis then, Hardt and Negri see their book as a draft realisation of the two missing volumes of *Capital*, on the state and on the world market, that Marx had planned but not written (2000:236). They pass through their own factory gates ... but the only trouble is that I don't think Empire is new, it has long been the enemy. And even if late, the most excellent analyses and brilliant insights providing demystification and ideology-critique are of little use if they remain only as spectacular dramatisation.

The drama must unfold. I am, I'm afraid, not sufficiently well informed of the factional obligations and patronage structures within which this book is written to know why some Marxists, and some concepts, are favoured and others are, with symptomatic dismissive asides, ignored or rejected. No doubt more microscopic sectarian scholarship would clear up the details of which characters are in and which are out – but the plot contains a variety of twists: somewhat rapid dismissal of the 'unidimensionality' of Marx's otherwise much used notion of subsumption; the Frankfurt School extension of this being not as clear as that of Deleuze and Guattari (Hardt and Negri 2000:25); Stalin accused of 'finally' turning the notion of communist revolution into national sovereignty (2000:112) (why is this considered so final?); Lenin's 'tortuous' thoughts running along 'the mysterious curve of the straight line' (2000:231) in analysis of imperialism, yet leading directly to the theory of Empire (2000:234); Samir Amin included amongst those 'theorists ... reluctant to recognise a major shift in global power relations' (2000:9); while conspiracy paranoia is directed against the 'sad' agents of the Third International (2000:411); and even world systems theorists are damned with a footnote reference with a bracketed *fort/da* routine referring to the 'in other respects quite impressive' work of Arrighi, Hopkins and Wallerstein (2000:429).

Selecting these citations is not meant to register the complaints of left fandom or of a sanctimonious scripture fetishist, reading texts as gospel and defending stone idols, but it is precisely around the points of dismissal that I think a critique of Hardt and Negri must be mounted. Wrong on any number of things, but rather than exhibiting the routine deconstructive arabesques and edifying, pointless, erudition of post-Marxism, this book is always audacious and engaging. Certainly some readers will insist that there is no break, no end of the dialectic, and no line in the sand, but at least discussions of these claims are possible because Hardt and Negri are not resigned – they offer vigorous and passionate argument, ambitious breadth and scope and – bonus – exquisite denunciations of the pallid, parasitic and rotten ruling class. Three cheers for this book. Yet. Comrades, what is to be done with these concepts? Up for debate is not the inviolability of the written tradition, but questions of the status of subsumption, of the political and administrative role of the nation-state, evaluations of imperialism now and in the past, the requisite format of internationalist organisation, and the political conception of Empire as a 'world system'-effect today.

In what may be an unguarded moment, Hardt and Negri also sing the 'Internationale', but only in a refrain. 'The "Internationale" *was* the hymn of revolutionaries' (Hardt and Negri 2000:49, my italic). These one-time songbirds now argue that because of changed circumstances – the advent of Empire – proletarian internationalism and its methods of organising have become obsolete (2000:50). The old methods of opposition to capital are outmoded, memories, residue. The proletariat was defeated and, paradoxically, this means the shape of the enemy has changed. On the basis of this change – decline of the nation-state, break from imperialism to Empire, real subsumption, a politics of hybridity and of rights – a new conception of political struggle is also declared.[1] This is manifest in a range of singular struggles and people's movements – the *Intifada*, Tiananmen, Los Angeles, Chiapas – which are understood to be related to capital in ways quite unlike the 'cycles of struggle' model which made sense of the contagious inspiration of anti-colonial struggles in the Philippines and Cuba, the events around 1917, those in the wake of the Chinese Revolution, or the African and Latin American liberation struggles (Hardt and Negri 2000:51). A horizontal cycle model is 'no longer adequate for recognizing the way in which contemporary struggles achieve global significance' (2000:57). Instead, a vertical and immediate articulation with 'the global level' is the character of singular, local and regional – untranslatable – struggles (2000:54–5).

Emphasising changed circumstances, Hardt and Negri see their definition of Empire as 'in step … with the development of the capitalist mode of production' (2000:xvi). This is an avowedly European and Euro-American conception which sees *Empire* as a contribution to the modes of production narrative – problematically, as I will argue below, because imperialism and the colonial theatres of accumulation are designated as 'outside'. This self-confessedly 'Eurocentric' genealogy of Empire might be reconsidered by way of thinking the politics of knowledge production and the constitutive power of terminology – codifications which prefigure. The protocols of Marxist historiography, Marxiological jockeying, sectarian sledging and academic triumphalism might be usefully rethought in terms that attend to the way the requirements of concepts, or of models or theory, produce descriptions and meaning – and blueprints for action.

So is Empire a break with imperialism as we know it? Hardt and Negri argue that various groups of theorists have been 'reluctant to recognize the globalization of capitalist production and its world market as a fundamentally new situation and a significant historical shift' (2000:8). This is so whether they have the world-systems theorists in mind, who argued that capitalism had always been an 'affair of the world-economy' (Wallerstein, quoted in Hardt and Negri 2000:417), or when they tackle a similar 'reluctance' exhibited by those who believe that 'capitalist nation states have continued to exercise imperialist domination over other nations' (2000:9) and that this, for Samir Amin, is a kind of 'perfecting of imperialism' (Hardt and Negri 2000:9). Such inadequacies in existing theoretical responses to postcolonial and post-imperial power give Hardt and Negri their real 'point of departure' (2000:9).

The break between imperialism and Empire hinges on the autonomy of the transnational corporation vis-à-vis the nation-state. Under what might rather be called 'millennium capitalism' (I prefer this terminology – capitalism encourages us to think it will last forever, but the seductions of celebration only mask the trick for now) the administrative work of the nation-state is displaced on to newly formed 'international bodies' of global civil society, non-governmental organisations (NGOs), the International Monetary Fund (IMF) and World Bank, etc. (Hardt and Negri 2000:307). This much is clear, but who is to say that this 'articulation' is unique? Is the post-state, minimalist administration, *laissez-faire* development of capitalism not something with an already long history? Is Empire really a 'fundamentally new form of rule' or, despite our authors' rejection, rather 'a weak echo of modern imperialisms' (Hardt and Negri 2000:146)? Is it not possible to see Empire as merely an extension of exploitation and brutality, structured via the tricks of surplus value extraction, operating within a continuing, if convoluted, history of accumulation?

The 'primary symptom' of the coming of Empire, for Hardt and Negri, is the 'declining sovereignty of nation-states' and their 'inability to regulate economic and cultural exchange' (2000:xii).

'In a previous period nation-states were the primary actors in the modern imperialist organization of global production' but now the nation-state appears 'increasingly' as an obstacle to the world market (2000:150).

Of course there is much to be said about the nation-state. It remains the case that the nation-state continues to orchestrate, and in effect shapes and operates, the sites through which struggles against capital can be waged. The nation-state continues to meddle in everything it can. It is the effective agent of the real subsumption that means the extension of capitalist relations to all aspects of our lives (even phone calls are charged to the second for an ever increasing number of the mobile-set). It is very useful in breaking down and delivering a segmented population as workforce for the labour markets. The nation-state remains armed to the teeth, and although transition and subsumption take myriad forms and the consequent heterogeneity, graphed on to an already existing multiplicity, can no longer be understood, and never could be, as a fixed model, there are as yet few transnational corporations as heavily armed (proviso: transnational corporations are not yet mercantile and mercenary in the way Clive and the East India Company were, but abundant evidence has shown that this does not disarticulate them from the machines of war).[2] Hardt and Negri seem to neglect the significance of the fact that it is the nation-state that protects meetings of the World Bank and IMF with water-cannon and tear gas. In other fields the nation-state is the 'poisoned gift of national liberation' (Hardt and Negri 2000:134), although I am not sure that Gandhi and Ho Chi Minh can so readily be named together in the same sentence (the one accommodationist, the other revolutionary) as critics of the 'perverse trick' that equates nationalism with 'political and economic modernization' (2000:133). The nation as defensive weapon in anti-imperial struggle and as vehicle of the autonomy and difference of local revolutionary struggle is not insignificant – the footnote reference is to Mao here (2000:438), but I am surprised that Mao's greatest contribution is ignored, in which he militated for continued revolutionary struggle against deviations and counter-revolutionary tendencies within the revolution. That Mao, and the Chinese communists, seem to have failed to outflank the 'boomerang' effect (2000:131) of capitalist restitution is a matter of record. The nation-state remains strong even when surrounded and infiltrated by the global. The nation-state must still be discussed. Taking into account many ambiguities, Hardt and

Negri recognise that 'the contemporary phase is not adequately characterized by the victory of the capitalist corporation over the state' but 'state functions and constitutional elements have been displaced to other levels and domains' (2000:307).

Hardt and Negri criticise postcolonial theorists 'because they remain fixated on attacking an old form of power and propose a strategy of liberation that could be effective only on that old terrain' (2000:146) – mentioning Edward Said, Homi Bhabha and Gyan Prakash. It might still be worth responding to the suggestion that postcolonial theory is a 'productive tool for reading history' but 'entirely insufficient for theorising contemporary global power' (Hardt and Negri 2000:146). It is not that I want to defend the term 'postcolonial theory' (on the contrary, I have said it appears to be not much more than a slogan for selling books), nor do I subscribe to any notion of the 'postcolonial' except insofar as it refers in a restricted and ironic way to the betrayal of anti-imperialist movements by nationalist elites (see Spivak 1999). (Nor do I advocate the same old 'strategy of liberation' – which one? – ascribed to Said, Bhabha and Prakash, and I will specify this in relation to Bhabha at the end.) However, the idea of looking to history as a key to theorising contemporary global power is not, in my view, exhausted. We learn from the past if we are attentive, we err if we gloss and misrepresent. So, in the context of the emergence of *Empire*, there might be cause to question an analogous concurrence in Hardt and Negri's model between the beginning of the imperialist phase and its end. This is perhaps knowingly tenuous, but if their presentation of the beginning of the imperialist period is carefully examined there are interesting clues to the significance of their claim that it has come to a conclusion. I hold the view that, in discussing the initial appearance of the imperialist state Hardt and Negri posit a significant difference between what would normally have been called mercantile capitalism and what might be called formal colonialism. These are not the terms they use, but they make much of the legislative interventions of the Dutch and British governments in colonial affairs in the middle 1800s.

No doubt there are more competent scholars of the transition who could do better here, and I am not really sure I can muster all the reasons to insist upon the significance of the ways transition to capitalism in Asia was bound up with Europe, or how Europe might be better seen as a kind of periphery to Asian capitalism (reversing world-system conventions as well, in order to recognise the location of accumulation and superexploitation), but I suggest this only as a speculative reorientation: the flashpoint of extraction and exploitation makes Asia the centre of accumulation, London only the site of the banks. The habitual constituting of capital with Europe at its centre continues to produce a Eurocentric knowledge even when the productive charge of capitalist accumulation has a financial, resource and labour power platform in the so-called peripheral zones. Is it possible to reverse the staging of this development and see, for example, the East India Company as the central player in the imperial theatre and not to disarticulate this from the realities of British colonialism? To do so might suggest new ways to think the 'reluctance' of continuist models of imperialism, Empire notwithstanding. Whatever the case, inverting the world in the mind does not yet redistribute wealth in reality, but it might give us pause to rethink the direction, as far as I understand it, and the manoeuvres required for Hardt and Negri to defend a 'quick and rough periodization' of the 'different phases' of the 'virtuous dialectic' between the nation-state and individual capitalists (2000:305). This dialectic constitutes a problem in terms of orientation (note that the dialectic is 'virtuous' because the state is the executive committee of capitalism in general). What is it that distinguishes the period of company rule – fully equipped with 'their own police, their own courts' (Hardt and Negri 2000:305), administrative structures, etc. – from the formal establishment of colonial governance? It is necessary, at this point, to rehearse the 'rough periodization':

> In the eighteenth and nineteenth centuries, as capitalism established itself fully in Europe, the state managed the affairs of the total social capital but required relatively unobtrusive powers of intervention. This period has come to be viewed in retrospect (with a certain measure of distortion) as the golden age of European capitalism.
>
> (Hardt and Negri 2000:305)

Note that the establishment of European capitalism was founded upon accumulation in the rest of the world (capitalism co-constituted with slavery, usury, mercantile plunder and other adventures). Possibly also the 'unobtrusive' interventions were viewed as part of the golden age because the brutal reality of massacre, ethnocide, slaughter, extortion, disease and death were less often reported (same distorted story today: one drink-drive car accident in Paris is headline news, bus or train disasters in Bangladesh are mentioned on page 17 and only if hundreds were killed). Expanding the citation, however, means Hardt and Negri continue:

> Outside the European nation-state in this period ... capitalist companies were sovereign when operating in colonial or precolonial territories, establishing their own monopoly of force, their own police, their own courts. The Dutch East India Company, for example, ruled ... with its own structures. ... The situation was the same for the capitalists operating in the British South Asian and African colonies. [Note, territories have already been renamed colonies.] The sovereignty of the East India Company lasted until the East India Act of 1858 brought the company under the rule of the queen. ... This period was characterized by relatively little need of state intervention at home and abroad.
>
> (2000:305)

If accumulation rather than the relation of state to capital were the framing perspective or, better, if superexploitation was, the difference that hinges on the revocation of the company's charter in 1858 might seem less significant. For Hardt and Negri the Indian rebellion of 1857 provoked the British government to intercede ('a direct response', 2000:306), but a cursory reading of even just Marx's *Notes on Indian History* (compulsory reading, prepared from an unedited manuscript of Marx by Progress Publishers, Moscow) suggests that the 1857 rebellion was only one of many struggles engaged by Indians against British interests in India over the entire history of its rule, and, more telling to the argument here, the question of government intercession was at issue in any case at least since the Act of Parliament of 1780, some 80 years earlier. Certainly from at least the 1770s the British government was heavily involved in company activities. A (sardonic) entry by Marx reads: '1771 Parliament interfered ... [but] through "providence" the assessors sent to Calcutta "lost their lives in shipwreck off the Cape of Good Hope"' (Marx 1947:89). Marx's sympathy for the appointed administrators of the state is no greater than, indeed the same as, his contempt for the plundering capitalists of the company, but the point is that the distinction between company and state looks less definite when the colonial site and metropolitan administration are taken together as co-constituted in the world system – the correspondences between the Lords and the Directors of the company, and the comings and goings in India House, would reveal the extent of envy, bribery and conceit which fuelled this long and mutually beneficial (for capital) involvement.[3]

There is then, to some degree at least, confusion as to the status of 'the Indian question' which revolves around the establishment of 'fully articulated' European administrations over the colonial territories in Asia. Is the formal jurisdiction of the nation-states the only aspect of guarding against crises that matters for capital in this period? What also of the long history of opposition to company rule? The conflagration following the 'Sepoy Mutiny', however significant that event may be, was not the first war engaged by British troops in India. Anticipating the circulation of 'cycles of struggle', it is clear more could be learnt about anti-imperialism (on rumour as a mechanism akin to 'cycles of struggle' see the discussion of Guha 1983 in Chapter 8 of this book).

Periodisation has a wider context of course, and Asia figures as central once again. The modes of production debate is far too convoluted to cover in detail here, but the significance of Marx's writing on India, and the issue of 'Oriental despotism' features in Hardt and Negri's argument and so deserves attention. Marx's journalistic articles for the *New York Daily Tribune* provide ample fodder for the working out of various positions around concepts of transition and historiography in Marxism. Hardt and Negri read Marx's recognition of the potential for liberation offered by global capital *and* his horror at the 'brutality of European conquest and exploitation' in the context of his writing about British parliamentary debate over the status of the East India Company and his situating of this in the history of British colonial rule (Hardt and Negri 2000:118–19). The issue here is that Hardt and Negri repeat as a constituent formula the passage which has Marx insisting that the arrival of British colonialism was, despite brutality, necessary for India to escape traditional forms of oppression ('Oriental despotism'). It is however, and contrary to *Empire*, not the case that Marx saw India's future as determined 'strictly' by Europe (Hardt and Negri 2000:120). There are several indications in the text that show that Marx is less 'unidimensional' and rigid than they contend. In clarification of his wider modes of production narrative Marx explained that the development offered in abstract in *Capital* was merely a 'sketch'. The polemic offered by Aijaz Ahmad against Edward Said cites Marx hoping for a 'socialist revolution in Asia, a nationalist revolution in India, and the break-up of the caste system' as 'preconditions for the "masses of people" even to start reaping any sort of "benefit from the new elements of society" introduced by colonialism' (Ahmad 1992:236). Even more significant perhaps, Spivak has made the point that Marx's mention of 'Oriental despotism', and discussions of the so-called Asiatic Mode of Production, belong to a 'speculative morphology' required in an activist's computation as justification for political action. Indulgent renderings with hindsight that excuse Marx for gaps in his knowledge will not do – even Hardt and Negri assert that his 'lack of information' is 'not the point' (2000:120). Spivak shows that the Asiatic Mode of Production was a 'crucial theoretical fiction' needed to 'set the machinery of the emancipatory transformation' of Hegelian idealism. The Asiatic Mode of Production is invoked and named (invoked not just by Marx, who probably used the phrase only once, Spivak 1999:71) but not as 'a "real" description of "actual practice" … [in this particular] … place or time' (Spivak 1999:88). When thinking transition, Marx did not need to think of transition from the Asiatic Mode of Production to capitalism. It is necessary to settle the account in *Empire*, but the process of formal subsumption is not one which requires the actual agents of transition (mercantile capitalists in the pay of the East India Company or seaworthy British government assessors) to theorise or even act according to a theory of transition. They do need to learn something of local conditions, if only to recruit comprador allies, but although theorists might not always avail themselves of adequate information, to the extent that an adequate assessment of these matters impacts upon political activity now, we do need to be as little misinformed as possible. The danger, Spivak points out, is that those who read the speculative morphology as a blueprint for social justice, in conditions where really existing Marxisms were surrounded by overdetermining hostile political and military opposition, will be forced to promote speculation as orthodoxy (Spivak 1999:91).

The point is that Hardt and Negri's accusation of 'Eurocentrism' in Marx serves to deflect attention from the political aspects of Marx's concern with the East India Company petition to the British Parliament for renewal of its charter. Did Marx 'far too easily' see only the choices of British rule, local domination or 'a path of insubordination and freedom' (Hardt and Negri 2000:119) modelled on Europe, or was he offering a possible projection and liberatory speculation as a part of a wider political history, consistent activism and emancipatory ambition? Hardt and Negri suggest that 'the central issue is that Marx can conceive of history outside of Europe only as moving *strictly* along the path already traveled by Europe itself' (2000:120, my italic). It is all too common to find

Marx fitted into this form of historical determinism, with consequent closure implied for political initiative (spontaneity at best). The clincher against such (unidimensional) distortion is contained in the all too infrequently read letter Marx wrote in 1878 to the editors of the paper *Otechestvennye Zapiski* warning that the chapter of *Capital* which described transition to a capitalist mode of production should not be 'transformed' from an historical sketch of the genesis of capitalism in Western Europe to a 'theory of the general course fatally imposed upon all peoples, whatever the historical circumstances in which they find themselves placed' (correspondence of Marx reproduced in Shanin 1983:136).

The orthodox reification of Marx that Hardt and Negri perpetrate is affirmed even as they suggest that Empire is, like capitalism for Marx, 'better than the forms of society and modes of production that came before it' (2000:43). Although they recognise that Marx was talking about the '*potential* for liberation' (my italic) being increased under capitalism vis-à-vis parochial and hierarchical local circumstances, they introduce a teleological tendency of their own and this, I argue, shapes both the questions and answers they deploy vis-à-vis imperialism.

So many years have passed to call into question the dubious book-ends analogy that, I am suggesting, Hardt and Negri set up between the history of the East India Company and the post-imperial Empire of the transnational corporations. The explanatory viability of this analogy might be explored by considering the degree to which there were mechanisms similar to the presently emergent administrative global civil society which functioned to manage the operation of mercantile capital, or by discovering at what period the transition to formal colonialism imposed such administration. Cultures of colonialism experts will be deployed to rake over the archival records. The key justification for pursuing this analogy however is strangely given by Hardt and Negri themselves when they say their 'first real glimpse of the passage to Empire' comes when they see that the 'global capitalist hierarchy that subordinates the formally sovereign nation-states within its order' is one that is 'fundamentally different from the colonialist and imperialist circuits of international domination' (2000:134). The subordination of a sovereign administration under a larger Empire is exactly what they describe as having occurred in the legislative containment of the East India Company – the key moment of the break returns.

Another way of understanding the national economy period of imperialist development is to note that it suited the cause of capital to arrange national economic units in relative autonomy and hierarchy. Nowadays the World Bank continues to make these arrangements with coercive alacrity – at one point tying loans to specific niche or sectoral manufacturing with the less 'advanced' technological modes of production allocated to one side of the international division of labour, high tech to the other, and at another point forcing open national boundaries for privatisation of 'national' industries et cetera. Urbanisation modifies this somewhat, but the distance between the elite programming class in Bangalore and their service personnel, (sweepers, rickshaw-wallahs), or even between micro-chip assembly workers in Kuala Lumpur (usually female) and building development speculators (usually linked to the Prime Minister) shows that neocolonial exploitation still thrives in conditions that I would call 'semi-feudal-cyber-colonialism' (see Hutnyk 1999).

Yet Empire is different. The new world order of *Empire* requires a new set of concepts to organise struggle. The model of struggle our authors offer differs substantially from the 'cycle of struggles' conception of apparently obsolete proletarian internationalism. The justification for this change is based on a 'break' which composes premature obituaries. Perhaps it is also orthodox understandings of the proletariat that have congealed (see Balibar 1994) in the ways I have questioned above. Nevertheless, rather than waste time trying to resuscitate the grubby 'old mole' that haunts Marx and imperialism (the mole is rumoured to be dead, Hardt and Negri 2000:57), let us continue to examine the concepts on offer in *Empire*.

# 7
# Difference and Opposition

Difference, subsumption, hybridity: in the first instance, the ways 'difference' and 'subsumption' were played out in the pre-colonial and colonial period would be a relevant basis for evaluation. What cultural aspects of the mercantile and imperialist periods are to be taken into account? (For an excellent examination of the cultural dimensions of transition, see Nugent 1993.) Hardt and Negri align themselves against the 'unidimensionality' of a Marx who 'had no conception of the difference of Indian society' (2000:120). In this they side with those theorists who deal with plurality and multiplicity (Deleuze, Foucault) allowing their analysis of subsumption to take in 'not only the economic or only the cultural dimension of society' (Hardt and Negri 2000:25). I am not convinced that transition, for reasons mentioned above, was so strictly conceived that culture and difference was not taken into account (on Marx and difference see Spivak 1999:78).

What of subsumption and difference now? Are these indicators of something new (the break) or are there continuities which should be stressed? Wasn't it colonialism that tried to subsume all aspects of the social life of others under new productive codes, to train the lazy natives, to co-opt the village headship, to create tribal allegiance (and difference) and national sentiments, et cetera? The idea of ruling by division, by forging identifications based on difference, was intrinsic from the earliest stage of capitalist expansion. I think the ways that capital thrives upon difference today, forging 'communities' of identification and segmentation which replace 'outmoded' allegiances or, rather, dangerously universal ones, appears quite similar to the ways new 'community' identifications had to be constituted by emergent capitalism to replace old feudal alliances destroyed when tenants, peasants and others were displaced from the land. The constitutive ascription of identity and community – whether racial, gendered, national or cultural – seems a consistent and necessary strategy of capital's administrative sector.

Hardt and Negri are fully aware that difference is used by contemporary capitalism, co-opted, contained and consigned to market via the Culture Industry. 'Long Live Difference' is the battle cry of power (Hardt and Negri 2000:138). They argue that a postmodern politics of difference 'not only is ineffective against but even can coincide with and support the functions and practices of imperial rule' (2000:142). This is old news for some; capital thrives on making differences and then taking them into account as equivalents in the trick of the market. Yet when a simple notion of hybridity is criticised, they can still posit a hybridity of a special type as potent. The ways hybridity works as a cul de sac for politics are well rehearsed – it implies a 'pure', belongs to the market, emphasises biological heritage, cannot found a programme (see Hutnyk 1998a). Capital readily co-opts hybridity and difference (and, as we shall see, Maoist sloganeering):

> The corporation seeks to include difference ... and thus aims to maximize creativity, free play, and diversity within the corporate workplace. People of all different races, sexes and sexual orientations should potentially be included ... the workplace should be rejuvenated with unexpected changes and an atmosphere of fun. Break down the old barriers and let one hundred flowers bloom.
>
> (Hardt and Negri 2000:153)

\*   \*   \*

In the second half of their book, Hardt and Negri become more and more utopian and finally present the 'multitude', its movement and rights, as the sublated possibility and potential within Empire that will save us all. There is more than a degree of optimism here, as a dialectical hope reworks the old promise that in Empire 'there is the guarantee of justice for all peoples' (Hardt and Negri 2000:10). The foundational power of Empire is the multitude: the peoples of the planet and their constitutive power. The main vehicle, it seems, for this power today is mobility. There have been many critiques of mobility as 'travel', and the ways in which this buzzword of postmodern theory has been deployed to carry creative ethnographic work as well as well-intentioned progressive sociology and diaspora studies is well documented (see Clifford 1997; Kaur and Hutnyk 1999; and 'Clifford's Ethnographica', Part 1 of this volume). Mobility is not always the comfortable luxury it appears to be in the brochures and holiday snaps of the privileged leisure classes.

To their credit, Hardt and Negri, with a characteristic contradiction, note the pain that comes with mobility. In discussion of the 'massive worker migrations' which called Empire into being, they note that such migrations 'are dwarfed by [migrations of] those forced from their homes and land by famine and war. Just a cursory glance around the world ... will reveal the desperate plight of those on whom such mobility has been imposed' (2000:155). The condition of possibility of the world market is the same 'circulation, mobility, diversity and mixture' that also 'overwhelms any binary division' and as 'uncontainable rhizome', it cannot ever be 'completely subjugated to the laws of capitalist accumulation' (2000:397).

In asking how a 'constituent political tendency within and beyond the spontaneity of the multitude's movement' might be recognised (Hardt and Negri 2000:398), the danger is that the form of the question may project a tendency, inherent in spontaneity, which needs rather to be actively organised. It is not predetermined.

The better question to ask comes towards the end of the book, and is 'how can the multitude organise?' (Hardt and Negri 2000:399). If a 'new type of resistance' is to be founded that would be 'adequate to the new dimensions of sovereignty' (2000:308), it matters very much that the periodisation of the 'break' shapes not only what would count as adequate but also what counts as object and context of resistance. If Hardt and Negri are pushing the wrong emphases in their periodisation, then their characterisation and rejection of 'the traditional forms of resistance such as the institutional worker's organisation' might require re-evaluation. Another path to explore would be how far proletarian internationalism might be from the congealed and orthodox (bureaucratic) 'trade unionism' that has too often come to be 'constituted' as the 'traditional' and 'institutionalised' forms of worker's organisation. Communist historians engage...

The point is that consideration of how to sustain organised opposition to the transnational corporations, the complicit civil society/NGO sector, and to Empire as such, without an internationalist organisation, and in the absence of 'cycles of struggle', is not addressed. Just where this book might have broached the party question, Hardt and Negri suggest quite a different content for the political struggle of the multitude. This takes on the form of a claim for rights. The multitude on the move provides the impetus for the first of these: 'the political demand is that the existent fact of capitalist production be recognised juridically and that all workers be given the full rights of citizenship'. This abstract demand can be reconfigured: 'The general right to control its own movement is the multitude's ultimate demand for global citizenship' (Hardt and Negri 2000:400). I have argued elsewhere against the discourse of rights, and it is sufficient to point out the compromise that the language of 'claim' and 'be given' structures into this prostration. A gift is never a gift ... (see Hutnyk 2000c). Rights constituted in law may be violated, and are more often than not violated across differences in power. They have some tactical utility, but the right to 'a social wage and guaranteed income for all' (Hardt and Negri 2000:403), the right to reappropriation (of the means of production) and the right to communicate (2000:410) all seem admirable but must be 'taken' not given, and taken in a movement which destroys the existing system, of wages, exploitation and ideological deceit. No matter what admirable rhetoric of 'unity managed by the multitude, organized by the multitude, directed by the multitude – absolute democracy in action' (2000:410), I still think we need to explore how the 'posse' might actualise this democracy in a way 'adequate' to oppose a capitalism armed with tanks. Note that a curious reference to contemporary rap groups is transmuted very quickly into something very unlike an armed gang and more like the metaphysical ontology of the Renaissance (2000:208) – I'm not convinced this escapes the Culture Industry at all.

From their first pages, Hardt and Negri write about the United Nations in terms of rights (2000:4). They offer a welcome critique of non-government organisations as self-elected representatives of 'the people' in global civil society. These NGOs who claim to represent those 'who cannot represent themselves' (2000:314), like the media when it positions itself as the 'voice or conscience of the People' (2000:311), are hardly 'democratic'. The media represents, and so 'hybrid networks of participation are manipulated from above' (2000:321). Even the militancy advocated at the very end of *Empire*, which is supposedly different from the 'formulas of the old revolutionary working class' (which were never so singular), also cannot be representative of the exploited (2000:413). The time to revisit the 18th Brumaire is again at hand.

Representation, and the right to communicate, have great importance. Our communicative competence is a subject for which interpretative historical and linguistic deployment is also necessary. One reason for such deployment would be to assess attempts to name the current conjuncture. Perhaps I have misrepresented *Empire* by forcing it into history. It might be possible to test this by asking if our descriptive-constitutive terms are adequate to the level of struggle required. This has multiple implications from the most obvious to the more obscure: has the 'industrial working class' really 'disappeared from view' (Hardt and Negri 2000:53)? A vanishing trick which is co-constituted with the related media black-out shrouding the sites of imperialist plunder on the dark side of the international division of labour (formerly the Third World or the South, now also at selected metropolitan suburbs). On the other hand, is a notion of Empire as speculative culmination and consequence of imperialism still somehow useful in the way that 'Oriental despotism' was useful to name a stasis that had to be interrupted in Marx's speculation (see Spivak 1999:97)? The notion of Empire might be convenient for fusing disparate struggles usually little noticed and not much more dangerous individually than internet hacking or symbolic protest.

So, the defining question for this book and the new thinking offered to make sense of Empire is that of how best to interpret and then organise the struggles against corporate imperialism. And how to do this so that it is not restricted only to being a community carnival co-opted and complicit with a global capitalism in search of 'release valves' to let off steam. The performativity of unorganised opposition, like erudite and edifying academic critique, is akin to what anthropologists call the potlatch, what Bataille called the accursed share and what Derrida calls pharmakon. I have in mind the balaclava-clad anarchist trashings of McDonald's stores in London at an anti-capitalist festival and in Prague on annual 'Surround the World Bank day'. 'More World, Less Bank' is a great slogan, but the McDonald's stores were trading again within days, the papers sold their front-page stories ('May Day Rioters Heckle Churchill Statue') and the Sony and Kodak camera supplies shops had a field day. How can the multitude organise the circulation of these struggles beyond the one-off flash?

As mentioned at the beginning of this section, Hardt and Negri offer up Tiananmen, the *Intifada*, Los Angeles, South Korea, Chiapas, etc., as examples of struggles that are no longer best comprehended within the 'cycles of struggle' model that animated understandings of the proletarian internationalist movements. Given mediation by the 'much celebrated age of communication', these singularities paradoxically become all but 'incommunicable' and cannot be linked together as a 'globally expanding chain of revolt'. These struggles 'fail to communicate' because they cannot be 'translated' into different contexts – other revolutionaries 'did not hear' these struggles as their own (Hardt and Negri 2000:54).

I am not sure that this is the case, though the white noise of the censor distorts reception. What would happen if we were to add Seattle, Prague, S11 in Melbourne, etc., to these singular struggles and consider these to have a direct or 'vertical' relation to the global level? What is more important, that these protests are against the World Bank and IMF, or that the containment of them – the tear gas and water cannon, is provided by the armed forces of individual nation-states?

Hardt and Negri lament, though only a little, the 'cycles of struggle' model. The new struggles are said to have 'gained in intensity' although this is perhaps more necessary for the notion of Empire than it is a descriptive or empirically verifiable reality. Intensity is so heavily mediated by channels of communication, the capacity to 'leap vertically' (Hardt and Negri 2000:55) relies crucially on a satellite uplink, operative internet connection, news broadcast programming priorities and interpretative fashions. The unorganised and spontaneous aspect of struggles like Tiananmen could be emphasised by interpretation – it may have 'looked like a weak echo of Berkeley' (Hardt and Negri 2000:56) precisely because on TV it functioned as a festival for CNN reportage. Station executives were just as interested in the Chinese government close-down of the uplink – the stain on our screens as the satellite went dead, over and over in slow motion – as they were in the 'democracy movement' of the Chinese students. The pixelation of the Los Angeles uprising, broadcast live from helicopters, began in the court room stop-motion analysis of the Rodney King beating tape. It is however less the case that these events are 'hypermediatised' on television because of their own intrinsic nature as spectacle – the students were also protesting for reform within the Communist Party, Rodney King was savagely beaten by the LAPD – and it is not necessarily the case that these struggles are 'written in an incomprehensible foreign language' for activists in other parts of the world (Hardt and Negri 2000:57), but that the writing, interpretation, concepts and code words favoured in relatively privileged mediatised and postmodern academic circuits is predetermined to ensure that these events appear as spectacle. The grim practicalities of battle in Chiapas, or neighbouring Guererro in Mexico, are a very great distance from the self-declared Zapatismo of laptop activists in Texas, Italy or Madrid – where it was possible in 1995 to buy souvenirs at the European Encentro such as a Zapatista balaclava, a Zapatista t-shirt, Zapatista baseball caps and – presumably for igniting cocktails – a Zapatista cigarette lighter. Similarly romantic revolutionary support for the rebellion in Bougainville in the Pacific, for Maoists in Nepal (cheering when the 'Communists take Everest – because it was there') or for Peruvian comrades in occupation of embassies, does not often translate into adequate comprehension of the levels of engagement involved. Jane Fonda's support for the Vietnamese was a spectacle of solidarity. It is no accident that 'just when the United States was most deeply embroiled in an imperialist venture abroad, when it had strayed farthest from its original constitutional project, that constituent spirit bloomed most strongly at home' (Hardt and Negri 2000:179). The anti-war movement, civil rights, Black power, student and feminist movements – the evil in Vietnam countered by love-ins at home. Live Aid and famine. Seattle and Structural Adjustment. It would be wrong to consider all revolts and all opposition processed through the media as contained, but it is also necessary to consider seriously the carnivalesque element of performative protest and the great disjunction of the 'uplink'.

There is of course some evidence to the contrary, but most contemporary forms of internationalist solidarity that make it into the mass media appear to work through formulas of romantic, sensationalist and exotic appropriation – political subjectivity today can present itself in attendance at world music and alternative festivals (Womad, Glastonbury, anti-capitalist carnivals); revolutionary consciousness is signalled by wearing t-shirts emblazoned with the image of Che; passing knowledge of one or two phrases from Subcomandante Marcos; a preference for veggie burgers over Big Mac and fries; and so on. It is always important to take seriously the new subjectivities formed on the basis of anti-corporate struggles and those mobilisations, usually called social movements, in favour of flexibility in work, in relationships, living arrangements, lifestyles, mobility, etc., and these, as Hardt and Negri argue, can be said to have forced capital to restructure. But new subjectivity is not enough to win – forcing capital to stop profiteering in one instance and being co-opted into a new mode of profiteering in another is rather less of a victory than might be required. Now we might well ask what was the difference between East India Company rule and the Raj? The new production of hybrid travelling queer subjectivities does not seem to have been so unwieldy that the cultural industries and institutions of the commodity system could not adapt and adopt these new subjectivities as principles for profit. Bataille's (1949/1988:12) suggestion that 'the sexual act is in time what the tiger is in space' hints at the terrible necessity for release. The shape this takes under capitalism is noted, in more prosaic terms, where 'Empire recognizes and profits from the fact that in cooperation bodies produce more and in community bodies enjoy more, but it has to obstruct and control this cooperative autonomy so as not to be destroyed by it' (Hardt and Negri 2000:392).

This control is built into the code words; but there is still a circulating opposition. Hardt and Negri write that the working class has disappeared from view (2000:53). They follow Debord's spectacular argument that 'only what appears exists' and note that the 'media have something approaching a monopoly over what appears to the general population' (2000:322). It would be conspiracy theory to think this was 'consciously and explicitly directed by a single power' (2000:323) but we could go further to insist on the possibility of informing ourselves of the criteria of accumulation, exploitation, ideological manipulation and representative misinformation that occurs in this Wizard of Oz cartoon, and which implies 'the impossibility of traditional forms of struggle' (2000:324). The victories of the previous century were not nothing; there were media and concepts that were not mere wizardry. And the work of books like this should be to extend the tools. The task is to understand the composition of class under current conditions, and this will require, I would argue, an operation to correct the myopic and racist blindness that fails to see how the proletariat has always been international, that the metropolitan city and the colonial theatre of exploitation have always been co-constituted, and that the identification of the 'working class' as a wholly economistic category was always an error. Why are these points no longer heard? We need to ask about the class interests of those who, living adjacent to the portals of new media, advocate a convergence of other-love, difference, rhizome, hybridity, connectivity and bandwidth, and yet claim solidarity with mediatised events filtered through the corporate screen. Looking to the production of subjectivity and abstract celebration of resistances, refusals and exodus is not yet adequate to win, even as it is a necessary step. There are also other moves to make.

If the time of proletarian internationalism is over (Hardt and Negri 2000:50) what comes to take its place? Surely both the declaration, and the search for substitutes, are premature if a wider view is taken – certainly the short period in which the rise of local and identity politics at the subnational level, and the period of contraction and reaction in the 20 years since *perestroika* are not yet enough to declare that the project of international proletarian unity is forever stalled. *Reformasi* struggles in Indonesia against Suharto, in Malaysia against Mahathir, inspired by the student and union organisations in South Korea, movements against Marcos and later Ramos in the Philippines, in Mexico against the PRI, and many more examples, are indicators that counter a too-fast transposition of de-industrialisation in the 'advanced West' to 'globalisation' as indicative of the end of proletarian internationalism. The interconnected cycles of struggle forcing reorganisation on the part of a capitalism that works across borders many postmodern theorists refuse to traverse. Evidence of this is that capitalism thrives on the co-constitutive exploitation of so-called periphery and centre. Why have analysts been so unable to break with the structuring myopia of these terms and only now come to realise the reality of the Empire against which so many have for so long fought? In one sense at least, *Empire* allows us to think these things anew; but there has always been Empire and there has always been an opposition to organise.

Organisation is the key, but for too many there is only spectacle and spontaneity, resting hopefully on the maturity of the multitude to come. 'The only event we are still awaiting is the construction, or rather the insurgence, of a powerful organization' (Hardt and Negri 2000:411). Organisation matters, but it must actually be organised, not simply named. The point at which more must be demanded from this book is again explicable with reference to Marx's writing on colonialism in India. In a footnote, Hardt and Negri find a 'resonance in Marx's articles' which they use to defend the views of Kautsky from Lenin's criticism. Did Marx pose a 'linear tendency of imperialist development towards the formation of a world market' (Hardt and Negri 2000:451) in a way that exonerates Kautsky for his 'reactionary desire to blunt the contradictions' of the situation of twentieth-century imperialism? The objection Lenin made to Kautsky's argument for ultra-imperialist subsumption was not that there was no trend towards cooperation of finance capital, but that this utopian future was used as an excuse to avoid action on 'the contradictions posed by capital's present imperialist organisation' (Hardt and Negri 2000:230). In his book *Insurgencies* (1999:230), Negri had already cited Marx on the necessity of organisation. Organised how is the issue. Is subjective rebellion and revolt – unorganised and spontaneous – more than a constituted singular eventuality ripe for recuperation? What this book might have done would be to sew the series of oppositional events together – to translate, communicate, organise. If the 1857 rebellion is interpreted as a singular event (as the 'Sepoy Mutiny'), to which the British state makes a founding response (it was not its first intervention), the ongoing opposition to British rule is spectacularised. This is only necessary if the 'cycles of struggle' model is to be jettisoned – theoretical demands force a rewriting – but when the rebellion and response is then read as significant for understanding of contemporary imperialism, it excludes from discussion the necessary problems of how to sustain and organise any 'cycle' of anti-Empire spectacular events. The discussion of an organised international solidarity that might work against co-option and complicity is not on the agenda, and has in fact been ruled 'outmoded' and dead. Even a grubby old mole could work out that of course we cannot look to the congealed institutions and mediatised formations for direction in this, however progressive some of them may seem: not the transnational, nor the postmodern, the hybrid, difference or history will ever be the vanguard. What may be, however, is a reconstituted proletarian internationalism informed by attention to a politics of knowledge production, rethinking how conceptual apparatuses shape our understandings and reclaiming Marxism and communism from misconception and reification – even as these are only the micro-theoretical versions of general ideological enframings, and our decisions must be tested in action, not by appeal to something like the true.

Perhaps we should learn more about the opposition to imperialism that comes from outside, at that moment of transition – the wars fought against colonialism from the earliest days of the East India Company through to the post-independence struggles against the Indian client state (Tebhaga, Telengana, Naxalbari, Bhirbum, for a start, see Banerjee 1984). These struggles were sustained and severe, our sanctioned ignorance of this anti-colonialism and its history, our Eurocentric focus and parasite carnivalism, our romantic naïve solidarities and our failure to organise adequately, condemn us to continued complicity if we forget.

At the end of section 1.1 of their book, Hardt and Negri offer as a 'final analogy' for their 'world to come' a reference to 'the birth of Christianity in Europe and its expansion during the decline of the Roman Empire' (2000:21). Two millennia on and Hardt and Negri would prophesy a new ethical and ontological basis for a subjectivity to challenge Empire. At the very end of the book the 'ontological power of a new society' (2000:413) is found in the god-bothering Christian figure of St Francis of Assisi. The terminology turns evangelical, but there is no need for hand-wringing and flagellation complaining that this book wants to be everything and to be everywhere – it had already proclaimed itself the update of unwritten bits of *Capital*. Fantastical utopian spontaneity and errors on any number of points do not prove irredeemable: Readers, strip this book of its holy costumery (St Francis), whip them into shape with disciplinary rigour (history, the party) and deploy them in organised squads. There is a world to win.

# 8
# The Chapatti Story

As I have argued, Hardt and Negri's *Empire* is a serious but flawed attempt to respond to the dilemmas of the contemporary 'struggle'. This response is to be achieved in part with speculation about hybridisation in terms of taking 'responsibility', and asserting control of identity formation, as a kind of politics. Mobility is offered as a way to combat Empire if it is possible to 'take control of the production of mobility and stasis, purities and mixtures' (Hardt and Negri 2000:156). A multitude in 'perpetual motion' subject to 'hybridization' (2000:60) is capable of 'smashing' all old and new boundaries and borders with a 'nomad singularity' and the 'omnilateral movement of its desire' (2000:363). Are the displacements, dispersal and exodus advocated by Hardt and Negri in *Empire* viable as metaphor or strategy for making sense of the contemporary? With this model of displacement, they suggest a general desertion from the global apparatus of power. Although this conception seems difficult to sustain if they also argue there is no outside, the characterisation of movement, circulation and flow has great appeal. Some may object that the valorisation of hybridity too often offers a strategy that is always already co-opted and complicit with an expansive capitalism – the movement of exodus with no outside is logically incoherent and offers either the danger of the deserters colonising still more aspects of life for capital or excludes the possibility of building a radically separate alternative. The latter requires more than the ad hoc abandonments of deserters, or the herd mobilisation of exodus – however hybrid and multiple the lines of flight might be. Is it not more likely that an older language, only obliquely mouthed by Hardt and Negri, might offer something new instead? It is to this we should now turn.

When evaluating theoretical debates it is good to remember how the displacement of concepts is another, sometimes overlooked, mode in the general disorientation of our times that sells us rightwards drift in the guise of a committed politics. My contention is

139

that recent theoretical discussions, disconnected from really existing Asias, have used that place as a sounding board or punching bag for ever more abstract and unhelpful speculations. This has been seen in the discussion of Empire and, I believe, can be identified again in another, parallel area of cultural studies theorising – one that Hardt and Negri refer to, however dismissively. In this chapter 'hybridity' is examined in relation to the ways that Homi Bhabha has adopted and modified the founding moves of the Subaltern historians. This example abstracts the specificity of Asia, under a spuriously celebrated hybridity, and what is displaced is the Marxist-Maoist-anti-imperial project that for many years was the only viable version of Asia outside of Orientalism. The fortunes and consequences of this displacement are to be (cautiously) evaluated and displaced yet further into what Spivak calls 'learning to learn from below' – what I think may be a reconfigured 'fieldwork' for a political anthropology or cultural studies.[1]

## SUBALTERN STUDIES

If it is the case that interest in the notion of hybridity within cultural and 'ethnic' studies affirms corporate hegemony and leaves the stratified South in flat shadow (Spivak 1999), then we might attend to one line of scholarship that has claimed to challenge this (post) colonial legacy. It is of course impossible and unhelpful to treat the entirety of the Subaltern Studies 'school' of writings as a coherent whole. Even to periodise early and late versions of the project would be to force some writers into categories they perhaps do not deserve to be in, for good or ill. The Subalternist body of work is diverse, and cannot be adequately summarised without reduction, but in terms of hybridity, the texts of its founding work have a key resonance. The way in which we might (selectively) get into this discussion is via one of the key theorists of hybridity who reads the subaltern scene. Homi Bhabha.

Among a plethora of 'culture clash' discussions around themes such as Westernisation (Srinivas 1962), monoculture (Lévi-Strauss 1955) and globalisation, it is particularly Bhabha's work that has found the notion of hybridisation useful in the colonial theatre. In *The Location of Culture*, he argues that colonial 'mimicry' is an effect of hybridity, 'at once a mode of appropriation and of resistance' (1994:120). Bhabha in particular elaborates on the multiple and divergent uses of translations of the Christian Bible, handed out by missionary evangelists in Hurdwar, India, in the early 1800s. Those who show interest in such texts may be feigning devotion or their prospects for conversion; there may be underlying calculations as to cheap combustibles; and so camouflage, mimicry, mockery and masking undermines the authority of colonial power. This is best seen in the demand for a vegetarian Bible, for example, since the one from the mouths of meat-eaters could not be clean. Bhabha argues that we should 'understand that all cultural statements and systems are constructed in [the] contradictory and ambivalent space of enunciation' – by which he means that communication is always a matter of interpretation. Only then can 'we begin to understand why hierarchical claims to the inherent originality or "purity" of cultures are untenable, even before we resort to empirical historical instances that demonstrate their hybridity' (Bhabha 1994:37). Does the example of mockery of the Bible lead to a politics capable of undoing imperial power? The mimic is the revenge of Macauley's minutemen – the turn of those who become accomplished in the ways of the master against that master. Bhabha is quick to point out, however, that hybridity is many things; just as hybridity is resistance, there is the 'hybridity of images of governance' (1994:134).

Hybridity appears, indeed, to be everywhere, and so this version of hybridity may have abstract and generalising consequences that undo Bhabha's intention to get at the specificity of colonial exchange. Kuan-Hsing Chen has argued that Bhabha's discussion of the hybridity of the colonised and the coloniser – in the essay 'Signs Taken for Wonders' – may de-historicise his 'objects' of analysis. The notion that ambivalences with regard to biblical translation two centuries ago – with the Bible used strategically as Word of God, and as wrapping paper – may have lessons for the present is an idea that should confront several questions: 'Has the "hybridity" phenomenon of 1817 continued to move on until now? What are the differences between then and the present? Under what conditions could hybridity work differently?' (Kuan-Hsing 1998:23). The continued productivity of studies of old colonial history for understandings of the present cannot be denied, but the specificity of the present is worth attending to also.

## THE GREAT REBELLION

Instead of asking how hybridity has changed, I intend to ask here why the term 'hybridity' has changed the subaltern project. This will be made clear. In his *Elementary Aspects of Peasant Insurgency*, which is after all identified as the ideological forerunner of Subaltern Studies, Ranajit Guha describes local acts of resistance that we will see become key moments of 'hybridity' in the reading of the same scenes in the work of Bhabha.

The debate hinges on Guha's reading of the 'revolutionary consciousness' of the peasantry, which is born of their shared 'subjection ... exploitation and oppression' (1983:225). In the context of his discussion of the 1857 Rebellion, Guha quotes Mao Zedong's 1928 argument that conditions of counter-revolutionary suppression in provinces that are adjacent to each other serve to unite the diverse elements of the peasantry in a shared and 'common struggle' (Mao 1928/1975:93). The people are united against the oppressor. Guha's discussion is of the ways that rumours circulate to establish and support this shared consciousness. The key story is of the greased bullets that soldiers were required to use in the Enfield rifle, with the defiling fat being an affront to religious sensibilities, and, as is well known, a 'mutiny' of soldiers in Meerut sparked off an India-wide insurgency. Of course, to see the events of 1857 primarily in terms of the rumour of greased cartridges only facilitates the colonialist view that it was a 'mutiny' within the military rather than a more wide-ranging rebellion and revolutionary fervour that caught the public mood, but there is no question that this confrontation has its role.

Guha is first and foremost interested in explaining the peasants' political organisation, read off from gaps and allusions in the colonial documents that work like parapraxes. Curiously, and in detail, he notes several examples in the historical records from 1855 (two years before the rebellion) of British patrols uncovering caches of arms – bows, arrows and drums (1983:233). These are indicators of peasant revolutionary consciousness as well, and though his focus is on the drums as 'nonverbal transmitters', arrows can also pass through the community as a call to struggle. Interestingly, a similar story concerns some chapattis that are passed from village to village as some kind of warning.

In reading this episode, Bhabha wants to emphasise the 'rumour and panic' involved, and suggests that the 'slender narrative of the chapatti' symbolises the wider contexts of the rebellion (1994:202). Following Guha, Bhabha wants to read the rebellion and the 'subject of peasant insurgency' as 'a site of cultural hybridity' – the rumour of chapattis indicates a panic that 'constitutes the boundary of cultural hybridity across which the Mutiny is fought' (1994: 206–7). The chapatti is a displacement of the Enfield rifle and its greased bullet, the ostensible trigger. For Bhabha, 'Panic spreads. It does not simply hold together the native people but binds them affectively, if antagonistically – through a process of projection – with their masters' (1994:203). He then identifies the British 'projection' of their own binding panic onto the story of the chapatti. The British did not know what to make of the stories of travelling bread.

Guha is careful to inform us that he finds 'nothing in the contemporary evidence to tell us what the circulating chapatti meant' (1983:239), even though they circulate rapidly and they are contemporaneous and in some way 'not altogether unrelated' (1983: 246) to the rebellion, and even if they only indicate, as some speculated, a response to the spread of cholera. It must be said that here Bhabha usefully notes that the coloniser is bound up with the colonised (co-constitution), but that he displaces the politics of this into the realm of translation is revealing: 'in the very practice of domination the language of the master becomes hybrid' (1994:33). The chapattis, drums, arrows and rifles become signs of hybridity as the 'address of colonial authority', in the discourse of the evangelical Christian missions, is threatened by 'the oppositional voices of a culture of resistance' (1994:33). This resistance is ambivalent so long as it remains talk. But, in a brilliant coda to his discussion, Bhabha evokes other rumours that spread panic, in particular about Christian conversion (hybridity) and an earlier mutiny, this time in Vellore in 1806, where the leather of belts and topis (hats) provoked panic (1994:210). The trouble is that we don't hear much of the mutiny as an organisational question. When Guha mentions Vellore it is not hats but stories of salt contaminated by the blood of pigs and cows (1983:267) that are the focus. What has happened to common struggle? Apprehension of loss of freedom through forced conversion to Christianity is identified, with a glance towards Marx, as 'a product of self-alienation' (Guha 1983:268; Marx and Engels *CW*III:339).

The key absence in Guha's narrative, but more so in Bhabha's distillation of the story, is the question of organisation that must necessarily be asked in terms of what is required for any 'revolutionary consciousness' to succeed against oppression. Clearly rumour is not enough, even if chapattis are part of the story; the arms cache has more political significance. The section Guha quotes from Mao, though he does not draw attention to it in the passage, is from Mao's critique of localism in a subsection called 'Questions of Party Organization'. Here Mao is writing against opportunists and 'blind insurrection' so as to build the Red Army into a 'militant Bolshevik Party' (Mao 1928/1975:93). Mao does not mention hybridity, but gives a subtle analysis of what is required for a political struggle that can succeed. His text, ignored at the time by the Chinese Communist Party leadership, then under Comintern influence, later became a key analysis of the character of agrarian revolutionary mobilisation.

Guha actually refers a number of times to exactly this Hunan-Kiangsi Report in his *Elementary Aspects* (1983:29, 48, 58, 67, 89, 135–6, 163). Indeed, he refers almost exclusively to this one text by Mao. In the retelling of the story by Bhabha, hybridity is admirably foregrounded, but what recedes is any chance of, or need for, a discussion of the shared experience of oppression that binds the peasants together sufficiently to organise an uprising. We are left with rumours, chapattis and only a faint echo of 'revolutionary consciousness'. This is not to say that the word of Mao is god. It is not unlikely that the Maoist text (it is in Volume One of the *Selected Works*, the same volume which has the essay 'On Contradiction' discussed in Part 2 of this book [Mao 1937/1975]) forecloses access to the position of the 'native informant' with the fabled romance of the revolutionary agent, but the advantage of recalling the ways this text is unwritten by hybridity might be that this foreclosure cannot always so readily be undone by postcolonial complicity in the metropole. Perhaps. It is certainly difficult, but endearing, to insist on Mao amidst identity politics and autobiographical opportunism.[2]

Early on in his book, Bhabha asks if the 'ambivalent borderline of hybridity' would 'prevent us from specifying a political strategy'. His later answer is that it would 'enhance our understanding of certain forms of political struggle' (1994:208), but he does not offer that strategy, cannot. What these texts show, on close inspection, is a cascading denial of organisational politics: from Mao, where the party question is explicit, through Guha, where rumour coexists with the rebellion of the class-in-itself (not for-itself), to Bhabha, where only the hint of the question of organisation remains and ambivalence is understood as the extent of politics. This trajectory can be faulted, however careful and elaborated, though it is perhaps no surprise that the party question is passed over in silence today.

The possibility of asking it is left open, but the text stops at enhanced understanding. Marx's 11th thesis springs to mind. A focus on the micropolitics of local hybridity and the trinketising amusements of stories about chapattis, vegetarian Bibles or topi hats, does not yet make a politics that can win, or allow a strategy for converting revolutionary consciousness into something more. How does the surfeit of trinket stories avoid commodity fetishism without articulation of questions of organisation and the party? Disarticulated and fragmented localisms seem easily beaten, at best they are coping strategies. How do we learn to learn from the insights of Subaltern Studies and move from understanding to something that does more than appreciate ambivalence?

## LEARNING TO LEARN

What displacements are entailed in those moves the Subaltern Studies project presented at its origins? The key issues that Gayatri Spivak identifies are the intervention in knowledge production that refuses to see subaltern insurgency as always 'pre-political' and the question of how religion or culture is transformed into militancy (Spivak 2000a:325–6). It is likely that the early phase of Subaltern Studies was not as clear about its Maoist credentials as it might have been. The citations in Guha aside, it is striking that in this context – subaltern insurgency, anti-colonialism in a rural sphere, the legacy of Naxalbari in intellectual work – that discussion of peasant organisation and struggle, and the texts of Mao, are subsequently ignored and absent. In a global scene now keen to foreground the rural as the site of assimilation by intervention, be it through the benevolent aid of NGOs through to the World Bank, or the anti-corporate activism of farmers who trash MacDonald's in France on behalf of farmers who trash Kentucky Fried stores in India, this absence of attention to a key set of texts on the forms of peasant organisation is revealing. Yes, there is a vague uneasiness about Maoism that names the Cultural Revolution as totalitarian; there is the restitution of capitalism in China, the horrors of Pol Pot and the deviations of '68 generation adventurism among the European Left, all of which do not commend a Maoist experiment to us (and the relation of the rural to the state is different, the corporations are not to be surrounded as were the cities, the protracted struggle is now that of the itinerant migrant sweatshop worker [see Dutton 1998:9]). On the other hand, reading with an eye for lessons of politics today, the historical successes of the Red Army in defeating the Japanese and the armies of Chiang Kai Shek, and the subsequent inspiration the Chinese communists offered other struggles such as those in North Korea and later Vietnam (they defeated the US occupation, it should be recalled), might still be instructive. These are blunt little red facts that would suggest that the texts of Mao deserve some study, at the very least leavened with the caution and distanced cold-eyed clinical evaluation of a Centre for Strategic Studies mind. Other less jaundiced approaches might find value there.

Does this demand a return to Mao? To suggest this is merely to point to the politics of the omission that handles other 'contradictions' and offers 'ambivalence' in the place that Mao once marked.[3] Anarchist anti-capitalists may profess international solidarities and a Guevarist aesthetic, but they do not read the works of the Great Leader. They are dissuaded from reading Marx on colonialism (see Ahmad's critique of Said [Ahmad 1992]), let alone those who tried to operationalise him in conditions far from the comforts of middle- class Europe. It is important to link up the struggles of rural insurgents in India and China with the global predicament of the present anti-capitalism, since the worst exploitations and oppressions are still visited on those rural fields – now become free trade zones filled with ex-rural piece-workers (see Ong 1999) or gene-modified crop plantations in the grip of intellectual property controls, at best. (The 'rest' are subject to annual devastating floods, displacement in the face of large dams – Narmada, Bakun; environmental disaster from mining – Bougainville, PNG; or disarticulation from economy and development as such, with mass famine or 'fratricidal' war as the only consequence – most of sub-Saharan Africa.)

What would be part of a return to Mao today, for those of us involved in anti-capitalist mobilisations? There would be the question of the party, of organisation. There would be issues of practice, of disciplinary conduct, of correct handling of contradictions and so forth, and perhaps most readily apparent, from the very first texts of Mao such as the very Report from Hunan that Guha cites, there would be the injunction to live among the peasantry and learn from their 'common struggle'. It is tempting to wonder if this could be reconfigured today as something like what Spivak (2000a:333) calls 'learning to learn from below'. I cannot be sure she would like to see this phrase made over as a formula in this way, but there is something in Mao's reports from Hunan that is intriguing both as good anthropology – he went and had a look for himself, i.e. undertook fieldwork – and good Marxist political practice – he started from the material conditions themselves. Of course there are many ways that both anthropological fieldwork and materialism have been derailed by ethnocentric and economist presuppositions, but Spivak's learning to learn from below specifically attends to this in the task of learning to learn. It is also well known in anthropology that the interfering anthropologist can be a nuisance, and taken for a spy. Negotiating these difficulties is worthwhile in a context that must recognise, for example, that the demands of international solidarity that fly through the Internet might also be inappropriate – the 'insurgent' group, or even the local NGO, has neither resources or time to dedicate personnel to running a website and answering outside demands for 'updates', nor for feeding an anthropologist for no return. Learning to learn also means paying one's way – the Red Army devised rules for this that did not rely on idioms of hybridity.

Learning to learn from below can only be something 'like' anthropology's fieldwork or Mao's peasant solidarity (and Subaltern Studies' archive), with the application of many qualifications, conditions, cautions. ... At the least, learning to learn from below perhaps could be a credo for rereading Mao in anthropology, sociology and cultural studies today. For those who need this to be spelled out programmatically, the task of teaching in these disciplines, then, could be one of promoting strategies for learning to learn from below as part of an organisational project that sees the liberation of all as a key to one's own liberation, and working together to that end. Learning to learn (even if not from the same below) cannot be a unidirectional flow, extraction, but must also entail attention to interaction. Reciprocity is on the cards as well as vigilance as to what the encounter produces (this word encounter is used intentionally; it recalls the police strategy of the staged assassination or 'encounter' with Naxalites throughout India in the 1970s).[4] Learning to learn is not neutral, nor without consequences that change all participants in the equation, whatever it adds up to. Learning to learn as a political strategy may mean a refashioned and quite mundane or colloquial communist practice, and as such it cannot really insist on slogans like 'Long Live the Helmsman'. But it would certainly be a refreshing alternative to banging on in the abstract about hybridity and resting content with a paralysing 'ambivalence'.[5]

## THE DIALECTICS OF HYBRIDITY

Bhabha writes:

> In my own work I have developed the concept of hybridity to describe the construction of cultural authority within conditions of political antagonism or inequity. Strategies of hybridization reveal an estranging movement in the 'authoritative', even authoritarian inscription of the cultural sign ... the hybrid strategy or discourse opens up a space of negotiation where power is unequal but its articulation may be equivocal. Such negotiation is neither assimilation nor collaboration.
>
> (Bhabha 1996:58)

Is it unreasonable to consider that the word hybridity may be a cover for not saying dialectics? Though at pains to stress a socialist ambition, a possible tone of anti-Marxism (ex-Marxism, or at least post-Marxism) is sometimes evident in uses of hybridity (or is merely a preference for other words?). This is found in exactly the place where it might be expected that Marx would be more productive – *The Post-colonial Studies Reader*, for example, managed 19 index references to hybridity (including hybrid poetics) and only four to Marx (no Mao, only one Lenin) – though dialectics does not necessarily have to invoke Marx.[6] In Bhabha's discussion, some passages resonate with the plausibility of a straight swap between hybridity and the Marxist notion of dialectics. The sentence: '[*dialectics* ...] unsettles the mimetic or narcissistic demands of colonial power but reimplicates its identifications in strategies of subversion that turn the gaze of the discriminated back upon the eye of power', makes just as much sense with the word dialectics at the front as it does with 'hybridity'.

Hybridity, however, is rarely articulated in terms of Marxist dialectics. Bhabha recognises that for Franz Fanon, those who 'initiate the productive instability of revolutionary change are themselves the bearers of a hybrid identity'. He is then able to go on to say that these people become the 'very principle of dialectical reorganization' constructing their culture from 'the national text translated into modern Western forms of information technology, language, dress' (Bhabha 1994:38). In the same essay, Walter Benjamin's notion of the 'dialectic at a standstill' is quoted (Bhabha 1994:18), yet this process, and 'commitment to theory' seem to be carefully disarticulated from that body of theory that would think dialectics as an internationalist revolutionary project. For Bhabha 'the problematic of political judgement' cannot be represented as a 'dialectical problem' (1994:24). He wants to take his 'stand' on the 'shifting margins of cultural displacement', and asks 'what the function of a committed theoretical perspective might be' if the point of departure is the 'cultural and historical hybridity of the postcolonial world' (1994: 21). He continues: 'Hybrid agencies find their voice in a dialectic that does not seek cultural supremacy or sovereignty' (1996:58). Faced with 'politics' Bhabha rhetorically asks: 'Committed to what? At this stage in the argument, I do not want to identify any specific "object" of political allegiance' (1994:21). What he offers instead is an 'inter-national *culture*' based not on the 'exoticism or multiculturalism of the diversity of cultures, but on the inscription and articulation of culture's hybridity' (1994:38). But notions of 'partial culture', 'shifting sands' and 'versions of historic memory' occlude another, and possibly more radical, politics. The ambivalence analysed in the hybrid threatens to incapacitate the politics of 'intervening ideologically' (Bhabha 1994:22). When Trinh T. Minh-ha writes: 'after a while, one becomes tired of hearing concepts such as in-betweenness, border, hybridity and so on. ... But we will have to go on using them so that we can continue what Mao called "the verbal struggle" ' (in Trinh and Morelli 1996:10), there might be reason to feel very hostile to notions of hybridity as translation and no return to Mao can excuse this. With Bhabha's admirable but hesitant intellectualisms, the idea of a revolutionary project that wants to win through to a sovereignty without necessarily instituting another totalitarianism is ruled out of court. All the while, the danger becomes one where the 'third space' that Bhabha describes can be taken to posit a new *stasis* as the place of hybrid articulation, and as such this is a space that is dangerously ready for calibration with the capitalist market. In the hands of opportunist entrepreneurs, dialectical hybridity and difference will sell well, and this leaves us ambivalent indeed, as we have failed to learn at all.

> To grasp the ambivalence of hybridity, it must be distinguished from an inversion that would suggest the originary is, really, only an effect. Hybridity ... is not a third term that resolves the tension between two cultures ... in a dialectical play of 'recognition'.
>
> (Bhabha 1994:114)

But what if it did make sense to look at the way hybridity has been discussed dialectically as flow? A dialectical politics that managed to see the term reclaimed from racist biology to do work for anti-essentialism, which itself reifies and must be countered, which becomes a new mode of essentialising, and which is then conceived as a verb – hybridisation – but which further excludes and so must be critiqued again. And none of this makes sense if it is not taken into the field, co-constituted here and there, and where we learn to learn, and still think that interpretation and under-standing is not yet enough, that openness to redistribution requires the mechanism of wanting to change it, and that, dialectically – we would still have this coda – there's 'a world to win'.

## CAPITALISM HAS TANKS

The displacement of Marxist categories in the discussion of hybrid-ity also gives an alibi for, and parallels the displacement and replacement of Third Worldist solidarity work and internationalist politics with a cosmopolitan 'postcolonial elite' politics. This joins up with a stay-at-home-lecturing-from-afar approach by the white Left, incapable of engaging a struggle against capital at home, co-constituted here and there. The here and there is forgotten in two complementary ways – and the second is more disappointing than the first, but both are concerns: (a) the postcolonial hybrids' self-concern in the face of metropolitan racism, and opportunity, also leaves the rest of the world in shadow; and (b) the metropolitan white Left's feeble attempts at solidarity end up as mere hectoring and lecturing from a position of assumed moral superiority, while leaving the presence and complicity of imperialist capital as man-aged from and organised in the very heart of the metropole unex-amined, and so also in shadow. Of course metaphors of shadow and space are subject to all sorts of distortion here – learning from below might mean learning from the Maoists, but they are up in the hills, or even mountains, threatening to take Everest, and not just because it is there. Space and the circulation of struggles, rumours, news – there are many examples where the simple geography of domesticated, agricultural-level analyses just cannot cope – see for example Hardt and Negri's mapping of Empire on vertical and horizontal axes (2000). Orthodox Marxisms abound with reified base-and-superstructure models, but even as the chapatti circulation story takes the mystified aura of the charmed circle in latter-day accounts, really existing struggles are never quite as neat as that.

The cascade that erases Mao as a possible theorist of hybridity is clear; what we would have if Subaltern Studies had retained a Maoist trajectory is less obvious. Was it career comfort that smoothed the way for this displacement? The library, conference circuit and the bookstore more amenable to discussion (and ego) than the cell group meeting? When called occasionally to account, the politics seem still to be there – there are many who can still talk the talk – but the march through the institutions of this political tendency has not carried with it a mass activist base, for all its successes. Is allegiance to subalterneity not the displacement of subalterns by postcolonial migrancy against which Spivak so often warns?

The advent of hybridity theory is the displacement of an anti-imperial political organisation into the glamour of the leftist publishing sector. Mao becomes as much a t-shirt slogan as complexity and ambivalence become the buzzwords. What becomes of learning about the actually existing conditions of global imperialism (from below)? Learning to learn how to do sociology and activism, anthropology and solidarity, Marxism and revolutionary politics together. Such ambitious dreams are necessary to displace capitalism which has tanks and helicopter gunships, oil contracts and hydro dam projects, tourism infrastructure and real estate deals, service sector pleasure peripheries and sweatshop work conditions. Mercantile global capital: not a new empire so much as empire renewed. The Raj is still red, white and blue, the stripes just run a different angle, there is still no black in the flag ('old glory' or the EU stars). Another theorist of hybridity, Paul Gilroy, maybe needs also to say 'There ain't no black in the stars and bars.' Yes, there are black stars – sports, hip-hop – and jazz bars a-plenty, plus Marines in Iraq, Afghanistan … (North Korea …), but the visibility or recognition of a few does not indicate an equitable redistribution of the spoils of imperialism, let alone its demise, Condoleeza Rice notwithstanding, or perhaps as case in point. The imperialists are armed with much more than foodstuffs, with tanks rather than flour and water, and the opposition needs to be organised, not just theorised or hybridised. Word needs to get around. Like the chapattis.

# Part 4

# Bataille's Wars:
# Surrealism, Marxism, Fascism

# 9
# Librarian

Burst of laughter from Bataille...

(Derrida 1967/1978:254)

I suppose we could imagine him in the library. He comes every day, but he arrives late. When the reading room is at its quietest and most austere, he suddenly laughs out loud. Can we imagine him sitting there reading Marx? Or must it always be Nietzsche and Mauss? It was Nietzsche who destroyed his Catholicism, it was Mauss who gave him a theme, but how about Old Beardo? In that library, in which he worked so dissolutely, he drew complaints from the patrons and was transferred to a different section for publishing dubious works of pornographic flavour. A maverick librarian, he has his own classifications, and he leaves for a bar with his friends immediately at closing time.

Reading Georges Bataille is a sort of gift off the shelves. A gift that – I want to convince you – repays effort. The use-value of Georges Bataille – that reading is not a waste of time, is not thereby a squandering. It may be destructive perhaps – what you thought was certain will be destroyed, uncertainty is revealed as a conceit – but this is not wholly frivolous. And on reading Bataille, I want to ask if there are ideas there that can help us make sense of and respond to the current geo-political moment that threatens us all.

Georges Bataille, according to his own words, was of a turbulent generation: 'born to literary life in the tumult of Surrealism. In the years of the Great War' (1957/1985:ix). The Surrealists, in the aftermath of horror, death, brutality and chaos in the trenches (which afflicted the French more systematically than either the English or Germans, who sent soldiers to the front, but did not have the front on their doorstep), wanted to move beyond the anti-art disenchantment of Dada and, from the mid-1920s, moved into the orbit of communism.[1] Bataille was not directly involved in Dada, and was technically peripheral to Surrealism, but his ascription of 'tumult' as his first context is not a surprise. For many others in France, the 15 years after the war were heavily marked by its consequences. In sociology, for example, Marcel Mauss was one of only a few of Durkheim's students to survive. In philosophy the future leading lights of Merleau-Ponty, Sartre and de Beauvoir were competing for the baccalaureate. In anthropology, Claude Lévi-Strauss was planning his escape to South America. Bataille was meeting his lifelong friends Michel Leiris and André Masson.

Of course Bataille's response to the First imperialist World War might not be the only figuring factor in his 20s – he was born in 1897 – but it is impossible not to speculate that war shaped his life and thought to a crucial degree. It is the thinking of war, or rather a militant thinking against war, that might be the best and most important theme that could govern a reading of Bataille.

So Bataille was born on 10 September 1897 and died in 1962. His father was blind and syphilitic and in 1914 had to be abandoned, unable to move from the house, in Rheims, when the Germans came and destroyed much of the town (Surya's biography of Bataille [1992/2002] reports 846 days of bombardment – excessive). No doubt this horror was just one among the reasons why Bataille, after toying for some years with the Catholic Church, was drawn towards the trajectory of Surrealism, with its ambition to re-enchant the world and its oblique revolutionary politics. Disabused of Catholicism through his reading of Nietzsche, his (Oedipal?) engagement with Surrealism started badly, and he feuded with André Breton from the beginning. Much has been made of the conflicted relations between Breton and Bataille, and there is no pressing need to dig into those trenches again. It might be worth giving a flavour of the conflict, however, by quoting the highest public manifestation of the exchange, where an amazing passage in Bataille's essay 'The Castrated Lion' takes revenge on Breton for spiteful comments directed at him in the *Second Manifesto of Surrealism*.

Breton had charged that Bataille wanted to 'avoid making himself useful for anything specific', he was obsessed with flies, an 'obnoxious' anti-dialectical materialism (?); and, a librarian by day, at night he 'wallows in impurities' (Breton 1929/1972:183–5). Bataille replied, in a pamphlet written with others excommunicated from

Surrealism: 'Here lies the Breton ox, the old aesthete and false revolutionary':

> I have nothing much to say about the personality of André Breton. ... His Police reports don't interest me. My only regret is that he has obstructed the pavement for so long with his degrading idiocies. Religion should die with this old religious windbag. Still, it would be worthwhile to retain the memory of this swollen abscess of clerical phraseology, if only to discourage young people from castrating themselves in their dreams.
>
> (Bataille 1994:28)

Bataille was later to express regret at these hostile words. As Breton had so generously noted – also an accusation – Bataille had trained as a librarian, and his dissertation was on a verse history of chivalry in the thirteenth century, submitted in 1922. In the early 1920s, Bataille published on sixteenth-century manuscripts and numismatics (the study of coins – prefiguring, in a way that must be decoded, his later interest in economic questions). Denis Hollier, whose book on Bataille, *Against Architecture*, generally excludes any discussion of Bataille's political economy, or his engagement with Marx and communism, beyond a few references, does make a good point about the 'perversity' of numismatists – they contemplate money 'not for what it is [the means of commercial exchange] but focussing on it an interest that is either strictly aesthetic or else documentary and historical' (Hollier 1989:124). Funnily enough, this aesthetico-documentary moment does open up a discussion of Bataille's politics in Hollier, after a detour through castration. In the later part of the decade Bataille wrote the pornographic novel *The Story of the Eye*, an anonymous publication signed Lord Auch (meaning 'God in the gutter'). This was perhaps the night-time Bataille, who spent much of his time in bordellos, or gambling. Sure, into this much of a psycho-analytic nature might be read – he was in analysis – and no doubt it would have to be related to the syphilitic father figure. The separation from the father during the war sets up the outcome of a kind of double obsession – a conflictual hatred of war, tending towards the Surrealists and Dada and a fascination-compulsion to understand and calculate its destructive excess. From his first book – on the war-ravaged cathedral at Rheims – through to his last, posthumous, book on sovereignty, war held Bataille in its fascinating, repulsive, grip.

A most interesting librarian to say the least, much has been said of the pornography – almost the sole focus of popular interest in Bataille, but a better read is the almost contemporaneous, equally racy, *Blue of Noon*, a novel about politics and the Spanish Civil War, written in the early 1930s but not published until 1957. Bataille had travelled to Spain in the years leading up to the civil war and wrote an engaging story about sexual ambivalence and communism that would repay investigation.[2] What is the use-value of the porno-graphic novel? I don't feel any need to defend that here – no doubt they could be defended – but it is possibly important that both nov-els involved travel to Spain. Escape from the stifling Paris was at stake, escape from (for) the father and from the war, and perhaps escape from his first wife, Sylvia Maklés (who later married Jacques Lacan). Looking for a way out, Bataille was a potential traveller, but his jour-ney so often seemed to stall. He also had plans to travel to Russia, Morocco, Tibet and China (he began learning the languages) but did not leave Europe. Instead he joined the Democratic Communist Circle centred around the old Comintern figure 'Souvarine'.

Souvarine was the revolutionary name, taken from a militant character in Zola's *Germinal*, of Boris Lifschitz, a member of the executive committee of the Comintern. Born in Kiev but having grown up in France, Souvarine travelled to Moscow in 1921 and stayed four years. He was among the first to defend Leon Trotsky when the Left Opposition came under attack and he was expelled from the party in 1924, soon after returning to Paris. He was not a blind devotee of Trotsky yet published letters from him in his jour-nal, the *Bulletin Communiste*, and also critiques of other communist leaders. He is said to have coined the term 'dictatorship of the sec-retariat' (in Surya 1992/2002:162) as an early critical description of Stalinism. He also published Karl Korsch and later, in a new journal, *La Critique Sociale*, published the first major political essays of Georges Bataille. Funded by Souvarine's mistress, Colette Pegnot, with whom Bataille would later live, it was in this journal that Bataille published key economic works, such as 'The Problem of the State' in 1933 and 'The Notion of Expenditure' in two parts, in 1933 and 1934. The first essay was a response to the rise of totalitarian states in Germany, Italy and under Stalin, and it questioned in this context how the revolution might do away with the state as antici-pated in that 'withering' phrase. 'The Notion of Expenditure' sig-nalled his interest in consumption and anticipated his later post-war works that took the Chinook word 'potlatch' as their axiom. As a critique of orthodox Marxist focus on production (we will see that Marx himself was not so narrowly constrained as regards circulation and valorisation), Bataille's 'expenditure' extended beyond Mauss and Malinowski's critique of mere barter (primitivism) to elaborate more strictly political-theoretical implications (this work is discussed in detail in Chapter 11).

So, the early 1930s were again all about war for Bataille, this time the anticipation of it rather than the aftermath. In the orbit of communist activists, Bataille's work turned to militant themes. Not all his efforts were devoted to politics, however; still working by day in the library (he was notorious for arriving late and the patrons complained that the doors were never opened on time – Surya 1992/2002:147), he also had time, with Leiris and Masson, to publish an art journal, *Documents*, which attracted much attention and discussion for its innovative and experimental – even sometimes 'monstrous' – tone.

*Documents* was published for two years from 1929 (15 issues) and Bataille apparently thought of it as a war machine against Surrealism and its alleged leader Breton – who had called him an 'excrement philosopher'. Breton was never mentioned, but philosophical it was, with a healthy dose of ethnography supported by Leiris's and Bataille's interest in Mauss. It carried articles such as 'Big Toe', 'Human Face', 'The Severed Ear of Vincent Van Gogh', several on taboo and filth, and short reviews or comments on theatrical events – 'the cemetery and mass grave of so much pathetic crap' (see the appendices of the volume *Encyclopaedia Acephale* [Bataille et al. 1995] for examples).

Like his good friend Michel Leiris, Bataille always had a complicated relationship with Surrealism. He later called himself Surrealism's 'old enemy from within' (in 1946; Bataille 1994:49), but had little time for contrivances such as automatic writing and the obsession with dreams and the meaning of chance (he'd rather gamble). His own obsession with regard to the surreal was with the eye as perspective and horror, with shock, contradiction and the uncontrolled – what he called heterology. This is what got him accused of being excremental; but Leiris too was documenting the satisfactions of the morning shit in his ethnographic studies (see Köpping 2002:189). Leiris travelled with Maurice Griaule on the Paris–Dakar–Djibouti expedition and wrote a detailed ethnographic report cum diary and subsequently several novels and a sustained autobiographical series (*Manhood*, 1946, the first of these, is dedicated to Bataille). His reminiscence in *Brisées: Broken Branches* is engaging, with gems like

Bataille's response to being invited by the Surrealists to a meeting to discuss the 'Trotsky case', which he refused to attend, saying: 'Too many idealistic pests' (Leiris 1966/1989:240).[3] Laughter and transgression are great interrelated themes; it was Bataille who introduced Leiris to Dostoevsky's *Notes from the Underground* and the two patronised bars and clubs together. Leiris worked at the Musée de l'Homme, near the Bibliothèque Nationale, and patrons could surely also hear there a sort of maniacal mischievous laughter, bordering on criminality, showing criminality to be merely morality. They acted on the motto from Dostoevsky's book: 'Nothing is true, everything is permitted' (a construction later significant for William Burroughs, attributed to Hassan I Sabbah, the Old Man of the Mountain). Bataille was to write several articles on humour and its darker sides.[4]

And Bataille was to keep this laughter up throughout his life. Quoting Antonin Artaud in 1951, Bataille writes: 'and the garlic mayonnaise contemplates you, mind, and you contemplate your garlic mayonnaise: and finally let's say shit to infinity' (1994:46). This was not incompatible with recognising Artaud's mental shipwreck. Bataille should not be considered callous or inhuman. There is enough of that in automatic reaction to his writings. Misconstruals abound. So many that it is impossible, and unnecessary, to itemise them all. It will do to show how specific interests and agendas fashion a Bataille for all seasons. The postmodern use of Bataille in the 1980s certainly encouraged the 'nothing is true, anything is permitted' approach to theory. Exemplified on the one hand by Nick Land, despite protestations and an elegantly wasted style (Land 1992); on the other hand, Jean Baudrillard probably takes things a step too far when he writes that, for Bataille, the 'economy has no meaning' and luxurious and useless expenditure is all that matters, and even this luxury is, in what the advocate of simulation means as a critique of Bataille, 'no more "natural" than economics' (Baudrillard 1976/1993:156–7). Michael Richardson's introduction to Bataille adequately, if somewhat heavy-handedly, warns against other postmodern manifestations of Bataille-mania (1994:4). Giorgio Agamben, normally so careful, seems to overstate the case for a versioning of Bataille as a kind of mystic. In his *Homo Sacer*, he suggests that Bataille's inquiries into sovereignty were 'compromised' by the errors of Victorian anthropology in the study of the sacred (Agamben 1998:75). Bataille had in fact read Frazer's *Golden Bough* early on, and no doubt picked up some funny ideas (that he was still citing in the

1950s).[5] With this taint though, Agamben then praises Bataille's 'exemplary' attention to what he calls 'bare life' – to the ambiguity and ambivalence of the pure and the filthy, the repugnant and the fascinating – he only regrets the inscription of this life under the sign of the sacred rather than the political (1998:112). Is Bataille a god-botherer unable to fully enact his Nietzsche and escape Catholicism? It would be another task altogether to follow the path of a sacred Bataille, suffice to acknowledge that 'sacredness is a line of flight still present in contemporary politics, a line that is as such moving into zones increasingly vast and dark' (Agamben 1998:114–15). I don't think this Bataille prevails. I might be wrong.

There are of course those who find Bataille too frivolous and too playful; others find him too exuberant, not dour enough; even his dark side is charged with eroticism. To counteract this it might be worth remembering Foucault's preface to Deleuze and Guattari's *Anti-Oedipus*; 'do not think you need to be sad to be a militant' (Foucault in Deleuze and Guattari 1972/1983:xiii). Bataille offers what he called a 'paradoxical philosophy' (formless institute, heterology, decodifying dictionary). He writes of the 'dishevelled joy of communication' (1943/1988:35) and of laughter as communication (1944/1988:139). His eroticism is aimed at redeeming the sexual organs from embarrassed laughter; he takes seriously the fine line between pleasure and pain, and finds ecstasy and horror, joy and delirium, blood, vomit and death as the coordinates of our life. Very human, he seems to have had much trouble with his teeth. In *Guilty* he is up all night with bleeding gums; his *On Nietzsche* includes this fragment: 'A toothache (over now it seems)' (1945/1992:108). The paradoxical philosophy had to be expressed in writing, yet 'writing … is deprived of wings' (Bataille 1994:130). The paradox: 'The leap beyond what is possible destroys what became clear: thus the impossible is the distressing contrary of what we are, which is always connected to the possible' (1994:131–2). This was at the heart of his laughing/serious appreciation of the poem of Jacques Prévert that he cites in 1946 and which is worthy of study itself in its inspired combinations of 'a Bengal nun with a tiger of Saint Vincent de Paul, an inspector of the round table with the nights of the Paris gas company, a member of the prostate with a swollen French academy' (in Bataille 1994:145–6). Of this, Bataille says the ruin of poetry is effected by means of an externally established determination – the exchange between couplets – that is akin to the writing triangles of Raymond Roussel (Bataille 1994:152; on Roussel and authorship, see Foucault 1962). The Bengal nun particularly grabs attention, as does the swollen academic French prostate. The legacy of this Surrealism, with which Bataille was so obviously infused and enthused, despite struggles, is one that continues in other groups that either Bataille set up – Acephale (one of its advertising slogans was 'If you are not crushed you must subscribe') and the College of Sociology (on this see Hollier 1988) – or groups that followed and might well be claimed to be the legacy of Bataille and a politicised Surrealism: most notably the Situationist International, but also such diverse irruptions as the YIPPIEs, fax art and some of the Reclaim the Streets protest performance politics of the anti-capitalist movement today...

It might be usual for an examination of Bataille to stop here, as many do, noting curiosities and assimilating his heterology to some trinketising catalogue of French diversions – cue the tunes of Erik Satie – but there is a serious underside to this legacy of Bataille: it is founded on an explicit politics, born of his encounter with Dada and Surrealism and the horrific legacy of war. Just as Bataille says 'Yes' to Dada's 'No' and Surrealism's mythmaking, Bataille brings a surrealist countenance to Marx and anti-fascist work. In the same way that his critique of Surrealism was made 'from within', so too is his critical response to Marxism and communism.

# 10
# Activist

I am amused, moreover, to think that one cannot leave
Surrealism without running into M. Bataille.

(Breton 1929/1972:183)

By 1935, Bataille was reconciled with Breton and working with him
in an anti-fascist collective called Contre Attaque. In Contre
Attaque, Bataille, Breton and Leiris participated in public meetings
and critique of the established communist parties (for their defence
of the popular front and its preservation of capitalism). Contre
Attaque's initial declaration begins with a proclamation against
nationalism, calls for the arming of the people and asserts its fundamental fidelity to Marxism (in Richardson and Fijalkowski
2001:114–15). As mentioned above, Bataille had initially been
drawn into the circle around Souvarine and had written articles in
the journal *La Critique Sociale*. It was not a simple matter of Bataille
becoming a Marxist, again what does it mean to be in this club that
even Marx did not want to join? Rather, Bataille got involved in the
political movements he regarded as most compelling at the time.
Among Bataille's writings in *La Critique Sociale*, for example, the
especially important 'The Notion of Expenditure' was conceived as
a critique of the orthodox Marxist focus on production and a
defence of the political significance of joy, desire, pleasure, excess
and waste which economy would rather exclude. The critique from
within at the start. Later in his life, Bataille admitted to Maguritte
Duras that he was 'not even a communist' (in Surya1992/2002:565).

Not ever? Duras asked Bataille, 'Can I nevertheless write that for
you communism answers the communal demands?' Bataille replied
'Yes you can.... But I repeat, I am not even a communist' (Bataille
interview with Duras in *France-Observateur* 12 December 1957).
Elsewhere the picture is carefully nuanced, as Bataille writes: 'I do
not want to forget that Marx's doctrine has always served as the
only effective application of intelligence to practical facts as a whole'

(1994:156). It is unnecessary to redeem Bataille to Marxism, but it is also not a matter of taking sides as when some commentators do not quite see the difference between Marx and orthodoxy. The strain is particularly pronounced in the art volume *Formless* by Yve-Alain Bois and Rosalind Krauss, where a discussion of Bataille and contemporary art has Bois speculating on the similarity of Bataille to Benjamin, but wanting to 'resist' such readings 'since this would be to push Bataille's thought towards Marxism, with which he was engaged only briefly (... roughly from 1932 to 1939)' (in Bois and Krauss 1997:48). To resist the brief engagement is a strange tension, since a few pages along from this 'rough' diversion it is the 'major theoretical text' from this period – the essay 'The Notion of Expenditure' – that Bois identifies as that 'from which almost all his later work developed' (1997:55). The evaluation of this essay will become still more important, but Bois clinches the deal with reference to other work: 'No Marxist could have penned' sentences such as Bataille's about gushing blood, violent death, cries of pain, et cetera (1997:49). Though in the same book in which Bois claims Bataille was not dialectical (1997:68), his co-writer Krauss notes Marx offering very similar language to describe 'the scum, offal, refuse of all classes' in his *18th Brumaire* (in Bois and Krauss 1997:246). It is of course not the point that Marxists never write about shit, offal and blood (how absurd a taboo would that be?), but that the orthodox Marxism that Bois is at pains to defend Bataille from might be one that he was in fact never associated with, not even for just a few 'rough' years, and, as the line in Krauss indicates, this was something he perhaps shared – at least in style – with Marx himself. It is worth recalling that Agamben praises Bataille's exemplary excrementa (Agamben 1998:112), just as Breton condemned it in the *Second Manifesto* (in Breton 1929/1972; no doubt the politics of shit would repay investigation – consider Dominique Laporte's inquiry into the town planning and sanitation edicts of the French state [1978/2000:7] or Mike Davis's comments on the 'Hyperion' sewerage treatment in Santa Monica Bay in his *City of Quartz* [1990:196]).

This excremental not-quite-Marxism, 'not even' communism, of Bataille, is what I would want to name an uncategorically bad Marxism, and it is of a different character to the Marxism of those Surrealists who gravitated towards Trotsky (Lewis 1990). Bataille's version of Marx differs again from the versions of French theorists after the war who found their own ways to embrace Marxism–Sartre, Althusser, even Lévi-Strauss says he was influenced, Derrida later jestingly 'returned', et cetera. Everyone is trying to specify and locate: the biographer Surya at one point calls Bataille a Trotskyist, but this seems far-fetched – remember his 'too many pests' quip, reported by Leiris. Whatever the case, Bataille's economic and anti-fascist writing deserves attention and gives a good indication of a variety of engagement and independence of thought arraigned against the 'sterility of a fearful anticommunism' (Bataille 1949/ 1988:168).[1] In the post-Soviet world, Bataille's Marxism being no '-ism' might indicate a plausible way towards what Félix Guattari and Antonio Negri project as the need 'to rescue communism from its ill-repute' (1990:1). In this regard, perhaps other communist connections among his co-writers around *Documents*, the Acephale group, and the College of Sociology also deserve to be thought of in terms of a bad Marxism that should not be airbrushed away into literary dilettantism – Aragon for example, and Leiris (whom I discussed in these terms in Part 1 of this book).This is the parallel to making too much of Bataille's 'mystic' side. Along these lines, even the Surrealists might be re-evaluated not only as the merchants of dreams – this does not mean that investigating Dali and his paintings of the bust of Lenin will uncover a political programme, but...(see the volume *Dada Turns Red: The Politics of Surrealism* [Lewis 1990]).

Bataille's version of Marx seems similarly careful in its reading to that emphasised in the discussion of responsibility and difference by Gayatri Spivak in her *Critique of Postcolonial Reason* (1999:78). Where she says 'ethics', Bataille says 'moral' or sentimental, as he recognises that Marx's originality was in working towards a 'moral result' through rigorously organised material intervention (1949/ 1988:135). The necessary and sufficient material change is directed, ultimately, towards what is a 'sentimental' end – 'sovereignty'. But because this effort was directed towards the 'elimination of material obstacles' (obstacles to the achievement of sovereignty, or to species-being?), orthodox interpretations saw only 'an exclusive concern with material goods' which missed his 'provocative clarity, his utter discretion and his aversion for religious forms' where truth was subordinated to hidden ends (Bataille 1949/1988:135). I am persuaded that the presentation of Marx's *Capital*, beginning with commodities, was not the same as the analytical whole, and a patient reading requirement that would encompass the expanding analyses of production, consumption, circulation, credit, valorisation and the global market might bring forth a different Marx. In the spaces between National Socialism and Stalin, Trotsky and

Breton, Acephale and Souvarine, before and after war, Bataille read this Marx.

This Marx is not the economist construct of orthodox Marxism, with its obsession with structure and superstructure, but Bataille starts out towards him by railing against the injunction, common in ideas about economics then in circulation, that leisure, play – and expenditure – were to be seen as 'diversions' (Bataille 1997:168). This was first broached in the 1933 essay that Bataille wrote called 'The Psychological Structure of Fascism', also in *La Critique Sociale*, where he asserts that Marx developed no 'scientific' analysis of the influence of superstructure upon infrastructure. These building metaphors have always been a little problematic, and Bataille does not break them, but he is more sensitive than most to Marx's use of metaphor – and, contra Hollier, it is perhaps his training as a numismatist that allows him to realise that money itself was less important for Marx than the equivalences between differences that it was used to measure. He takes seriously the key point about the relations between things being an expression of congealed relations between people – commodity fetishism: 'it is only if I remain attached to the order of things that the separation [of beings] is real' (Bataille 1949/1988:192) and 'consumption is the way separate beings communicate' (1949/1988:59). Even when writing of fetish in a different sense, as in the valorisation of 'Big Toe', it might be an error to think that the analysis of commodity fetishism was far from his mind – the celebration of things previously ignored is a process of subsumption. Similarly, the almost obvious insistence of Marx that even old Robinson Crusoe, alone on his island, was formed as a social being, was shared by Bataille: 'Every human is connected to other humans, is only the expression of the others' (2001:236).

The issue of activism and organisation cuts through here. Not just in the obvious case of the organisation of the Democratic Communist Circle and Contre Attaque – though the significance of anti-fascist activity in 1933 and 1935 should not be missed – but in so many cases the issue of the group or the community comes to the fore. The creativity of the collective is asserted as greater than that of the individual, and this is reason enough to prefer communism – Bataille uses the example of myth-making to illustrate his point (Bataille 1994:106).[2] Of course the group is more productive – the essence of the social – but the political group led by an inspired and original intellectualism is something else again. Bataille suggests that the theorist probably just as important to him as Marx was

Friedrich Nietzsche – he was first to defend Nietzsche from National Socialist misappropriation. Like the Surrealists between the wars, Nietzsche wrote as if motivated only by the desire to 'found an order' (Bataille 1994:109), and this desire has affinities with the foundation of a political party. Bataille's groups are not so different.

In his essay for *La Critique Sociale*, 'The Psychological Structure of Fascism', Bataille considers the necessity of the proletarian classes becoming aware of themselves as an active, not passive, even as a revolutionary, class. Bataille's call is for a 'conscious proletariat' (1997:143). He writes even more militantly in the essay 'On the Popular Front'. He calls for subversion, against fascism, and this is urgent because thus far – 1933 – only the indifference of the proletariat had saved democratic countries from turning fascist. No doubt Bataille has his errors of historical detail, but he was certainly right to think later that his ideas were unlikely to be heard – the notion of an intellectual cohort exhorting the working class to revolt has always carried its own class contradictions.

An enemy also from 'within' communism perhaps. At the beginning of *The Inoperative Community*, Jean-Luc Nancy, working through the meanings of the word 'communism' – a place of happiness and 'community beyond social divisions' is one emblem – cites Bataille as one of those who pointed out early that 'the states that acclaimed it have appeared, for some time, as the agents of its betrayal' (Nancy 1991:2). Nancy does point out that the 'schema of betrayal' is less tenable than it once seemed, as the ideal of a pure communism, untainted by realpolitik, is now difficult to project ('not that totalitarianism was already present in Marx', he quickly adds). Nancy accuses subsequent commentary on Bataille of being governed by, 'despite everything, a meager and all too often frivolous interest' and he underlines 'the extent to which his thinking emerged out of a political exigency' (1991:16). We might hedge a bet on the psychological structure of Bataille himself: the politicisation resulting from the First World War transfers his energy into activism against fascism, which in turn energises the concern for, and critique of, totalitarian communism in the interests of another possible communism (and not sterile anti-communism).

Bataille and anti-totalitarianism deserves to be read carefully, not only because he was among the first to offer a sustained intellectual critique, and not because his psychological insights are superior to others, say perhaps Adorno, with whom there are useful similarities. Bataille's critique of fascism in particular was contextualised; he recognised that it would not do to go to war simply on behalf of capital. In 1935 he wrote:

> ... at the same time, while dread mounts from day to day before the immanence of physical extermination ... we know ... that stupid imperialism precisely engendered this fascism that we mean to fight while marching in ranks assigned to us by generals and industrial magnates.
> (1985:164)

Imperialism and industry were at the heart of fascism and war, but the task of a politicised anti-fascism was more than national defence. It should be clear that this was a part of a wider practical-intellectual project – one not embarrassed by action – yet also not a patronisingly insipid engagement for the sake of the engaged theorist's ego. The critique from within has the ultimate interest of a more adequate communism. In his book on Nietzsche, for example, Bataille points out that the idea that anyone would subordinate their thinking to the demands of a party was appalling (1945/1992:xxii). To think that being in a party would demand this is feeble itself, an abdication of any critical principle of the party and the responsibility of membership which requires people not to be automatons. Any party member who abandons thought should be dismissed as unreliable and dangerous – a lazy follower who only deserves to be led by the nose. This is the material of the popular front essay, but it is also prefigured in the essay on fascism, where heterogeneity is identified as that which must be assimilated or excluded from homogeneous – democratic – society. As Bataille noted in 1933, a distinction may be drawn between those differences which can be negotiated and those which a state must suppress to retain power: a distinction between a parliamentary model of negotiated compromise and military suppression. Some differences are too different and must be overruled or the state overturned – hence the double deceit of democratic politics on the one side and despotic violence on the other – two strategies (see Bataille 1997:124). The problem is that it is Hitler who breaks laws, and his is a heterogeneous, hypnotic force, an authority based on a projected unity under his leadership, godlike, with devotees, a cult. It is the 'uniting of the heterogeneous elements [of society] with the homogeneous elements' that is specific to fascism (Bataille 1997:140). And a party – or an army – that assimilates and demands obedience, rather than develops a conscious proletariat, is one that spells trouble.

The attempt to construct a model of heterogeneity and homogeneity as a diagnostic for politics resonates with the later 'war machine' and 'nomadological' primitivism of Deleuze and Guattari (in their *Mille Plateaux* 1980/1987). Yet the neat models were a cul de sac of sorts, which Bataille recognised yet was compelled to explore in the context of fascism and totalitarian bureaucracy. In a 1935 lecture to a Contre Attaque meeting, he argued that if insurrection 'had to wait for learned disputes between committees and political offices of parties, then there would never have been an insurrection' (in Bataille 1985:162). This might echo Souvarine who, recall, had coined the phrase 'dictatorship of the secretariat', but Bataille's target was those 'professional revolutionaries whose party activity amounted to both disparagement of the spontaneity of the people and distrust of the intellectuals'. These 'so-called revolutionary agitators' would like to 'eliminate' the 'brutal' and 'convulsive', 'human tragedy that the revolution necessarily is' (Bataille 1985:162). Perhaps there is behind this again a more sentimental and scatological Bataille, the blood gushing once more, but the critique of revolt via meeting procedure is well taken. In the event, this so-called revolutionary was also much ignored. Contre Attaque foundered after two years. Bataille moved on to other projects with a more academic bent – the College of Sociology – and again into the library, so that by the time Hitler's war started, he seemed resigned to sit it out – not only for health reasons.

# 11
## Anthropologist

... celebration of a militant communism.

(Habermas 1987:228)

On either side of the Second imperialist World War – if we take his health problems of 1942 as a marker, then symmetrically seven years either side – Bataille published his most important economic studies. In 1933 'The Notion of Expenditure' and in 1949 *The Accursed Share*. During the war a period of introspective writing – *Inner Experience, Guilty, On Nietzsche* – while all the while 'working on a book on economics', which, as even Bois tells us, was the key work of his later life. Michael Taussig gives a generally accepted assessment of the significance of this work in anthropology vis-à-vis the exchange theories of Malnowski and Mauss et al.:

> ... against more restricted views of the undoubted importance of exchange in grounding social life ... this emphasis on giving for the sake of giving, on giving as expenditure regardless of return, was Bataille's contribution to social theory.

> (1999:268)

It is idealism to reify exchange and expenditure and not examine the specificity of capitalism's 'restricted economy' in the context of Bataille's attempt to escape the curse of this accursed share. A case in point that should modify the idealism of this would be to consider the 'gift' and 'consumption' of workers' labour power, nominally purchased by the capitalist, who then gets the surplus produced by that power for free. Taussig distinguishes the 'art' of 'profitless spending' from 'the restricted economy of capitalist profit-maximisation' (1999:81) – and, with Bataille, has in mind here the more restricted notions of exchange of those who do not see an alternative, whose vision of the social rests complicit with the idea that exchange determines production (Clifford 1997 is my example in this book; see Part 1). Such interpretations forget that Marx wanted to take production and exchange, consumption, circulation, etc. together, so as to overturn the process of exploitation (*aufheben*) and emancipate creative life from exactly those restrictions. Bataille says as much in the introduction to *The Accursed Share*:

> ... the extension of economic growth itself requires the overturning of economic principles – the overturning of the ethics that grounds them. Changing from the perspectives of restrictive economy to those of general economy accomplishes a Copernican transformation: a reversal of thinking – and of ethics. If a part of wealth (subject to a rough estimate) is doomed to destruction or at least to unproductive use without any possible profit, it is logical, even inescapable, to surrender commodities without return.
>
> (1949/1988:25)

Anthropology had long been fascinated with the idea of 'potlatch'. Mauss wrote *The Gift* in 1926 on the basis of reports from other anthropologists like Malinowski (on the kula gift exchange of the Trobriand Islands) and on the festivals of destruction of the indigenous North American potlatch ceremonies. This text inaugurated what Lévi-Strauss identifies as a beginning of theorising in social science:

> For the first time the social ceases to be the domain of pure quality – anecdote, curiosity, material for moralising description or scholarly comparison – and becomes a system, among whose parts connections, equivalences and interdependent aspects can be discovered.
>
> (1987:38)

Bataille had attended Mauss's lectures in the 1920s and, with the already mentioned essay in *La Critique Sociale*, began a lifelong exploration of notions of expenditure, reciprocity, exchange and the problematic of the gift. The gift is about ostensible generosity, it is that which is to be given generously, in excess of utility, given beyond what would be a utilitarian or reasoned calculation of value. The gift establishes social ties, reciprocity implies an ongoing relationship. In anthropology and related disciplines the well-worked theme of the kula finds the Trobrianders engaged (seemingly forever) in a series of exchanges – of shells and necklaces – which bind trading partners together in a circle of reciprocal gift relations – these are the obligations of the gift. For Malinowski, the kula is a serious game of both calculating exchange and of excess, debt and luxury (but for the Trobrianders?). Kula shells and necklaces are prized objects of renown, but the social relations kula secures are trading relations, and all manner of other exchanges accompany the kula trading trips (Malinowski 1922). The gift here is also contradictory in that it is never only a gift – as many have pointed out, including Jacques Derrida – if a gift is to be a gift there must be no exchange, no debt to be repaid, no reciprocity, not even the idea of a payback – there can be no gift, there is only the exchange of gift and counter-gift (1991/1992:7). It is impossible to give without return. Even charity returns something to the anonymous giver. The kula and the potlatch is more like a contest, as most exchanges seem to be – destructive. As Dan Ross argues in an unpublished paper, the gift is the mythical virtuous side of a calculation that, in other respects, takes the form of the gamble, another kind of exchange, that is about chance, but unreasonably – as everyone knows – it doesn't pay off, one does not escape the calculus of credit and debt (1992). For Derrida the unreason of the gift is that it is always a debt that is invoked – he suggests that any calculation or legislation of the gift, or, in another example, of hospitality, is impossible – hospitality must be freely given in excess of what is expected, it cannot be calculated (2000:22).

For Derrida, who ascribes to Bataille a 'Hegelianism without reserve' (1967/1978:251), what the gift gives is time – the possibility of taking time before repayment, whether that be a return gift or an even more extravagant potlatch. For Deleuze and Guattari, who mention Bataille only in passing, the gift inscribes, it writes, it records. In the context of a discussion of ethnology and bourgeois colonial economy they write:

> The essential thing seemed to us to be, not exchange and circulation, which closely depend on the requirements of inscription, but inscription itself, with its imprint of fire, its alphabet inscribed in bodies, and on blocks of debts.
>
> (1972/1983:188)

For Bataille, the gift and potlatch are a part of a calculus which suggests the necessary expenditure of an organism that, generally, receives more energy 'than is necessary to maintain life' and:

> ... excess energy (wealth) can be used for growth of a system ... if the system can no longer grow, or if the excess cannot be completely

absorbed in its growth, it must necessarily be lost without profit, it must be spent ... gloriously or catastrophically.

(1949/1988:21)

It is important again to note how Bataille distinguishes between the general and restricted, with the bourgeois manner of giving the most limited: 'Where accumulation is concerned, the one who gives loses what they have given, but in the traditional world their dignity grew in proportion to their material loss' (1991:346). This may hint at romanticism, derived in part from that reading of Frazer and Mauss, and forgetting colonial disruptions. But would it change the reception of Bataille's work if it were understood that his notion of the 'ultimate' necessity to consume without return (1949/ 1988:22) is distinguished from individual examples of destruction – coffee overboard etc. – in a way that can in fact be reconciled with the contradictions of the capitalist circuit of production in Marx? Although he explicitly disregards the significance of individual examples – accidents – in favour of the 'totality of productive wealth on the surface of the globe' (1949/1988:22), he writes of 'the final dissipation'. It is here that the trick of the gift is most explicitly revealed in a political way, as part of a programme.

In a restricted economy, destruction serves primarily to reaffirm the position in the hierarchy of the one who destroys most. Reciprocity of course is an ideal in the notion of exchange as it must imply a notion of equivalence in value. That value equivalence is a matter of calculation is one of the key tricks of commerce. Hierarchy and exploitation do not calculate this ideal except to subvert equivalence as the deceit of the market where money is used to stand for a general equivalent and the various interests come to trade do not do so from equal positions. Is it this idealism Bataille wished to fight? The desire to solve this paradox of reciprocity which is never equal is perhaps the same sentiment that leads people to project human qualities (good, evil) in idealised form on to a deity (cf. Feuerbach 1841/1972). Bataille hints at something similar in his wartime introspection about sacrifice:

The forces which together work at destroying us find in us such happy – and at times such violent complicities – that we cannot just simply turn away from them as interest would lead us to. We are led to contain the fire within us ... without going to the point of delivering ourselves [Bataille had mentioned the Hindu who throws himself under a festival cart], we can deliver, of ourselves, a part: we sacrifice a good which

> belongs to ourselves or – that which is linked to us by so many bonds,
> from which we distinguish ourselves so poorly – our fellow being.
>
>                                                          (1943/1988:96)

In a system obsessed with things, the absolute and sacrificial ideal is curiously not things, but profit. Having banished God and insisted on materialism, capital still reifies a deity of abstract and awful power. Where what Bataille calls the moral result of Marxism is to be achieved through subjecting things to a regime of governance that enslaves things and not people, instead capital has developed into the unrestrained liberation of things from any rigorous control, while humanity remains enslaved (1949/1988:135–6). Against sacrifice and complicity, against the restricted economy, Bataille wants to release a self-consciousness that would not be deceived into engaging in false transactions. He denounces the ignorance of the generally 'catastrophic destructions' (1949/1988:24) just as he condemns 'shameless attempts at evasion such as charitable pity' (1997:129). What is needed is to face up to the fact that 'the choice is limited to how the wealth is squandered' (1949/1988:23). Bataille recognised that the compulsion to produce an excess is not inevitable – but equilibrium is also not compatible with capitalism, as Marx's analysis of the tendency of the rate of profit to fall had shown. There are, however, the possibilities of choice of expenditures: destructive war, or expansion of services, frivolous dissipations (like brothels?) or 'the rational extension of a difficult industrial growth' (1949/1988:25). In an introductory essay Bataille was not going to dwell on the undeniably interesting possibilities and specific instances, he was concerned instead with exposing general parameters and working for an escape from the poverty of accumulation. It was 'Bataille who showed that the glorious and transcendent sovereignty of the sun-king present[ed] to all [that] their common sovereignty had only ever taken place held and enslaved within the installation of bourgeois power, of market economy, of the modern state' (Lacoue-Labarthe and Nancy 1997:131).

The trick of restricted economic systems is the conflicted hypocrisy of claims to equality mouthed by those whose privilege to speak rests upon an inequality they will not admit. The structure of fascism, ruling class stupidity, illegitimacy, bourgeois delusion and lack of courage is clear in the self-centred opportunism manifest in the failure to face up to the ongoing crimes of that same privilege[1] – bureaucrats claiming unrestrained universal forces as excuses for their repressive rules, and showing no restraint in claiming specific rights when they break these rules themselves. The advent of war is a curse of a sacrificial expenditure out of control, just as is the exploitation of slavery, including wage-slavery. The curse of restricted economy can only be lifted by a consciousness of the process, and in this light it seems disappointing that all that can be proposed instead of war is a general raising of the living standard (Bataille 1949/1988:40) – but after all, this would be something, wouldn't it? No doubt what is raised must also be education, and autonomy – sovereignty, the freedom to squander for all, not just the rich – but something in the formula of the gift – its duplicity as debt, returns to haunt. Bataille had also argued that social security and wage claims increase the share of wealth that is allocated to non-productive labour and this would apply to efforts – after the Second World War, the Marshall Plan – to raise the general standard. There would be less for the bosses' luxuries, but also less to devote to the development of the means of production. 'The share allotted to present satisfaction [bosses' luxury and welfare] increases at the expense of the share allotted to the concern for an improving future' (Bataille 1949/1988:154). Wage claims are part of the negotiation of a system that needs to be abolished, not improved. Shopping (for a better deal) is indeed a form of civil war.

A further difficulty with Bataille's formula lies in 'The Psychological Structure of Fascism' where his notion of sovereignty in the end undermines the coherence of his political programme. In 1933 Bataille identified fascism as 'no more than an acute reactivation of the latent sovereign agency' (1997:135). The etymology of fascism has to do with 'uniting' or 'concentrating' according to Bataille, and this is used to show how fascism is the activation of the masses under a sovereign leader (the power of the charismatic king, or the Führer, based on a unity of military and religious legitimacy with – like Louis Bonaparte in Marx's *18th Brumaire* – a populist public support). Jürgen Habermas is critical of this ambiguous fascination with fascism as unity, and questions his proximity to the Weberian religious explanation of capital – as well as insisting that Bataille could not be dialectical (Habermas 1987:229). Be this as it may, Bataille was clearly a militant against the war, there is no doubting his engagement in this regard:

> … we can express the hope of avoiding a war that already threatens. But in order to do so we must divert the surplus production, either into rational extension of a difficult industrial growth, or into unproductive works that will dissipate an energy that cannot be accumulated in any case.
>
> (1949/1988:25)

And even after the war he maintained a theoretical interest in ways to escape restrictions. In the second volume of *The Accursed Share*, Bataille speculates on alcohol, war and holidays as the choices for expenditure. He is not so naïve as to think that a larger participation in erotic games would help avoid war (nice thought), but he does rethink the ways of avoiding war: 'we will not be able to decrease the risk of war before we have reduced, or begun to reduce, the general disparity in standards of living' (Bataille 1991:188). This 'banality' is what Bataille sees as the only chance for an alternative to war, and it is possible even in the midst of the Cold War.

The trouble was, faced with war itself, Bataille retreated to the library.

Bataille's contempt for and fascination with fascist 'community' must – Nancy says – be behind his withdrawal (Nancy 1991:17). Unlike Marx in the *Brumaire*, Bataille's analysis fills him with unease and inevitable failure in the face of 'a paradox at which his thinking came to a halt' (Nancy 1991:23). It is this interruption that left Bataille susceptible to the postmodernist revision that drained any sense of a political programme – the fight against fascism – from his work.[2] He was confined to the library, resigned, introspective, and in the end left passing books on to others with a whispered recommendation (the review *Critique* was the last publishing venture he started, and it continues today). Spiralling into the conflagration of the sun, which gives energy without (obvious) return, he later wrote:

> The planet congested by death and wealth
> a scream pierces the clouds
> Wealth and death close in.
> No-one hears this scream of a miserable waiting.

And then:

> Knowing that there is no response.         (Bataille 2001:221)

And, finally, from the 'Notebook for Pure Happiness' written towards the end of his life:

> The only escape is failure.         (Bataille 2001:223)

> Everything that we know is true, but on condition of disappearing in us (we know better in ceasing to know).
> (Bataille 2001:247)

# 12
# Provocateur

Have I not led my readers astray?

(Bataille 1991:430)

Bataille cannot be left to rot in the library.

How useful an experiment would it be to try to 'apply' Bataille's notion of expenditure to politics today? Klaus-Peter Köpping asks questions about 'modernity' that arise explicitly from his reading of Bataille as a theorist of transgression, addressing political examples such as Bosnia, Serbia, Croatia and Indonesia (2002:243). A more extravagant general economy framework for such questions might take up the massive accumulation that is the excess of an arms trade promoting regional conflicts as integral to sales figures on the one side, with the performative futility of massed anti-capitalism rallies and May Day marches that fall on the nearest Sunday so as not to disrupt the city on the other. Expenditure and squandering today, in Bataille's sense, might be seen in both the planned obsolescence of cars, computers and nearly all merchandise, as well as in the waste production and fast-food service industry cults and *fashionista* style wars, tamogotchi and Beckham haircuts that currently sweep the planet. No doubt it would be too mechanical to rest with such applications, too utilitarian, but the relevance is clear. The use-value of Georges Bataille is somewhat eccentric and the deployment of pre-Second World War circumstances as a comparative register for today is of course merely speculative. No return to the 1930s (colourise films now). Yet, taking account of a long list of circumstantial differences – no Hitler, no Moscow, no Trotskyite opposition – is also unnecessary since it is only in the interests of thinking through the current conjuncture so as to understand it, and change it, that any return should ever be contemplated.

The importance of French anthropology – Mauss – as well as psychoanalysis and phenomenology, cannot be underestimated and all are crucial in Bataille's comprehension of the rise of fascism.

Can these matters help us to make sense of political debates in the midst of a new world war today? That the intellectual currents that shaped Bataille's analysis were post-Marxist did not, then, replace the importance of Marx. Today the comprehension of Bush's planetary terror machine still requires such an analysis, but one that can also be informed by the reading of Bataille's thought as shaped by the intellectual currents mentioned above. In a period of capitalist slump, crisis of credit, overextended market, defaulted debt and threatening collapse, the strategy of war looms large. Even before the events of 11 September 2001 in New York, Bush was clearly on the warpath with missile defence systems, withdrawal from various international treaties and covenants, and massive appropriations for military and surveillance systems. The imperialist element is clear and sustained – the aggression against the Palestinians, the adventure in Afghanistan and the war on Iraq (to defend papa Bush's legacy) obviously have roots in the imperialist mercantile tradition – plunder and war in pursuit of resources, ostensibly oil, but primarily armaments sales. If this is potlatch, it is of the destructive kind that Bataille feared.

The possibility of an alternative geo-political solution other than war should be evaluated. But it is a matter of record that, under the Bush family regime, the US–Europe alliance has not been interested in pursuing any programme of reduction of disparity, a few suspensions of Third World debt and UN summits notwithstanding. When Bataille searches for an alternative to war in some 'vast economic competition' through which costly sacrifices, comparable to war, would yet give the competitor with initiative the advantage (1949/1988:172), he holds out hope for a kind of gift without return. That he showed some enthusiasm for the Marshall Plan after the Second World War as a possible model for this might need to be ascribed to the exhausted condition of post-war France, but he soon revised his assessment. The Marshall Plan was not as disinterested as Bataille implied; it facilitated circulation and recoupment of surplus value as profit. The Cold War and nuclear proliferation turned out to be the preferred examples of reckless waste in actuality – as recognised in volume two of *The Accursed Share* (Bataille 1991:188). Today, redistribution is not considered an option, and – after the slaughter of millions – the threat of Asian communisms (China, Korea, Vietnam) can be ignored. The war on Islam (known variously as the Gulf War, Zionism and the War on Terror) appears now as the primary strategy (combined with a war on South America, mistakenly named as a war on drugs, and a war on immigration disguised as a security concern).

The secondary strategy is a newly hollowed out version of liberal welfare. In 1933 Bataille had written of the bourgeois tendency to declare 'equality' and make it their watchword, all the time show-ing they do not share the lot of the workers (Bataille 1997:177). In the twenty-first century, Prime Minister Blair of England has made some gestures towards a similar pseudo-alternative. At a Labour Party congress in the millennium year he spoke of the need to address poverty and famine in Africa, and no doubt in quiet moments still congratulates himself on his pursuit of this happy agenda; a little over a year later a large entourage of delegates and diplomats flew to Johannesburg for another conference junket – the World Summit on Sustainable Development (for sustainable profit). The party accom-panying Blair and Deputy Prescott included multinational mining corporation Rio Tinto Executive Director Sir Richard Wilson (*The Guardian* 12 August 2002). Rio Tinto is hardly well known for its desire to redistribute the global share of surplus expenditure for the welfare of all.[1]

If there are no gifts, only competitions of expenditure, what then of the effort of Bataille to oppose fascism? It is not altruistic, and yet it is the most necessary and urgent aspect of his work that is given to us to read for today. Is fascism a charity-type trick? A deceit of double dealing which offers the illusion of more while giving less? Something like this psycho-social structure of fascism appears to be enacted in the potlatch appeasements of the propaganda spinsters surrounding Blair. The New Labour and Third Way public offering is ostentatiously to be about more health care, more police, more schools, but Blair spins and rules over a deception that demands allegiance to a privatisation programme that cares only about reduc-ing the costs (fixed capital costs) of providing healthy, orderly, trained employees for industry, of short-term profit and arms sales to Israel, of racist scare-mongering and scapegoating of asylum seekers, refugees and migrants, of opportunist short-term gain and head-in-the-sand business-as-usual. Similarly, the gestures of multi-millionaires like George Soros and Bill Gates in establishing charity 'foundations' to ease their guilt is not just a matter of philanthropy, it is a necessary gambit of containment (and these two in particular bringing their cyber-evangelism to the markets of Eastern Europe, South and South-East Asia). The liberal rhetoric of charity and the militant drums of war are the two strategies of the same rampant restrictive economy. Carrot and stick. Team A and team B of capitalist hegemony – the critique of the gift is clear, a gift is not a gift but a debt of time – and this is not really generosity or hospitality. The same can be said perhaps of war – it is not war but profit, just as the gift reassures the giver of their superior status, the war on terror unleashes a terror of its own; war does not produce victories but rather defeat for all. Bataille shows us a world in ruins.

11 September 2001 has been made into the kind of event that transforms an unpopular (even unelected) figure into a leader under whom the nation coheres in a new unity – much as Bataille saw Nuremburg achieve for the National Socialists. Of course I am not suggesting Bush is a Nazi – he hasn't got the dress sense – but people are betrayed by the trick of a 'democracy' that offers pseudo-participation once every four years, and this time in a way that has consequences leading inexorably to a massive fight. The kowtowing to big business with a rhetoric of social security has been heard before – it was called the New Deal (or welfare state) and was a deception almost from the start. Where there was perhaps some contractual obligation of aid in the earlier forms, today the trick of the buy-off bribery of service provision is contingent and calculated according only to corporate strategic gain. While we lurch towards endless war, governments reassure us with the watchwords of security that really mean death and despair to those on the wrong side of the wire. The largest prison population ever (under democracy or any other form of government), mass confinement for minor offences (three strikes), colour overcoded death row (Mumia Abu-Jamal etc.),[2] arrest and detention without trial or charge, celebratory executionism and worse. The incarcerated souls in the concentration camps of Sangatte,[3] Woomera,[4] Kamunting[5] or Guantanamo[6] are wired in and offered up as sacrificial gifts to the rule of new judicial-administrative fascism. A toothy-smiling Christian cult of death and technology, spun carefully via press conferences and TV sitcoms – television has given up any pretence of journalism in favour of infotainment. Does the US administration dream of a new post-war era where, once again like Marshall, they could come with a plan to rebuild upon ruins? This would indicate the exhaustion of the current mode of production, which, with an 'information' revolution promised renewal, but was quickly stalled. Whatever the case, the enclosure of the US and Europe behind fortress walls does not – experience now shows – ensure prophylactic protection, and ruin may be visited upon all. It was Bataille who said perhaps only the

'methods of the USSR would ... be equal to a ruined immensity' (1949/1988:167–8). Polite critiques and protest have no purchase – orderly rallies against the aggression in Afghanistan, against asylum and immigration law, against the destruction of Palestine, etc., get no 'airtime' (instead, 'political' soap opera like *The West Wing* is the current equivalent in ideological terms to the Cold War's Bomber Command). Every leader that accedes to the 'War on Terror' programme and its excesses (civilian deaths, curtailment of civil liberty, global bombing) is an appeaser. This is akin to the dithering of Chamberlain in 1938, only this time the opposition activists are fighting in a 'post-national' arena and Stalin's slumber will not be broken, the Red Army cannot run interference, there is no Churchill rumbling in the wings, the fascist empire will prevail without militant mobilisation across the board. This is the appeaser's gift – betrayal into the 'ranks assigned to us by generals and industrial magnates' (Bataille, 1985:164). The unravelling of the tricks of social welfare, of 'asylum' and 'aid' programmes, of 'interest' even (the narrowing of news broadcasts to domestic affairs), of tolerance, the hypocrisy of prejudice – all this prepares us for a war manufactured elsewhere. After the breakdown of the gift's tricks, fascism is the strategy, the obverse side of capital's coin. In this context, the geopolitics that enables, or demands, appeasement of the imperious corporate/US power is the restricted destruction we should fear, and we should fight in a struggle that goes beyond national defence, wage claims or solidarity. The discipline of the Soviets and of Bataille could be our tools.

Bataille reads on in his library. We are left speculating with him, rashly charging in with ideas that a less excessive, less exuberant, moderation might withhold. But there is no more important time to consider the efforts in the arts to fight militarism out of control, and, as Bush drags the world into permanent war, it is worth asking why Bataille's surrealistic opposition to Hitler was inadequate. Is it because there are no more thinkers in the party? Is it that subversion is uninformed and its spirit quiet? Chained to the shelves, it is not enough to know that appeasement of the military-industrial machine is the obverse side of liberal charity. Why are we still unable to acknowledge this is the path to devastation? What would be adequate to move away from appeasement to containment and more? What kind of sovereign wastage would Bataille enact today? Against the 'immense hypocrisy of the world of accumulation' (Bataille 1991:424), the answer is clear: we should 'condemn this mouldy society to revolutionary destruction' (Bataille 1997:175). The Bataille of *La Critique Sociale* might argue for a glorious expenditure as that which connects people together in the social and recognises their joint labour to produce themselves, and this must be redeemed from the restricted economy that insists on expenditure for the maintenance of hierarchy. If he were leaving the library today, the Bataille of anti-war Surrealism might say it is time for a wake-up knock-down critique of the barking dogs. The castrating lions of appeasement must be hounded out of town. Back in your kennels, yelping pups of doom. Fair call, Georges Bataille.

# Conclusion: The Cultivation of Capital Studies

Left academics, sad lot that we are, love to conjure with Capital. Turning tables turn our heads (Derrida séance), we take up objects as fetish items with a guilty pleasure (not what Marx had in mind), subtly snide sectarians and contrary comrades with a penchant for the bludgeoning footnote. There is at least an enthusiasm for reading that can be discerned, though discerning is not the be all and end all of these texts. These final paragraphs evaluate the foregoing critique and suggest, as promised in the introduction, a bad Marxism that conjures Marx differently.

Concluding thoughts can offer little more than an eclectic roundup that never measures up to the detail of what went before, but I want to insist upon a dual aspect to bad Marxism. On the one hand I identify: (a) the complicity of avowedly leftist theorists and Left activists in a quietism even as both 'camps' seem more active and committed than previously; (b) a trinketisation rampant in cultural studies theorising that restricts the scope of Marxism to stunned contemplation; and, on the other hand (c) the importance of an open kind of 'bad' Marxism that works through these stunted critiques to something more adequately engaged and open. There is then a recap of (d) some of the key points that arose in the main sections of the book, drawing out implications and how it all fits together; to allow (e) a sketched analysis of where we are now with regard to capital and anti-capitalism as a project. With some consideration of (f) the party question where the role of theory in cultural studies and anthropology is tested again in the light of (g) our need to study (class composition, imperialism, etc.) and to teach, and (h) (gee whizz) to change the world.

\* \* \*

## COMPLICITY

Book publishing and the Research Assessment Exercise replaces research and politics; high-profile dilettantes come to represent – and draw condemnation for – wider positions; the culture vultures' conference-circuit star system rambles on and on, and must be blamed for a failure to be adequate to the rightwards reaction; co-option and complicity – clever erudition without much to say. Among the post-, neo- and ex-Marxists; the abdication of feminism; commercial lifestyle-ism of sexual politics; isolated minority 'exceptions' to the rule, without a mass base – where is the institutional effort that encourages broad layers of people committed to and actively involved in the theory and practice of liberationary struggle?

There is a place, then, for a sharp critique of the academic lifestyle of cultural studies theory-heads. The conference and restaurant luxury of even the modest professor must be described as jet set. Sure, not much caviar and Möet, nor sun lounge poolside cocktails, but certainly a different level of comfort than most office- or factory-bound wage slaves experience. What is the point of doing theory for frequent-flyer points? I want to make this explicit. It must be more than instruction or some sort of practical exercise regime for toning minds – if that is all there is, then purpose lies elsewhere. Egoistic investments no doubt play a part – the desire to be known for thinking, writing, teaching. Prestige and glory – though these are limited today. Institutional allegiance and its corporate agenda – a shallow but real commitment it must be said – has meant the revolutionary project is not seen as immanent by academics any time soon.

So this is why the version of Marx most popular in the academic arena comes across as so rarefied. The contextual conditions clearly draw upon much wider factors, such as a complicity with power and politics that extends beyond the small world of cultural studies. Do the organised and party formation Lefts do a better job? This book does not examine the party schools explicitly, but notes a productive tension where orthodox guardians of the tradition opt for primers and swift assessment in an aversion to theory and debate that seems very familiar. A critique of everything would demand a party of a new type; and a Marx that was not just an oracle. Possibilities persist in the rampant intelligence that fights the global order with a toolkit from Old Beardo – 'comrades, to the schools' – but the existing Left sects are not preoccupied with a project of research and engagement. Often their activism is primarily interested in recruitment drives and declarations of the number of people who filled out membership forms at the most recent summer campaign workshop. Dubious twists of the alliance configuration and volatile variations of focus keep everyone on their toes, but only avid readers of the activist press have much of an idea of where the discussion might be at. And none of this really filters into the academic scene, for good or ill.

I would suggest that organised leftist thought has fared not much better than the liberalist academic versions of Marx discussed in this book. To schematise, we might distinguish different modes of complicity if we were to consider the implications of the last great hope of 'cultural politics' and examine its adventures in both the constituencies of the party political Left and the institutionalised academic 'Left'. Opportunism is hardly new, but here, on the one hand, the institutional, career and publishing successes of avowedly leftist academics has seen an unashamed accommodation with scholarship and rigour – not bad things in themselves – that further sees anti-racism morph into pro-ethnicity and pro-hybridity, activism into posturing and punditry, the slow work of politics into gesture and press conference. On the other hand, Left segmentation in organisational politics can be characterised as a display of self-righteousness and the self-declared self-importance of micro-sects that utilise tortuous arabesques around the divination of the correct line, and/or entrenched identity and culturalist positions, to avoid the necessary reassessments.

Surely there are reasons not to do this, but let us mark out two camps anyway, hoping to show the dual bifurcations of reified abstraction where closer engagement might offer more:[1]

Institutionally based academic Marxism is:

more or less secure in academic employment, state sponsored via pay, grants and awards, accommodationist comforts, nice office, secretarial support;

mildly sectarian, defends only its own domain from the onslaught of managerialism, which sometimes co-opts;

self-marginalising, egoistically eccentric, has a propensity for bushy eyebrows;

co-opted by institutional obligations and participation in the teaching factory, and mutely resents this;

conditioned in terms of its ambitions by the emergence of designer, coffee-table glossy publishing (yes, I do want one of those, with the soft matt full-colour cover);

theoretically focused without obvious purpose as erudition does not
necessarily imply engagement;

focused on cultural politics at best, cultural studies more likely;

telegenic, or at least wanting to get invited onto morning news
radio, as celebrity;

often single-issue oriented in any take-up of cultural politics, individual links with 'new social movements' if any, and almost always
several years out of date;

anti-institutional, anti-Left, fanatically campaignist at best, viru-
lently anti-party and idealist/indulgent/irrelevant most of the
time;

without a mass base (heaven forbid).

Outside academia, Left organisational Marxism can often be:

isolated into trotocentric sects around 'line' or issue with a prehis-
toric dinosaur cast of mind;

inadequate in terms of its dialogue with new social movements;

opportunist, parachuting in on other campaigns to recruit, and
self-righteous in its lack of self-criticism;

collapsed, in terms of party form, through endless rounds of micro-
splits and divisions (wafer-ism);

sectarian in extreme form, especially Trotskyite truth-sayers;

incapacitated by anxieties over the heritage of Stalin, the consequences of the Krondstadt or the collapse of the USSR;

elitist, sometimes quite bizarrely cultist, with rapid shifts of 'line'
left unexplained to all but the inner clique;

single-mindedly focused on texts as if scripture (to varied degrees);

often unemployed or underemployed outside party activity, with
cadres supporting themselves with part-time labourwork or fragmented work in voluntary sector;

existing in adversarial and draining conditions, burnt-out or fanat-
ical and wild-eyed in its commitment, exacerbated by the dwin-
dling number of supportive venues, the decline of Left bookshops,
etc.;

without a mass base (but wants this).

No doubt it is too simple to divide things in this easy way: on
the one side a cluster of secondary sources, recitations of dogma,
routines of the already familiar; on the other a rampant intelligence,
unconstrained and exploratory, a little crazed, but alive. Where too
are we to place the anti-capitalist, anti-G8, gay, environmentalist,

feminist anarcho-vegan, dedicated human rights, anti-weapons trade (and I do not mean weapons 'inspectors') and other primarily activist and campaign versions of the 'Left' in this equation? And in any case the organised 'camps' can be divided again: among the repetitors there are those who evoke the classics as renewable through puzzles, teaching machines, logic bombs and further a proud tradition of questioning and knowledge. This tendency hints that conservatism is a consequence of structure. Among the innovators there are several splits. Cynics and opportunists, whose radical conservatism is disguised in an egoistic avant-gardist self-image, jostle with truly unstable visionaries who shine and burn, before they fall. Additionally, too, there are those among us who oscillate between these varied ideal types, conservative in the morning, radical in the afternoon, crazy in the night, flamboyant on the weekend. And everyone makes their way through the world more or less on their own in the company of others. This applies, too, to making one's way through political work and even through thinking about political work. The point is that a reading practice against these (fictive) polarisations can perhaps help define a more adequate, nuanced range of alternatives for the party and for the academic, together. A melding that the unorganised social movements – feminism, identity politics, environment – have pointed to but rarely found. There is an illustrative avoidance to be enacted, a dialectic that moves us.

The particular studies of particular authors in this book then have no more general relevance than any particular example of the general condition of socio-political being that we all find ourselves in. Impressed as I am with the social, I find it singularly difficult to think of it in any other way than that already made famous in the Marx line Clifford so liked, about making history in conditions not of our own choosing. We might try to choose how we receive these influences – the dead might bury the dead here. But we must know by now that, through the necessity of standing on shoulders to see, we are surely obliged to offer loud and sometimes irreverent critique if we are to get those shoulders to heave. Time to be offensive, but not just to offend.

### FOR BAD MARXISM

Thus, with a sideways glance at the implications of the ways the culture industry and the teaching factory mark out the complicity of cultural studies as capitalism, I still think there is a place for theory, and theorising with Marx. With Bataille on the loans desk, I believe critical readings of Marx must be part of any radical curriculum. In this regard, the readings offered here might be welcomed as partial, provisional and prospective. There are inevitably omissions, but the alternative to not making a start on bad Marxism would be to neglect the most influential social scientist of them all, and I find that particularly obscene. In the foregoing parts of this book we have seen how several 'returns' to Marx have precisely not been good. Hence the obvious sense of bad Marxism. But I also mean bad Marxism in another sense, and wish to set this out here. There is not only much to learn from Clifford, Derrida, Negri et al., but also from an inverted bad or maverick Marx, one that Old Beardo himself might have cherished. The Marx that sometimes arrived drunk at demos as well as the Marx that argued every fine point late into the night – not to mention the Marx of the stunning insight and the inversion of common complacencies.

There are no doubt some built-in ironies here. I guess I have in mind the sort of things that the sectarian gremlins will necessarily shoot us for, come the revolution. Walter Benjamin, though some think he was a bit flaky, also recognised that support for the party was necessary, even though probably the party would be forced to ban him from doing his sort of criticism. Benjamin has been described as the kind of Marxist you can take home to meet the parents – my view is that his unfinished Arcades project has been the excuse for still more trinketisation as eclectic readers too readily scour the text for details but conveniently ignore the theorised intelligence behind the (incomplete) arrangement.

The trick is to refuse to rest in the easy accommodations of academic privilege or sectarian slaggings off (however embattled these 'really existing' positions may now appear) and instead to use the productive incommensurability of both 'camps' to invent a bad Marxism that lives, reads and mobilises – offers the gift of thought to guide actions against trinkets, time, theft and death. I do not read these texts just for pleasure; I do not read them without. If the party of the new type is to have any coherence, it must be open to intellectual challenge. The revolution is not just an idea (to be sold and sloganised), and it is not without ideas. Cultural studies theory – travel, time, empire, gift – is part and parcel of a bad Marxism that wants to learn, and so the texts must be engaged.

Bad Marxism could be a critique of orthodox simplicities (and Maoist, Stalinist, Trotskyite ones too of course), and it is also, as we have seen, mostly a critique of the bad versions of Marx now deployed by postmodernists, postcolonial 'ex-Marxists', Johnny-come-lately returnees and the ideologues of trinketisation. From Derrida's spirit versions through to those of Ernesto Laclau and Chantal Mouffe (so-called post-Marxism makes me squirm), it could even be a critique of Stuart Hall's cautious Gramscian inflected 'Marxism without guarantees'. Here the bogey of 'orthodox Marxism' was reified in ways that were conditioned by the necessities of the British Left scene (the need to combat the simplicity of the sects) and then Hall went on to present what I would consider a more sensible Marxist position as a critique of that orthodoxy. A somewhat understandable move I guess, given the swamp in which the New Left, and emergent cultural studies, worked in the UK, but the context means the presentation of 'Marxism without guarantees' as the solution comes across as a more radical departure than it might be for those who bother to read Marx – there were never any guarantees.

I want to affirm that the only guarantee is a bad Marxist insistence on the ruthless critique of everything. This requires vigilance against what Giorgio Agamben calls the reconciliation of intelligence with television. He sees this proceeding through compromise: of freedom of speech with advertising, of 'the working class with capital, science with opinion, democracy with the electoral machine' (Agamben 2000:138). Compromise and collaboration softens people up before the handover to the Nazis, as Adorno also foresaw: 'Critique is essential to all democracy' (1998:281). It is essential to the separation of powers model of reciprocal checks and balances and essential to the maturity of a citizen able to have opinions despite coercive force and complicity with authority. Mistrust of critique – as divisive, subversive – is totalitarian. Anti-intellectualism is its secular form, military discipline its model. Yet only mouthing critical words also borders on complicity. Totalitarianism is unsympathetic to those who do not work or obey. The compromise of a half-hearted criticism softens us up for the slaughter. Critical thinking is overextended where it just lip-synchs the words, diluting its purchase as merely the rumour of opposition – this is bad Marxism too, the need to act corrects it.

Critique of everything aside, it is also not possible to make sense of capital without looking at particular social formations, in the global context, which determine how capital is accumulated, how its accumulation and exploitation is differentiated, and how relations of production are organised, filtered, multiplied. The corporation, the welfare state, the culture industry, et cetera, are not culturally neutral forms, and vary according to the ways differential – even hybrid – capital is organised by and organises around culture. It is also the case that 'philosophical' Marxism has a context – as was noted in the introduction, and I hope demonstrated throughout. In the end what this requires is a critique of the way that Western Marxism has 'paradoxically inverted the trajectory of Marx's own development'. Anderson suggests that whereas 'the founder of historical materialism moved progressively from philosophy to politics and then economics ... the successors of the tradition ... increasingly turned back from economics and politics to philosophy' (1976:52). Whether this trajectory can be sustained given Marx's turn towards anthropology in the latter decades of his life is unclear, but it does seem likely that we can credit the point that the 'successors' trajectory away from economics and politics is a consequence of the shift of Marxism from working-class organisations to academia and its subsequent contemplative stance. The advent of cultural studies 'as' capitalism manifests in the struggle over bad Marxism in theory. The significance of this is illustrated when the class structure of education is considered. There is no need to be reminded that structures are, for Werner Bonefeld as much as for Marx, 'historical forms of existence of class antagonism'. Bonefeld writes, 'History is the history of class struggle, as Marx declares in the *Communist Manifesto*; however, as he adds in the *18th Brumaire*, under conditions imposed on human activity through the results of former struggle which serve as a premise, as a new basis for this struggle itself' (1992:125).

Philosophically embroidered cultural studies Marxism must itself be evaluated as structured in this way, and as a class relation, as ideological, as political in purpose and position. This does not mean an ossified and simple notion of class must be used, but certainly class struggle is carried on in the debating of, and the practices of, cultural studies theory as industry. Class is useful if thought about in the double sense of both markers of status-based resource privilege and as a system marking differential usage, distribution and expropriation of resources. It does not make as much sense if rigidly restricted to a bipolar opposition of the kind necessarily sketched in the polemical opening of the *Manifesto* nor within rigidly maintained notions of nation. The working-class hero is best thought of as a far more diverse identity than that of the cloth-capped union man. For sure, the idea of class struggle makes less sense today in a national context but retains all its urgency and coherence if the international division of labour is, rather than ignored, taken as a key part of the calculus. Gibson-Graham et al., show the necessity of moving away from the essentialist class narration that fixes the subject of working-class agency in the image of the white heterosexual male (2000:8–9). It could be argued that the nation-bound class struggle in a place like Britain becomes a fashion show, a parading of accents and check shirts, the adoption by the middle class of cockney inflections and punk kids dressed in ripped designer jeans. Being working class is nothing if it is merely fashion. On a wider canvas, however, the picture is more troubling, the immiseration of a global proletariat proceeds apace. In the small world of the global publishing industry there are examples – the celebration of British or Indian authors are national sources of pride, yet the mechanics of the book trade require bumper sales to the market in the US for viability, while production is often handled 'off-shore' (off whose shores?) in the cheaper labour enclaves. When a London-based publishers print in Asia, costs are kept down; circulation and just-in-time delivery, plus the Amazon dot com phenomenon, ensure that the trade remains competitive. A division of labour prevails; the nationally identified and located author serves as local window dressing.

Which is not to say the nation has no power, nor military might with heavy weaponry. Cultural studies theorising is not the only site of struggle that matters. It is, however, also not just peripheral. Adorno contends that Marx leaves the primacy or determining status of either forces or relations of production unresolved, and thereby suggests 'that the balance between them changes according to the state of the conflicts within society' (2000:13).[2] Benjamin and Korsch had argued similarly about the base and superstructure model, the one as an expression of the other (Benjamin 1999:483). My take on this is that struggles over intellectual matters are not innocent of wider engagements. Even the footnote asides betray political investments, and in this stream accusations of 'bad' Marxism as a way of silencing debate is an old routine. Divinations of correct-line Marxism act as a form of censure and as assertions of correct behaviour or discipline. The use of citation and counter-citation in hegemonic maintenance is not something ever completely avoided, the mystification of authority and pedagogic demonologies are also symptoms – there are so many contests and contexts. Given all this, I am inclined to see debate over the line as evidence of vitality and leave it to the secret tribunal of the central committee to decide in the very last instance where we 'really' went wrong, so long as that grim finale never actually comes. In the meantime it is plausible to point to some of the places where things seem to be going astray in the present, and to debate them. To do this in the limited domain of cultural production, and specifically cultural studies theory, is only a specific instance of a generally applicable tenet. The critique of orthodox Marxism needs to be made, but anti-Marxism is what it becomes if care is not taken to insist on another possible Marxism, one that declares itself open to critique.

So if I want to put forward a bad Marxism that engages with the faults and deviations of specific versions of Marx, I also want to resist the idea that bad Marxism implies good Marxism. This is poppycock. The bad is already doubled and tripled, and the good – let's leave that to Platonists and accountants with their columns and reckonings. There will not be here a good Marxism, or rather the attempt to conjure it up will necessarily fail – and not to worry, there is a grand heritage of failed Marxisms, all hoping to be on the way to success, but there can be no final reckoning I reckon. The idea is that bad Marxism secures critical engagement as a key component of Marxist critique. Is this tautological? Probably. So? The good thing about this notion of bad Marxism is that, being a bad Marxist, there is not – at least on the face of it – a danger of instituting an unchanging hegemonic good Marxism in the prescriptive, blueprint sense, as Spivak has shown (1999). Being bad at Marxism means our ideas cannot be immediately deployed into the kind of project that institutes something that will not be able to budge (as if this were the only problem with, or the only way to name the problem of, totalitarian orthodox forms). Yet, let us at least insist on this, that bad Marxism must always be directed to a critique of Marxism in the interests of a better Marxism. Dialectically.

I want to join. I want to join a Marxism that is so rich as to accommodate all manner of rogues and dilettantes, monsters and magicians; and yet it is still worthy. Who could argue with this if not even greater rogues and monsters? There is no reason to believe the hype that demonises, since there can be no recognition of some ultimate authority – a god – who would sit as chair of a council of evidence to sift through the files and punish us for getting things wrong. Or rather, the consequences of being wrong are to be debated. In any case, the correct-line police could hardly perform that police action.[3] And what, after all, is wrong with a project that sets out to improve everyone's lot? We are already so engaged, some more than others.

## RESIDUAL COMMENTS ON THE BAD MARXISTS

The linking thread, or one of them, across these chapters is the dual problematic of fascination and paralysis. In the face of an increasing abundance of trinkets and the analysis of trinkets, the trinketising analysis stops analysing: stasis, blockage. What looks like theoretical sophistication to all intents and purposes, is unable to theorise in a way that matters, indeed, becomes an impediment to any theorising, as well as to action. A bad Marxism would rather interrupt.

The consequence of trinketising versions of Marxism, abstracted from political projects and shorn of urgency, relevance, is not just that Derrida can be read as 'the deconstructability of every structure of ideas' (Massumi 2002:37) or that Bataille can be remembered primarily as a theorist of the gift and excess, with the gift decontextualised and excess sensationalised. There is rather a systematic malaise that fragments and desiccates all culture and meaning. In the trinketisation that infects both the commodification of cultural and knowledge production, there is a resigned shrug, a gesture that signals defeat, a giving up. And this is not any heroic shrug like that of Sisyphus returning down the mountain, or the look of incomprehension shared between Lévi-Strauss and his cat. Rather, it is a pathetic giving up of the loser who thinks he or she still has some degree of credibility. The poseur is not even a *flâneur* in this foreshortened world of trinkets – even wonder and awe in the museum or before the pyramids is half-hearted … another Lonely Planet moment ticked off the list.

So often theory, latching on to the trinket, the isolated quotation, the metaphor or fetish object, slips too quickly into this dilemma when dealing with the social project of Capital. If time really does equal money, in that it is the general equivalent into or through which, as money, all things are translated, then the insight from *The Poverty of Philosophy* that there are several speeds of capital might suggest that more complicated calculations of equivalence and translation need to be taken into account. The general sense of the equivalent now clearly should not be taken to be too homogeneous. Circulations of value and valorisation attain irregular speeds and, in practice, an assumption that disregards the differentials is as abstract and as potentially misleading as the simple oppositions – plebeian and serf, use and exchange, base and superstructure. That the presentation of abstract analysis might necessarily have elevated the sketch to the status of empirical description, and hence model and blueprint, is to be guarded against (Spivak 1999). The search must not be for the accurate calculus of equivalents, but for the tools to interrupt and tamper with the system of calculation itself, at least insofar as it furthers the rule of moneybags and his (mostly his) kind.

The question of organisation harried Marx when working out the presentation of *Capital*, and of the *Manifesto* for that matter, and it is this that leads much theory off track. The problem is not so much what to do in terms of organisation, but the way the making of the text becomes subordinate to the purpose for which it is made, how it takes on a spectral life of its own. Or how the authorial voice comes to stand for something more authoritative. Gayatri Spivak often points out that Marx wrote *Capital* in an effort to provide the working class with the 'x-ray vision' to see through the trick of commodity fetishism and so to combat the increasing incursion of commodified social relations into more and more parts of life. The 'destined reader' of Marx's text is a 'member of the German Social Democratic Workers Party' (Spivak 1993:108). Today, as for Marx, the question of capitalist expansion has an internationalist resonance to do with the matter of how 'Chinese Walls' are battered down by the bourgeois mode of production. Is it – has it 'always' been – the case that trade and commodity production compels that mode's adoption, or is it rather that the force of arms compels the 'expansion' of trade? This is the key issue that confuses James Clifford when meditating upon Fort Ross. We should remember that it was a fort. In the Chinese case, the British used cannon to open up China to the opium trade. Clifford worries about the violence of the Californian-Russian fort and the trade in otter pelts. The bombing of Cambodia by B52 flying fortresses morphs, after the Cold War, into the Contra and Drug Wars of South America, the Black Hawk downings of the Sudan, the gift of charity and bombs to Afghanistan, the occupation of Iraq, the 'containment' of North Korea – all part of an armed camp mentality marching across our screens. Clifford makes a fetish of the pelt, but forgets, as he strokes it, the socio-political relation that commodity fetishism as concept was designed to reveal.

It is the trinket shorthand versioning of Marx that allows both the fast and loose dismissal on the part of opponents and the self-limiting stupidities of orthodoxy that becomes totalitarian. And cultural studies theorising falls into this trap when it renounces organisational politics and a constructed threat of the 'dangerous regime' it fears in such organisation. Thinking that restricting oneself to the trinket guards against the transgressions of 'really existing socialism' cannot lead far. But when Derrida thinks organisation he asks: 'Don't you think it's urgent to rise up against a new anti-Marxist dogma?' (2002:109) and says of the Party 'I hope it won't come back ... we must remain vigilant' (2002:112). This bad Marxism closes possibilities, restricts the party to one homologous form, forever fixed in some 'horror' arcade of camps, Stalin, Kronstadt or cultural revolution (choose one or all). What such a vigilance refuses to consider is a party formation that would not lead inexorably to totalitarian crackdown – but the equation is already fixed. This anti-communist tilting at shibboleths works with a monological notion of time that Derrida would more often than not disavow. Elsewhere, he wants to critique any tendency to 'settle down, and "read Marx carefully" ' so as to 'give him the recognition he deserves as a great philosopher' (Derrida 2002:112). But he goes no further when exactly such a philosophically compliant Marx should be replaced with one unshackled and released from conservative constraint. Surely even Derrida would have warned of the deception of this gift, which settles Marx down, as philosopher, not activist, and which imagines only one orthodox Marxism, one form of party, and condemns them.[4] There is not just a haunting spectre of Marx here, rather another wax exhibit in the house of the macabre. Derrida confirms the conservative character of his ghost story, that he will tell over and over, when he affirms: 'I don't believe in the return of communism in the dominant form of the party (the party form is doubtless on its way to extinction, more generally, in political life, it is an afterlife that may last a long time, of course)' (Derrida and Stiegler 2002:26).[5]

Today 'so-called primitive accumulation' appears to be ensured via government-backed military campaigns, ushering in uncontested 'development' contracts to Halliburton and the like. Marx's comments on violent accumulation in the latter part of *Capital* have to be recalled in this context. The analysis of Empire must take into account the ongoing superexploitation of mercantile or pirate capital not so much unregulated by the state as carefully not regulated – a kind of facilitation by neglect.[6] Three years into the 'war on terror' Empire does not look very different from before; it continues, only with more destruction. The current Empire is rather older than Hardt and Negri admit: the erection of the Empire State Building confirmed the transfer of imperial power to the USA long ago and, as King Kong of the jungle already knew, the twin target was that building and possession of the dream-date white girl. The destruction of the World Trade Center towers in New York in 2001 does not confirm their analysis, but rather mocks it with calculated identification of the symbolic recognised by the monkey-monster long ago. The tower is a camp, already long identified with power (the ring must be destroyed).

With more interesting consequences, Hardt and Negri's conception of hybridisation and a mobile multitude deserves attention. I think their valorisation of the multitude is not a nostalgia for the mass movement politics we may need (unities across differences in a 'common struggle'), but an attempt to put a positive spin on what, when blocked by the passports, visas, border patrols, immigration laws and detention centres of the state, is a limitation on the social character of work. The mobility here – more radical than Clifford's travelling theory and diaspora, but nevertheless under-theorised – must remind us of the integrated labour force that Marx thought would anticipate the political awakening of the proletariat: 'Workers of the world, unite', he wrote. Instead, the bourgeois counter-reaction fosters a general anxiety about multitude as a threat to bourgeois capital. Cultural hybridisation is explained as a consequence of urbanisation, and so the old routine of the unwashed hordes swamping the metropolis raises its ugly head as motive for policy and legislation. Travel theory has much more importance than is usually acknowledged, but only if we attend to its 'bad' side, the blockages to 'flow', the discontinuities and uneven exchanges. The multitude is an optimistic and emergent, even tentative, category that Hardt and Negri offer as the condition under globalisation of what used to be called the socialised worker under nation-states. This conception posits a smoother space to globalisation than is warranted, even taking into account their cautions. The nation-state and the corporate conglomerate might be better understood as a continuation of imperialism with the characteristics of mercantile plunder. Examination of actually existing class composition today might show that Empire is not everywhere, and does not tend towards evenness – the mobility of workers is not a constant or even comparable mobility (tourism is not labour migration; it is neither blocked travel nor flight capital, and it is not urbanisation). That Hardt and Negri valorise movement could be applauded if it came with organisation, but without such discussion the terms readily replicate the 'little England' anxieties of Enoch Powell and Margaret

Thatcher (or the anxieties of West Coast American professors worrying about the influx of 'Japanese' capital). Since blockages to exodus are the more common experience for those not of the traveller (middle) class, that is, the more or less indentured worker drones of labour migration,[7] it is the case both that the multitude is not simply on the move and, inversely, its movements are indeed political, but require a greater level of organisation if they are to defeat the border patrols. In this context, the Bush–Blair transnational junta is as much about playing the nation-building game of mercantile imperialism in the interests of transnational corporate profits (building contracts, oil deals, arms sales) as it is a racial-evangelical *jihad* of fundamentalist Christianity on the march. The failure of theorising to engage adequately with the coordinates of this *jihad* is what makes bad Marxism tragic.

It is the disaggregated mass of people that the Communist International of Marx sought to organise, providing analytical tools – *Capital* – that remain fruitful. But without transmuting a necessarily obscured and abstract future communism-to-come into the trinketisation that Hardt and Negri perpetrate. Swapping the organisation of the International for an abstract and obscure multitude-to-come cannot be a Marxism that succeeds. With this limiting and bad Marxist mode of commentary, the small-scale, anarcho-consensus network-hybrid lines of flight intensities and multiplicitous multitude-ness of the anti-capitalist movement can seem so amorphous that they mesh with a hybridising, differentially decentralised, mobility of mercantile and global capitalism as such.[8] The anti-globalisation protests in Prague, Seattle, S11 in Melbourne and the like are not yet the hope that Hardt and Negri desire, but rather the unformed expression of angst by the children of global rule unable to live with the brutality of that rule. A rule that was exposed by moves to global market and welfare state roll-back in conditions that have not yet undone national oppressions. Without organisation, this leads inexorably to defeat because of an inability to pose the question of what is adequate to win against capitalism-with-tanks. A bad Marxism that valorised critique of everything as the ethic of the anti-capitalism movement might avoid doom and impotency because it does not rest only on a moral critique. Insofar as what Hardt and Negri offer (and Clifford, for that matter) remains a moral critique, it retains a residue of Christian salvation, a salvation for 'everyone' (who chooses Christ), but salvation nonetheless (some Christians were communal after all). The trouble with salvation is its reliance on a saviour who will not arrive, reliance upon an outside power, an imaginary god. A communist would not suffer this morality but would devise ways to achieve what is needed, not wait for its delivery from afar.

The seeming contradiction of nation-state versus global market is resolved in the hypocrisy of the appointed apologists in various seats of power. When threatened by those over whom they rule by exploitation, they claim at once to be for the ideals of community, participation, inclusion – so that the world 'community' or the 'united' nations share the responsibility of force – and exercise a class rule exposed and raw in ways that they would otherwise be loath to admit as their modus operandi. When threatened by one of their own they abandon these ideals and fight for privilege and singularity – exemptions and exceptionalism expressed in tariff controls, trade quotas and protection. Sometimes the ruling class present themselves as offering the gift of benevolent leadership on behalf of all, sometimes as the only and exclusive power. Why both? Because different circumstances requires different defences of their constituent and constant interest in profit. Accumulation remains the goal, even of expenditure.

However, the critique of global capitalism is always a possibility, and bad Marxism would struggle forward to insist again that the old slogans of unity and organisation have some purchase in such dire circumstances. The point of theory here is to intervene, to transmute globalisation into something better than its mercantilist Empire-reinforcing brutal forms. Bataille saw this even towards the end of his life, when he wrote optimistically of communism: 'In today's world nothing is more familiar than communism. Everywhere in the world, communism has commanded attention as a fact or as a possibility ... there are few human beings left who don't have some idea of it' (1976/1991:262). Published nearly 30 years ago, this comment still applies today – and we could say something similar about Islam; both have been demonised in the same way, despite radical differences, indeed often oppositions. It remains the case that 'everyone has heard the word; sometimes associated with hatred, sometimes with devotion, more rarely with indifference' (1976/1991:262). What would social theory look like if it were to take up Bataille's call from long ago? The 50 years of the Cold War have been worse than the 1930s context in which he wrote his most incisive critiques of fascism and expenditure. As Bataille puts it: 'a banality that everyone already knows is that, quite simply, there is no chance of being able to decrease the risk of war before we have reduced or begun to reduce, the general disparity of standards of living' (1976/1991:162). After the setbacks of the 1920s, the socialist parties did not rebound but rather adopted a limiting social democracy. Depression and economic hardship prevailed. Only the likes of Bataille insisted that one did not have to be 'crushed'. Not hearing that call, and allowing such space to be compromised, invited the totalitarian fascist-nationalist reaction, latent in European culture. This seems commonly to arise within a recently defeated power. Not that the defeat of Germany in the First World War is the same as the US defeats in Korea and Vietnam, but Bush does have the stature that may give some pause for thought and the detention camps in Cuba look ominous. A compromised retreat from engagement into theory, into the library, into contemplation is, in the long run, bad for theory, the library and for contemplation in the face of such reaction. The destruction of the planet precludes the isolated pleasures of the happy scholar alone in a (square) cell.

## WHERE ARE WE NOW WITH REGARD TO CAPITALISM?

The always-entertaining Slavoj Žižek has, several times, pointed out that 'we can enjoy coffee without caffeine, beer without alcohol, sex without direct bodily contact' (2002:174). His comment captures something of the frustration that might be understood if Marxism as presented in theory, as discussed here, were the be all and end all of Marxism as such. I would add that this is Marx without Marxism. Similarly interesting is Žižek's point that 'doing nothing is not empty, it already has a meaning – it means saying yes to existing relations of domination' (2002:194). This was said while discussing Bertholt Brecht's 1930s remark, on the show trials, that if those on trial were innocent then they deserved to be shot. For me, this suggests that to sit around reading theory and doing nothing but be pleased with the correctness of citations and the display function of your book collection might be the less clever choice (despite all those glossy covers and Zone volumes). No matter how proud you may be with your name-dropping and conversational skills the Culture Industry still has your number.

The commercialisation of everything: the extension of information technology to all parts of our lives ('above all email'), the calculation of all time as money, the production of hi-tech elites/skilled workforce and the formation of an underclass (free in a triple sense, in that they are free of all possessions, free to sell their labour to anyone who will buy it, and free to not labour at all, since there are not always jobs).[9] The decline of welfare, the segmentation of work-forces, the internationalisation of the repressive apparatus (in the form of the UN forces, and in the exchange of police technologies through forums such as COPEX,[10] in the occupying armies, the terror legislations, the Patriot Acts and surveillance powers) and so on.[11] In many of these examples what can be discerned is not so much a new mode of Empire as another reconfiguration that attempts to reduce necessary costs of production and/or extend the productivity of labour wherever it resides. Such aims are the never changing ambition of capital: to get the workers to work more for less. That this now extends across the entirety of social life, so that a reduction in welfare spending by the state is the equivalent, in the former period, of a decline in wages, indicates the logical, and exploitative continuities of this process. Increased exploitation may appear as speed, but to call it so rests content with the mystification of the market and the phantasmagoria of progress.

It is not through mere technological advance nor through speed that this extension comes about, and it still remains to be analysed how today relations of gender, class and race, and then of aesthetics, literary appreciation, university teaching, quiz shows, lottery, travel, tourism, nostalgia, even history, should be calculated as costs of production. World Bank and finance capital shore up unstable governments in the wake of social unrest in South East Asia, such as that organised by Reformasi in Malaysia and Indonesia and the workers' movement in South Korea and the Philippines. Here we necessarily need to take into account mergers, protection, tariffs, deregulation, financial flows and MBA managerialism, which are factors too detailed for a book of this type even as the injunction to do more than analyse remains. There is, and will be in such studies, a refusal of speed, a refusal of low aspiration, of fear of the technological, or of loss of tradition, an overcoming of the superficial divisions of racism, ethnicism, essentialism, absolutism, as well as a refusal of the hegemonising sameness and blandness of ever more diverse culture markets. Sally, let's dance. And dance at a time when the triumphalism of capital brooks no opposition, when plunder and accumulation in the old imperialist sense are back on the cards, and when all this is underwritten by aid programmes, expert advice under the guise of development assistance (trade facilitation), and liberal patronising religio-arrogant, anti-racist, 'friends-of-the-Third-World' charity (the kindly face of racism). In such circumstances all talk, and not just poetry or theory, is barbaric unless it fights.

Now, I don't want to be confined to retreads of the old Masters, but it is also plausible to think of Adorno's work in relation to the heightened anxieties about technology and speed that prevail in some quarters. Adorno permits us to think about these matters carefully first of all by denouncing the anxiety itself that seeks to justify. He says that today intellectual work:

> … is done with a bad conscience, as if it had been poached from some urgent, if only imaginary occupation. To justify itself in its own eyes it puts on a show of hectic activity performed under great pressure and shortage of time.
>
> (1951/1974:138)

This sounds more and more like the conditions of academic production in the mass teaching factories of the 1990s. He continues, 'It often seems as if intellectuals reserved for their actual production only those hours left over from obligations, excursions, appointments and unavoidable amusements' (1951/1974:138), so that the whole of life comes to look like the worst of jobs. Against this, refusal of the speed mythos of capital would dislocate hegemonic flows to create moments and spaces unavailable to the consumptive rhythms of the next, next, next. Reading more carefully, slowly, Adorno says that dialectical reasoning is mad: 'Was it not bigoted and talmudic to insist, in the midst of the exchange economy, on the difference between the labour-time expended by the worker and that needed for the reproduction of the worker's life?' (1951/1974:73). A mad bad Marxism might include a dialectical reason which 'when set against the dominant mode of reason [is] unreason', as only 'fools tell their masters the truth'. The work of Adorno, though, is not foolish, it is to 'help this fool's truth attain its own reasons' (1951/1974:72).

Adorno looks to the future where 'the remnants of a division of labour which the radical curtailment of working hours might leave in society would lose the horror of shaping the individuals throughout' (1966/1973:278–9). It is time to further the ways in which we refuse to be accomplices to a leisure time that is only recovery for work, for an unemployment that is only reserve army idleness, for an identity that is only the abstract and simplifying categorisation of a hypostatised and meticulously policed exuberance that might otherwise transform our lives. Reading Marx badly and against the schools and protocols might suggest some of this, however much such reading must still be argued, debated, challenged, engaged.

This is the dilemma though: critique is caught in academy or sect, art is corrupted in the halls of culture, literature by the bookshop and the sales pitch, sculpture corroded by long sentry duty as memorials to power – any suggestive element within these forms has long been contained or punished. Even the criticism of criticism is a privilege (Adorno 1966/1973:41), which accounts for the transaction that authorises a book of ideas. There is little room for articulation in the quiet and guarded corridors of complicity.

*   *   *

Ships in distress signal their latitude and longitude, as did the Romanian surrealist group's Gherasim, Luca and Trost in 1945 in 'Dialectics of the Dialectic' – apparently an influence on Deleuze and Guattari's *Anti-Oedipus* (1972/1983). Just because there is no time to decide which ship,[12] or to ensure that the ones chosen for travel are not overburdened, leaky, have a crazy captain or show upon the radar screens of the Royal Navy, this does not mean we cannot map the coordinates of a critical interest today – the plotted points around which a bad Marxist might organise academic work in the present, addressing, for example, the commodification of everything, including time. The continued advance of forms of globalisation of exchange (uneven). The unabated polarisation, within the west and across the south.[13] Massive development of the means of communication (patchy).[14] The war economy. Pharmaceutical cash in on HIV, global environmental catastrophe. Subcultural creativity of geeks, deviants, reprobates, organ grinders, et cetera.

The composition and potentials of anti-capitalist and anti-imperialist forces are a focus; communication and control among both capital and the varied oppositions deserves attention; the circulation of struggles in Nepal, China, the Philippines, New Zealand, Peru, Columbia, Mexico, Angola, Eritrea, Palestine, Kurdistan, Ireland, South London are instructive – there is much to learn. Pedagogy within the institution and beyond might deserve more effort, looking for the grounding of such pedagogy in the slow work of transformation and learning to learn what this requires; honing subtle skills and habits of mind that do not close down, and that 'counter' opportunism and co-option.

Class struggle tends towards global reconfiguration and further polarisation – communications, travel, migrancy, meaning/media, regulation, terror laws. The reconfiguration of the relations of production entails new alliances, national ethnic and religious; new needs, new possibilities; differences, niches, identity (ethnographers to be deployed). Commodification of criticism, plus complicity and publicity circuits of star academia tends towards alienation and celebrity fetishism, trinkets, citations, position. The portrayal of resistance as eclectic, exotic, romantic and reactive, or easy, could be contrasted with an engaged and patient willingness to debate complexity without falling for the convenience of novelty or curiously loaded buzzwords. Trinketisation is just the circumstantial effect of a general fetishism that must be analysed. A potential and possible emancipation festers before the ideology of the hybrid and the marketing of difference. Fragmented, rhizomatic capital thrives exactly where intellectual activism must focus upon the emancipative capacity of global development and organise to transmute its prospects into the real. The contradictions that must be hurdled include those between workers and capitalists, between capitalists and capitalists (they fight each other once they have secured the field for operations), between production and consumption, between the forces of production and the relations of production, between capitalism and feudalism, capitalism and communism, comprador and class, organisation and theory, reader and text, mission and outcome, signifier and sign. Though this by no means exhausts the series, it is displacement of contradictions like these that constitutes the class struggle.

## THE PARTY (OF THE NEW TYPE)

Learning from Bataille, a party-organised open (bad) Marxism worth its anti-capitalist credentials must address inequality and maldistribution of wealth – the increasing affluence of the rich. That the rich enjoy their luxuries and live simultaneously in proximity and out of reach of the poor, in both London and Lusaka, in Brixton and in Bhubaneshwar, in Zaire and New Zealand is based on capitalist exploitation of a systematic type. Everyone knows that the workers of the First World economic 'bantustans' are perhaps slightly better off than those in the South, but relative prosperity is founded on the greater appropriations of the ruling class. Only complicity with, and co-option to the cultural sheen of that ruling class prevents the rise of truly multi-sited anti-capitalist solidarities.

There are ways that the current conjuncture has to be met with an open and inquiring countenance. That this may take slow reading and investigative work is only the necessary recognition that capitalism has enjoyed a longer gestation than the conditions described above, and though it blocks a still recent opposition it cannot last forever (more than 500 years of plunder and only 70 years of the first soviet experiment – the next awaits). In the interim it is important to recognise the lived reality of struggle requires an equally flexible mind. For example, no one should be surprised to find the labour theory of value is not the be all and end all of Marx. It was not even so in Marx's own layout. Again, the commodity form is the subject of Chapter 1, money of Chapter 2, circulation comes later, and rent, and struggle, et cetera. There are even unwritten chapters, and of course more than 150 years since *The Manifesto* and *The Poverty of Philosophy*. If speculations on the spectral economy, and on postmodern informatics, advertising and cyber-values, not to mention sexualities, perversities and panopti-cons were not mentioned in the calculus of Chapter 1 (though in some interesting ways maybe they were anticipated), this is not yet an excuse for dumping the Marx text in the cupboard for gnawing by mice. Old Mother Hubbard would be less than pleased to find the larder of critical thought as bare it is these days.

Samir Amin reminds us that the critical project continues:

> For me socialism means more than the abolition of private property (a negative characteristic); it has a positive meaning of alternative labor relations other than those defining wage status, alternative social relations allowing society as a whole (and not an apparatus function-ing on its behalf) to control its social future. This in turn means a democracy far more advanced than the best bourgeois democracy.
>
> (1994:173)

Advanced? What is the advance projected here? Is the circle of struggles around anti-capitalism a possible renewal of critical work that might lead to an internationalist solidarity to reconfigure the world? Such solidarity must do more than solve the crisis of over-production by means of income redistribution, but that would be a start in that the burden of crisis is conventionally transferred to the south by international capital. Alongside this redistribution a new cultural revolution is required – can the anti-capitalist movement provide it? Is the solidarity of the multitude both an economic and cultural force in the class struggle? Only solidarity between progres-sive social forces in the North and anti-comprador forces in the

South can achieve the redistribution that will overcome the regular crises of capitalist overproduction. That internationalist solidarity is not in a good state makes crises devastating as the northern capitalists relay pain and suffering, via so called structural adjustment and their comprador allies, away from themselves, in a failing coping strategy. Globalisation without a redistribution towards income parity and an international regulating mechanism that will limit overproduction, can only mean damaging boom and slump, which the imperial powers will shift, in terms of burden, on to the South every time. War, dumping, extraction, sweatshops – all this means that solidarity begins 'at home' in a way that requires more than theory, but must be theorised.[15]

One day a year festival processions in the midst of the metropole may be a gesture of solidarity with struggles like Chiapas, but it does not make Zapatisas of us all. The Communist Party of the new type has to earn the trust of wide sections of the public rather than just a few dedicated sect-dwellers. It can only do this by providing a relentless educational service, informative articles in its press, news unavailable elsewhere and perspectives on the news. Openness to debate, commitment to struggle, support for a better life for all through revolutionary politics and the cultivation of a renewed internationalist culture of the Left. Without patient work of this type, the perception of a series of defeats of the past will remain in the minds of potential supporters, rather than the as yet unfulfilled potential.

> 'Openness' here, refers not just to a programme of empirical research – which can elide all too conveniently with positivism – but to the openness of Marxist categories themselves. This openness appears in, for instance, a dialectic of subject and object, of form and content, of theory and practice, of the constitution and reconstitution of categories in and through the development, always crisis-ridden, of a social world. Crisis refers to contradiction, and to contradiction's movement.
>
> (Bonefeld et al. 1992:xi)

## THE NEED TO STUDY/TEACH

As a coda, I am tempted to consider this credo for teaching: Believing that it takes time and study to come to know ever less about a place, the task of education is this endless struggle with ignorance and growing ignorance (my own and others'). We might aim, at the very least, for a better and more specified stupidity. Alongside this, an injunction to intervene where one can by way of instituting mechanisms that facilitate the struggle against ignorance. No doubt Adorno is correct to complain that no amount of enlightened education can prevent the appearance of those 'bureaucratic desktop murderers and ideologues' who dream up policies and programmes of reactionary character. But he also holds out hope that such enlightened education might manage to forestall the conscription of those asked to carry out the orders of the ideologues (Adorno 1998:204). This alone requires the anti-war and anti-capitalist movements to find a place within the curriculum of progressive education. There is a place for study, reading, research, and several speeds at which to go have a look for yourself. A possible project for a Marxist academic could include the transfer of diagnostic and analytic critique into liberation-driven investigation as part of an organised political project. What is it that bad Marxism needs to know? The conditions inside the detention camps? The conditions of sweatshop labour? The character of cybercolonialism? The long history of empire? Just who holds power and why are they lying? The deceptions of charity, development, aid, gifts? What can be done to undo the atrocities in Palestine, Iraq, Afghanistan? Who has the wherewithal to limit the profits of the pharmaceuticals industry, to link up struggles for global health, environmental justice, universal quality of life (health concerns 'at home' cannot exclude health concerns of the globe)? What might get us past the endlessly static debate over the primacy of race, class or gender? What is the dictatorship of the proletariat and how is this organised worldwide? What is the nature of class composition today – in the nation, the region, the planet? Are trade unions a compromise or concession? How is resistance sustained? What would be adequate to win against capital? How might an organisation defeat capitalism-with-tanks, without becoming a manic tank master too? What form of organisation? What mode of struggle? Which theory and which debate? There is much to do.

\*   \*   \*

The obligatory six-point programme:

1. Fetish and trick – requires dexterous analysis not grinning appreciation.
2. Trinketisation – requires contextualisation, recognition of systematic institutionalisations.
3. Contextualisation – requires an ethnographic engagement with enframing (with all its methodological hang-ups born of Malinowskian fieldwork and its disintegration, have a look for yourself, learn to learn from below).
4. The curse of sanctioned ignorance – requires slow work for transnational literacy.[16]
5. The public secret of institutional complicity – requires mainstreaming, articulation, visibility.[17]
6. Visibility – requires a politically transformatory project.[18]

# Notes

## Introduction: Cultural Studies as Capitalism

1. In an essay called 'Jungle Studies' I wrote of anthropology in a way I would adapt for cultural studies today:

   Let's for starters assume there is a discipline called anthropology. Furthermore, let it be an wholly institutionally-based global system of knowledge about the peoples of the world, organized with researchers and research projects, teaching programs and degree structures, publishing houses, theoretical schools (more than one, more than a succession of paradigms), methodological precepts, debates, tenure, career, course guides, reading lists, footnotes – and let this whole agglomeration be, if not the most important and central among the knowledges, at least not totally decimated and paralyzed by anxiety and reflexive crisis or post-colonial/post-modern angst. ... Let us then invoke the proper names and crucial texts ...

   (Hutnyk 2002a:15)

   I think it is in the same spirit that Victor Alneng writes of cultural studies as:

   ... also an institution, a policy, a fortress, a panoptic tower, a solitary confinement, a commodity (not least), an escape, a procedure, a brand name, a breadwinner, a career goal, a call for papers, a cocktail and a cocktail party gossip, an excuse, an alibi, an identity, a surplus value, a subterfuge, a possibility, an end, a beginning ...

   (Alneng, email correspondence, August 2003)

2. For my take on these specific filters, see *The Rumour of Calcutta: Tourism Charity and the Poverty of Representation* (Hutnyk 1996), *Travel Worlds: Journeys in Contemporary Cultural Politics* (Kaur and Hutnyk 1999), *Critique of Exotica: Music, Politics and the Culture Industry* (Hutnyk 2000a) and *Dis-Orienting Rhythms: The Politics of the New Asian Dance Music* (Sharma et al. 1996).

3. See Stephen Nugent's discussion of the 'courtship', 'alliance' and 'incompatibilities which militated against [an] easy melding' of cultural studies and anthropology (in Nugent and Shore 1997:1).

4. Howard Potter reminds me of the collection *Fieldwork and Footnotes* (Vermeulen and Roldán 1995) where 'Vermeulen notes that the nationalistic/occidental history of British anthropology (Kuper et al) demonstrates a degree of "presentism" and then suggests a different genealogy', whereby the historians and linguists such as August Schlözer are responsible for the emergence of both *Völkerkunde* and *Völkskunde* at Göttingen between 1771 and 1782 (respectively, 'knowledge of peoples in general and of a people in particular'). Between the 1720s and 1780s, some of

Schlözer's colleagues worked for the Imperial Russian Academy of Sciences, conducting expeditions intended to map the Empire with regard to the histories, geographies, languages, customs and manners of its peoples. Schlözer is credited with assimilating the results of his colleagues in his work at Göttingen (Vermeulan 1995:44). In the same volume Schippers further suggests that through the influence of the Göttingen work there developed the tradition of *etnografija* in both imperial Russia and the USSR, that is, the study of 'primitive peoples' (1995:240) or 'primordial communities' (Pershits 1980:86). Enter Morgan and Engels, and their influence on Soviet ethnology (Kuper 1991:71), and Maine, Lubbock and Marx (Krader 1974). This offers an oriental/subaltern alternative to Gledhill, but while broadly agreeing with the colonial/imperial beginnings, it 'shifts the historical ownership eastwards, and backwards by a century' (Potter, email correspondence, August 2003). We might also attend to the work of Klaus Peter Koepping on Adolf Bastian (Koepping 1983).

5. A point that has been often critiqued, corrected and shown as debilitating by Karl Korsch as cited in Benjamin's *Arcades* (1999:483) and Adorno (2000); more recently Žižek (2002) and in Part 4 of this book, on Bataille.

## PART 1   CLIFFORD'S ETHNOGRAPHICA

## 1   Clifford and Malinowski

1. Malinowski travels in order to displace travel accounts. Stagl and Pinney write:

> The ethnographic monograph is commonly regarded as the literary form which most corresponds to Malinowski-style fieldwork. Both are said to have been born together and to have replaced the over-ambitious syntheses of travel reports by 'armchair anthropologists'. This is no doubt a simplification encouraged by Malinowski himself.
>
> (Stagl and Pinney 1996:122)

2. The classic monographs such as *The Nuer* and *Argonauts of the Western Pacific*, which 'all anthropologists read in training' become vehicles for 'all manner of detached theoretical debates, autonomous from the ethnography and no longer substantially constrained by it' (Marcus 1988:69–70).

3. Of course, Clifford has always been concerned with travel; his first book *Person and Myth: Maurice Leenhardt in the Melanesian World* was a detailed study of a well-travelled figure. Though at pains to show that the missionary Leenhardt was some sort of anti-colonialist, when for example he writes that the formation of the Institut Française d'Océanie was an opportunity to show that 'colonialism is something other than a money-grubbing enterprise' (Leenhardt in Clifford 1982:192), Clifford perhaps does better to contrast this with Michel Leiris' anti-colonial position, also discussed in that book (Clifford 1982:197). Leenhardt appears more as an apologist for a worthy and civilisational version of colonialism, while Leiris offers a much sharper anti-colonial view, but there are at least substantial and sustained analyses and historical detail in *Person and Myth*

which make it possible to read against Clifford's maybe too-generous narrative. Such a reading could be usefully informed by his later examinations of the way authority is claimed in ethnographic texts.

4. And so many other criticisms it's not funny: that cut-up experiments are *passé*; that only tenured professors can experiment (Rabinow already made this criticism in the *Writing Culture* volume itself – and Clifford supposedly set up an experimental ethnography series for graduate students with the University of Wisconsin Press, but he does not refer to many, if any, such texts in his bibliography). Also, that there is no political programme that would be adequate to win; that the project produces a new ideology for hybridising capitalism, etc.

5. Instead, I am concerned to ask why and how, with what political effects, and in what way the discussion can contribute to action on racism, exploitation, imperialism. Ask what interests are served by going on with reflexive anxiety and 'suicidal rejoicing' for the end of anthropology (Richardson 1975:527 – now a very old quote)? Instead, a drive to analyse, explain, inspire, change the world (naïve? but the struggle is grim :-) ).

6. See Hutnyk (1987:60), 'The Authority of Style', which was an early attempt to summarise the first moves of the Writing/Culture critique. Salute to the seriousness of John Perry and Malcolm Crick of Deakin University.

7. See Hutnyk (1989:105), 'Clifford Geertz as a Cultural System', which took an early stab at the cult of names in ethnography – Geertz's initials (CG) elevated on his covers to icons (Geertz 1988) like those of E-P, R-B and L-S. Immortalities of the alphabet.

8. Note the conflation here of travel and travel writing, to which Clifford is blind. I thank Steve Clarke for pointing this out.

9. See Phipps (1998), but as a counterfactual see ethnographies under fire, most interesting in Genet (1986/1989), with commentary by Swedenbourg (1995).

10. Rapport speculates that the photograph of Malinowski with the limepot in his lap, which graces the cover of the reissue of *A Diary in the Strict Sense of the Term*, is very much staged, only the anthropologist wears a kula armshell and 'it appears ... that he has been adorned with them, sanctifying the scene like some idol: "Posed before the niggers" [27.1.1918]' (Rapport 1990:5). Malinowski himself calls his own photography a 'capital blot' on his fieldwork. He admits to having treated photographs as secondary and unimportant, a 'serious mistake' to make. He put photography 'on the same level as the collection of curios' and had no 'appetite or bent' for the task. For more on photographs see Kratz (1994) and Hutnyk (1996: ch. 5).

11. He ' "pawed" and perhaps more (the *Diary* was censored by Malinowski's widow before publication)' (Newton 1993:7). Of course such exploits could be left out of the written text, even before the widow censors, by the man capable of being simultaneously engaged to two professor's daughters, in Melbourne and Adelaide, and, if Baldwin Spencer is to be believed, possibly others (Wayne 1995:88, 98). It is

thought that Spencer opened Malinowski's letters and reported various indiscretions to the Stirling family (Wayne 1995:138). Perhaps a fair deal, since it seems Malinowski may have been going through Spencer's mail from F.J. Gillen (Roswell 1996), and gleaning the notion of participant observation from the Central Australian postie (and accomplice grave-robber, letter from Gillen to Spencer 13.3.1896) (see Mulvaney et al. 1997:41, 46–7, 104). The story of 'pillow-talk' ethnographic instruction on the part of concubines in the field remains a hidden one, even as Clifford cites two recent examples (though leaves one out of the bibliography, referencing only Rabinow 1977 – which was rather tame I thought – omitting Cesura 1982; a more steamy episode might be found in Wade 1993). Clifford's observation that Leenhardt was scandalised by Malinowski's *Sexual Life of Savages* and saw such work as 'a subversive movement devoted to moral relaxation and based ... in Moscow' (1982:147) is highly entertaining. However, Leenhardt's accusation does not, in reality, make a comrade of the Pole. Clifford himself seems a little shocked by the book, promoting it in order of sequence in another comment comparing Leenhardt's rather dull book titles with Malinowski's *Sexual Life of Savages*, *Argonauts* and *Coral Gardens* (1982:147). It is perhaps often the case that Malinowski's sex life gets raised beyond its importance.

12. This formulation anticipates the neologism 'writing culture' by 70 years (Rapport 1990:6). We discover from Malinowski's letters (Wayne 1995) that in his diary Malinowski was rewriting and reviewing his life prior to arrival in the Trobriands.

13. I owe John Gledhill thanks for many discussions on these points.

14. As a hint to how I would think through this, I have learnt, as ever, from Gayatri Spivak, who computes:

> ... even as circulation time attains the apparent instantaneity of thought (and more), the continuity of production ensured by that attainment of apparent coincidence ['apparent' used twice already] must be broken up by capital: its means of doing so is to keep the labour reserves in the comprador countries outside of this instantaneity, thus to make sure that multinational investment does not realise itself fully there through assimilation of the working class into consumerist-humanism ... the worst victims of the recent exacerbation of the international division of labour are women.
>
> (Spivak 1987:166–7)

15. On Malinowski's arrival see Thornton (1985:13); on Geertz, consider how Indonesian politics is invisible in the much-taught cockfight article (Geertz 1973). For their sins of self-display, Geertz calls Rabinow, Crapanzano and Dwyer 'Malinowski's children' (quoted in Clifford 1988:113). This, I guess, makes Geertz himself the mother's brother and Clifford the mother's brother's son. Dear diary: See, I did pay some attention in my kinship class. The mother, as Steve Clarke kindly pointed out, is missing. Of course, it's Elsie Masson, confined to her sickbed, the invisible hand in this heritage, rewriting, annotating,

correcting, Bronio's books. Though it could also be the Elsie that Clifford briefly extracts from a William Carlos Williams poem, only to have her disappear, in *Predicaments* (see Marcus 1991:136).

16. Admittedly, Clifford is only one person who produces books (though his productive activity is also shared among research assistants, copy-editors, typesetters, binders, packers, truck drivers, salespersons and promotional corps), and it is also not the case that he is typical of his type. In the current conditions of academia it is clear that many of those who may have been inspired by Clifford's work could not get academic jobs, especially not in anthropology departments. An entire generation of students, even two, has not entered the academy at a time when in many countries student numbers have expanded exponentially, while funding in real terms has plummeted. The old guard has remained, beset by its own woes of increased teaching load, administrative duties and commercialisation (increased fee-paying student offerings, education as export earner, etc.), bunkered down to protect their own patch and trying to stave off the cuts, and to defend – and then attack in a curiously calculated backlash – the postmodern anthropology that Clifford has come to represent.

17. Shows are culture. Clifford comments elsewhere on the 'long history of "exotic" displays in the West' (1997:197), precisely after he reports favourably upon the low-budget sculpture display organised by an anthropology student (Jim Mason), who recruited Melanesian artisans to work on decorating a corner of the corporate Palo Alto Stanford University with a 'New Guinea Sculpture Garden'. Cheap entertainment here may be contrasted as exploitation in one register and a real-politically useful media exposure for artists in another. A similar complex was also offered when rural craftspeople were brought to Washington D.C. for an 'Indian Mela', using the occasion to raise concerns about begging laws in India (Clifford 1997:196), while the Smithsonian Institution no doubt basked in the glow of bargain multicultural arts.

18. I am resisting this temptation to diarise myself, but as I am writing this in Heidelberg, what to make of the complete Masewa canoe from Kiriwina (1988 *erworben* [i.e. collected in 1988]) I glimpse through the window of the Völkerkundmuseum, Palais Weimar, closed for the summer? Trobriand canoes indeed travel far. Young notes that contemporary Trobrianders are said to recognise that Malinowski has stolen their heritage (Young 1979:17). The practice continues. In relation to Bosu's access to world media, jobs, and 'right of reply', I wish I did have permission here to report Clifford's lament that Bosu doesn't get to write letters of recommendations either ('off the record' letter to author 1998).

19. Even the journal *Documents* ends up being of little more significance than as an example of 'an unfinished collage' (Clifford 1988:133). Collage itself is not all of what was political about the publication of the journal by Bataille, Leiris et al., and nor can the elevation of this as some sort of 'method' (despite belated denials, [Clifford 1991]) out of any context serve as much more than a gimmick. *Documents* and the College of Sociology could be credited with more seriousness than this. Collage,

of course, could be political. Though not always necessarily so. Whatever the qualms about how badly Clifford has rendered surrealism, it is well known that political debates over collage, (Max Ernst, Picasso 'Still Life with Chair Caning' [1912], Carrà 'Interventionist Demonstration' [1914] and Duchamp's collage cum curio cabinet 'The Large Glass' [1915–23]), and the closely related, perhaps more calculated, montage, have a very long 'political' pedigree. For discussion I am indebted to Scott McQuire and Don Miller (see McQuire 1995, 1997b; Miller 1992).

20. In a review of *Trobriand Cricket*, Weiner suggests that: 'For Trobrianders, there is nothing unique about playing to the camera' (1977:506). Malinowski suggests that to the English cricket is about sportsmanship, to a Kiriwinian it is a cause for quarrelling, passion and gambling, and 'to another type of savage, a Pole, it remains pointless – a tedious manner of time-wasting' (1935:212). I refrain from noting how many times in a row the English have now lost the Ashes (are they becoming Polish in the face of the Australian attack?). The urn should be despatched forthwith. Of course nationalism requires all manner of intellectual myth-making investments. The struggle over the nationality of Malinowski, and indeed over the national claim to have discovered the 'fieldwork method' is itself full of contention. Witness the refusal of British publishing houses to print a text (mentioned above, note 11) which was to claim, in part, that Malinowski's investigations in Baldwin Spencer's rooms – Malinowski was a house guest for a time – were formative for his ideas about fieldwork and 'living among the natives' (Roswell 1996:12–20). The nationality of Malinowski – a Pole with Austrian citizenship, in Australia, engaged and later married to an Australian nurse (whom English commentators continue to call British) and settled in Italy, working in the UK, is of course fraught. Ernest Gellner offers the best response to the question while making a point about Malinowski's cultural rather than political nationalism, telling us that Evans-Pritchard had told him that Malinowski 'firmly turned down the suggestion that he should rename himself McRasberry' – *malina* being the common slavic name for the fruit (Gellner 1985:7).

21. For me, the most interesting and concise illustration of what is at stake comes from the relationship between two Soviet filmmakers, Dziga Vertov and Sergei Eisenstein. The maker of *Man with a Movie Camera* coined the phrase 'Kino-Glaz' ('cinema-eye', 1923) for his cinema. Eisenstein, with the Proletkult group, whom Vertov found 'hopeless' (Leyda and Voynov 1982:14), was more interested in montage and the possibilities of gaining a political effect from calculated juxtaposition. He responded to Vertov by describing his film technique as 'Kino-Fist'. You are either with the programme, or a dilettante. Marcus suggests that from a methodological perspective, 'Vertov's work is an excellent inspiration for multi-sited ethnography' (Marcus 1995:106). Eisenstein unquestionably is worth more than this one slogan, Kino-Fist, but this may suggest another sort of multi-site anthropologising: in his autobiography he writes:

In subject and composition, I never try to limit the frame solely by the way things appear on the screen. The subject must be chosen thus, turned this way, and placed in the field of the frame so that, besides mere representation, a knot of associations results that mirrors the mode and sense of the piece. ... Light, camera angle, the cutting of the shot – everything is subordinated not merely to representing the subject, but revealing it.

(Eisenstein 1995:30–1)

22. Malinowski inscribed the fly leaf of the copy of *Argonauts* he gave to Elsie with the words: 'To my collaborator, who had half the share at least and more than half the merit in writing this book' and he signed this revelation, 'Its nominal author'. The letters reveal that Elsie continually contributed additions to Malinowski's texts (Wayne 1995:26, 30.4.1927). The dedication to *Coral Gardens* also acknowledges her.

23. I do not want to elevate some list of the 'revolutionary' interruptions to fieldwork beyond this incantation, but I do note that a number of anthropologists have interrupted fieldwork to become revolutionaries. I call decolonisation a failure because, in Spivak's phrase, it's a bitter joke; so-called postcolonialism is a hoax (see Hutnyk 1996:36). This new buzzword is often promoted by comprador elites and publishing-opportunity-conscious propagandisers for a revisionist colonial history and business-as-usual. On Naxalites, see *Critique of Exotica* (Hutnyk 2000a: ch. 7).

24. Absurdly, Thornton suggests that Malinowski's reading of Nietzsche made him a postmodernist before the rush (Internet posting anthro-l, October 1995), but the letters suggest that Nietzsche's influence was not so great, an 'insignificant ingredient' (Wayne 1995:63, Bronio to Elsie).

25. However, probably today's fieldworkers would be less prepared for trouble should things become unsafe in their chosen site. Look at what happens to unwitting adventure tourists in Kashmir and Cambodia (see Phipps 1998). This is the dilemma at the heart of calls either to codify methods of training for fieldwork or leave possibilities (dangerously, interestingly) open.

26. What is offered here is a suggested way to read ethnographic work in a context. This is quite a different task to thinking about how to write such a text oneself. I cannot imagine that Malinowski or Clifford were/are well placed to anticipate and second guess what their texts might become, what agendas they could serve. These texts may not have been intended as allegories of the political, but by being available to the reading requirements of different times they become so. Chapter 2 looks for the symptoms.

## 2   Fort Ross Mystifications

1. This last essay stands in the structurally important place that was occupied by the much discussed Mashpee chapter in *Predicaments*. See the special issue of *Social Analysis* for debate, especially Marcus 1991, and Strathern 1991.

2. Or more pertinent to this particular discussion of Fort Ross, Clifford asks: 'Is it possible that historical reality is not something independent of ... differently centred perspectives?' (Clifford 1997:319), and if not,

then it matters that Clifford's perspective for writing a – however complex and uncertain – history (meditation) on Pacific trade is centred in UCLA, Santa Cruz. He says it has become 'harder and harder to sustain a unified, inclusive historical consciousness capable of sorting and reconciling divergent experiences', complaining that Marx did not decentre Hegel's 'synthetic historical realism' and doing so would be the 'philosophical project of Nietzsche, and the practical task, still unfinished, of decolonization' (Clifford 1997:320). I am tempted to wonder if those (Nietzschean cadre?) fighting ongoing US imperialism – in the Philippines, Central America, the Gulf etc. – find decentring Hegel a particularly urgent 'practical' task?

3. Sex travels violently – and in the context of Clifford's attention to 'intermarriage' between colonists and locals it is possibly worthwhile to pursue the following digression: noting that Lévi-Strauss was aware that the 'untouched' Nambikwara that he met in the jungles of South America had been decimated by sexually transmitted diseases. In Australia, that early participant observer F.J. Gillen wrote that he had 'always thought ... that syphilis was common to these people [Aboriginal Australians near Alice Springs] long before they came in contact with the White man' and he ascribed it to rapid spread of the disease from the North or South due to the 'custom of exchanging women' (Gillen to Spencer 23 March 1897, Mulvaney et al. 1997:152). In this instance Gillen was agreeing with the German ethnologist Eylmann who had visited him at his post (the editors of the letters suggest in a note that the disease discussed with Eylmann may have been Yaws, which shows similar symptoms). However, the speculations of those involved in this founding fieldwork scene are worth noting: Gillen and Spencer's 'informant and collector' the police constable Cowle reported, after a discussion with Eylmann regarding the lighter skinned Natives who lived near the Missionary station, that perhaps the water of the area had 'a bleaching effect' (Cowle to Spencer 9 February 1897, Mulvaney et al. 1997:160). Later Gillen lampooned the idea that such fair skinned children resulted from eating Mission flour and he modified his views on syphilis, writing: 'For a long time it has been growing upon me that these people were at one time more numerous – I don't of course believe that they degenerated morally etc ... their numbers have been decreased by the introduction of syphilis from outside ... there is not the ghost of a shadow of doubt and with their peculiar customs the rapid spread of the disease throughout the continent would only be a question of a few years' (Gillen to Spencer 22 October 1897, Mulvaney et al. 1997:190–1). He did however report to the South Australian Select Committee of the Legislative Council in 1899 that he thought Aboriginal peoples had acquired the disease from 'contact with the Malay race who traded on the north coast of Australia many hundreds of years ago' (SA Parliamentary Paper No. 77, qn 2191). It seems these speculations may have at first been provoked by a point in the Anthropological Institute's Notes and Queries on Anthropology (1892) which was sent to Gillen in 1897 and included the instruction: 'It is of importance to observe whether syphilis exists in any newly explored country where there had been no intercourse with Europeans, direct or

indirect, or where the intercourse has been very limited' (*Notes and Queries* 1982:81, cited in Mulvaney et al. 1997:191n). Cowle eventually died from degeneration of the nervous system due to 'tertiary syphilis' (Mulvaney et al. 1997:441n).

4. Especially worthy of a subalternist rereading would be the reference in Clifford's text to the anti-conscription, anti-white rebellion around the Koné police station and nickel mine in 1917. Clifford reports 11 whites killed and an unknown number of Canaques slaughtered in a year-long repression of the rebellion (Clifford 1982:94–6). This was not the only rebellion, and earlier severed heads of executed rebels were sent back to the Paris Anthropological Society (Clifford 1982:124).

5. As elsewhere, these epidemics 'decimated' local populations (Clifford 1997:305). No doubt also syphilis played its grim role (see fn 3). The obvious question that could be asked here is, where were the men? Dead at the hands of Long-hair Custer and his vicious spawn.

6. When only the code words of ideas are taken up by a parasitic theory-writing project that proliferates everywhere in order to sell product it is important to ask about uses. Where in the reception of these texts from France, where various writers emerge as 1990s postmodern culture heroes, is a serious assessment of the influences on their work of political engagement, struggle, militancy and activism? The occlusion of a radical politics occurs often when theory travels. Clifford does seem to have mellowed since 1982, where comments on two pages of the Leenhardt book suggest a Leiris-style politics was once more pronounced. He writes that, 'a tone of elegiac regret is no longer sufficient' in the face of anthropology's colonial involvement, and 'If anthropological research no longer proceeds as it did in 1878, the general political, moral, and epistemological issues … remain. Is it possible to study the other without asserting power over them?' (Clifford 1997:125). 'The forms of imperial dominion have not been simple. Naked oppression of other societies has co-existed rather easily with generous aesthetic appreciation of their modes of life; economic exploitation has seldom impeded the development of scientific understanding' (Clifford 1997:126). Yet, 'If there are signs that things are changing in the dynamics of ethnography, these changes cannot be conceived as independent of the continuing deployment of neo-imperial power' (Clifford 1982:125). My take on this would be to point out that scientific understanding in the form of generous, now self-reflexive, concern is not much more than more of the same, and the formula of a changing ethnography may only indicate the complicit adaptation of theory to contemporary requirements: thus the changing dynamic of anthropology may very well suit the changing dynamic of international capital. Changing how anthropology is done does not necessarily mitigate the exercise of power, however generously difference is marketed.

7. His chapters on the Soviet Union in *The Accursed Share* are impressive examples of the political possibility of anthropology. His views on Stalin and the deviations of the CPSU may be also wrong on any number of counts, but at least he was expressing views and engaging in debate pertinent to the times. In a different way my section on Bataille in this book reclaims the kinky red librarian.

8. Does he think maps are somehow too final? Were they not always only partial, like his dream of 'full accountability'? A total map would be equivalent to the terrain, and as in a story by Borges, you could go and live in it (see Hutnyk 1996:124–5).

9. It might be worth noting here that uncertainty is not 'undecidability' and should not be taken as some sort of malevolent import from post-structuralism. Derrida notes that undecidability demands a decision, a politics (Derrida 1994/1997:219). The question has to do with the degree of analysis upon which you decide, and why decisions are taken. To ignore this politics is not abstention, but conservatist status quo.

10. The next section of this book offers my reading of Derrida's Marx very much influenced by the work of Spivak.

11. The designation 1867 which I use for *Capital* is fiction however, as this passage itself was not in the first edition. It was added to the second, much revised, edition of 1873 (see Marx 1867/1976:4). (Ps. to Spivak: writing under a time and space restriction, it would be useful to read the 'sinnlich übersinnliche' passage which follows, if only to recover the elided 'gesellschaftliche' before 'Dinge'. See Spivak 1995a:11, Marx 1890/1975:86. Also, in the translation of the passage Clifford uses, the metaphor of the mirror appears to have been omitted, and so an opportunity for a reflective pun missed.)

12. 'The exchange of equivalents occurs (but it is merely) the surface layer of a production which rests on the appropriation of other people's labour *without exchange*, but under the *guise of exchange*. This system of exchange has *capital* as its basis. If we consider it in isolation from capital, as it appears on the surface, as an *independent* system, this is mere illusion, though a necessary illusion. It is therefore no longer surprising to find that the system of exchange-values – the exchange of equivalents measured in labour – turns into the *appropriation of other people's labour without exchange*, the total separation of labour and property, or rather that it reveals this appropriation as its concealed background. For the rule of exchange-values, and of production producing exchange-values, *presupposes* alien labour power as itself an exchange-value. i.e., it presupposes the separation of living labour power from its objective conditions; a relationship to these – or to its own objectivity – as someone else's property; in a word, a relation to them as *capital* ... If labour is once again to be related to its objective conditions as to its property, another system must replace that of private exchange, for as we have seen private exchange assumes the exchange of labour transformed into objects against labour-power, and thereby the appropriation of living labour without exchange' (Marx 1857–58 Pre-Capitalist Economic Formations, http://csf.Colorado.EDU/psn/marx/Admin).

13. See Hutnyk 2000b for discussion of Marx on this. Malinowski notes near the beginning of *Coral Gardens* that the pearl trade 'has produced a revolution in native economics' (Malinowski 1935:19), yet Trobrianders did not all flock to become pearlers because this would impinge upon the established rights of one section of the population, and in any case they were little impressed with the inducements offered. He continues: 'The only foreign article which exercises any purchasing power

on the natives is tobacco ... The Trobriander indeed shows and expresses a ready contempt for the European's childish acquisitiveness in pearls ... the greatest bribery and economic lures ... cannot make the native give up his own pursuits for those foisted upon him. When the gardens are in full swing "the god-damn niggers won't swim even if you stuff them with kalomo and tobacco" as it was put to me by one of my trader friends' (Malinowski 1935:19–20).

14. Spivak quotes Marx to suggest that exchange value is a 'parasite' on use value: 'This character (of exchange) does not yet dominate production as a whole, but concerns only its superfluity and is hence itself more or less superfluous ... an accidental enlargement of the sphere of satisfactory enjoyments ... It therefore takes place only at a few points (originally at the borders of the natural communities, in their contact with strangers) [*Grundrisse* 204]' (Spivak 1987:162). Natural? Despite this anachronism, the significance for anthropology is clear.

15. Here the often noted metaphorics of the camera waits to be exposed (see McQuire 1997a).

16. The relation between buyer and seller in industrial capitalism 'has its foundation in the social character of production, not in the mode of exchange. The latter conversely emanates from the former. It is, however, quite in keeping with the bourgeois horizon, everyone being engrossed in the transaction of shady business, not to see in the character of the mode of production the basis of the mode of exchange corresponding to it, but vice versa' (Marx 1893/1974:120).

17. As has often been the case, Spivak's careful readings of Marx are instructive again here. She makes a similar point re Derrida in 'Ghostwriting' (Spivak 1995b). See the next section.

18. I would add here, the importance of Ludwig Feuerbach's critique of Christianity in this regard, and of the difference between is and ought, the still relevant concerns of the *Economic and Philosophical Manuscripts*, among other things (see Hanfi 1972).

19. Perhaps such points might mean Clifford would need to be more circumspect in his dismissal of, for example, the comments of Julie Marcus and the claims of some of his feminist critics (Marcus 1991) and that maybe the introductory comments in *Routes* about Philippina domestic labour could be more systematically investigated.

20. In a section that I think is best left discussed in a footnote, Clifford speculates on species-centrism and wonders if otters have a consciousness of historical change (Clifford 1997:326). Offering a critique again of Hegel and a certain 'Western' reason which 'is no longer adequate to the heterogeneous experiences of environment, continuity, and change', he feels able to ask about 'non-human temporalities which intersect with but are not reducible to human history. An impossible translation exercise' (Clifford 1997:327). And an eminently silly one – and not even half way as eloquent as the model offered by Claude Lévi-Strauss in communication with a cat at the end of *Tristes Tropiques*.

21. I discuss transition more fully in the section on *Empire* later in this book – I seek a reading of transition that would not fall into orthodox

estimations of a strictly eschatological progress in Marx (see Shanin 1983) and which would attend to the possibilities, and likely limits, of utilising the notion of transition to hold together an array of contemporary movements – telematic, social, political.

22. Or is it the case that Marx is one of those grand theory total system Stalinists that we should loathe and despise? Curious symmetries of revisionism operate here. Stalin rewrites. But so does Malinowski, and presumably Clifford – those diary entries are 'worked up' texts. And Marx revises too. Indeed, Spivak has suggested that it is useful to see *Capital* as the worked up version, suggesting that both a 'continuist' example of Marx's scheme of value, and a discontinuous one, reside in his texts. (Scholarship looks for continuities and glosses over the cracks [Spivak 1987:292]): 'intimations of discontinuity [in Marx] are most noticeably covered over in the move from the seven notebooks now collectively called the *Grundrisse* to the finished *Capital 1*. It is a secondary revision of this version that yields the standard of measurement' (Spivak 1987:155–6). Thus measuring value by means of an orthodox formula is not the only story to come out of Marx's work. This is so for formularists like Clifford and his truncated 'exchange makes production', or even for more sophisticated considerations of labour power as that whose use creates value, even greater than it costs – appropriated by the capitalist – taken to market – exchanged – recouped as profit – reinvested – circulated – crisis – restructuring – crisis, or even ($C = c + v + s$, $M - C - M'$, $P' = s'\, v/C = s'/c + v$ and so on). The book *Capital* is full of reminders that the presentation is schematic. Just as *Capital* is more complicated than a cursory reading suggests, so too is Malinowski's *Argonauts*. In this light, it is the contrivance of including 'diary' entries as ethnography that pretends to a 'fidelity to the real' and does so in a way that is more duplicitous than that of functionalist empiricism. Why would anyone today accept such an offering at 'face value'?: 'look, I know texts are constructed, so here, let me offer you one which is not'. Its a trick. Rejecting Marx for continuist grand totals is to abandon the usefulness of his text, and those concepts which seem to still hold considerable explanatory, heuristic and politically contingent qualities for scholarship today (even if it often seems the institutional constraints are too many: the scholar must also tamper).

23. Anti-Bolshevik? Elsie too. For example, Masson campaigned for and voted in favour of conscription in 1917, saying that the Australian workforce had 'been infected with the idea that the war was being carried on for the benefit of Capital' (Wayne 1995:7, Elsie to Bronio). This same orator (she had been speaking at the Yarra Bank soapbox forums) later attends National Socialist rallies in Germany 1933, though does not profess support, and is clearly critical of Mosley's British black shirts in 1934 (Wayne 1995, Elsie to Bronio 30.4.1933, 18.6.1934).

24. Marx, we can note, was never as simplistic. For debate about whether the necessary evil of capitalism was always necessary, see Shanin's book on the late Marx's optimism for the Russian revolution to come (Shanin 1983).

## 3   Fever

1. It seems a draft sketch of what became the *Manifesto* was produced by Engels on a train from Manchester to London as he made his way to the Communist League meeting of November 1847. This was added to slightly rewritten sections from the drafts *Poverty of Philosophy* and the *German Ideology* in December. The first three sections were written up by Marx in Brussels before a letter came from London on 26 January demanding the finished text – under threat of 'further disciplinary action' against comrade Marx. The finished text was then sent 'a few weeks before Feb. 24th' (correspondence in Marx and Engels, 1990–2004). I guess we should assume by return mail at the beginning of February 1848. This, I think, means Marx spent the 'festive season' correcting the manuscript. Thanks to Richard Barbrook for demanding the specifics on this point. Ho Ho Ho.

2. It was 'perhaps' plausible to ask such questions in a specific moment – 150 years, 1,000 days before the millennium, alongside Derrida's *Archive Fever* and at a conference on 'Time and Value'. There seemed no more auspicious opportunity as this essay was presented as 'Forgotten Marx and Speed-hype in Capital: The Poverty of Philosophy' at the conference 'Time and Value', Lancaster University Institute for Cultural Research, in the Politics stream convened by Mick Dillon and Jeremy Valentine. It had an earlier manifestation as 'Speeding Marx in Derrida' at the Human Sciences Seminar of the Philosophy Department of Manchester Metropolitan University, and I especially thank Joanna Hodge for her comments. With regard to the auspicious, Donald F. Miller has been working on time for ages, and in a certain way this work is wholly indebted to conversations with him many years ago. More recently I have benefited from reading the work of Eugene Holland (1997), Ian R. Douglas (1997) and Nigel Thrift (1996), as well (inversely) from listening to the plenary presentation at 'Time and Value' of Liz – 'I used to think that when I was a Marxist' – Grosz.

3. I would read Freud's several comments about his teacher, colleague and 'dear friend' Fleischl von Maxrow's cocaine poisoning death carefully here. Is his concern for von Maxrow, for his own reputation – having suggested he take cocaine, but not anticipating intravenous use – or is it with regard to his own patterns of consumption? Whatever (Freud 1900/1976:187, 192).

4. An altogether more impressive discussion of the ways 'electronic media have both extended and transformed ... [and] ... produced significant pressures on both private space and public sphere' is in McQuire (2003:103) where the transformations of privacy are traced back to the 1920s.

5. Benjamin Franklin said that time was money. Though I think Marx convincingly shows that money is time, in the *Poverty of Philosophy* he wrote that 'time is everything' (Marx and Engels, *Collected Works* 6:127).

6. While Derrida suggests that email transforms the 'entire' space of humanity 'in quasi-instantaneous fashion' (1995/1996:17), Spivak offers

a corrective when she writes of how 'circulation time attains the apparent instantaneity of thought … the labour reserves in the comprador countries [are kept] outside of this instantaneity' (1987:166–7; see Part 1, ch. 2, note 14). Spivak's work is very important here, and worth a short aside to argue that while telecommunications research accelerates the technological means of extending relative surplus value extraction and not absolute, the obsolete forms of technology are dumped in the 'Third World' where, across the shifting boundary of the international division of labour, a kind of negation of the negation operates this boundary to ensure that superexploitation thrives. (This is a paraphrase, and ever so slight departure, from Spivak 1987:167.) Suggestions that enthusiasm for theory production, subsidised computerised information retrieval and cultural studies should be subjected to scrutiny given the implication of these forms, as a part of general telematics, in 'entrenching the international division of labour and the oppression of women' have rarely been taken up, and so often the 'dark presence of the third world' (Spivak 1987:167) is ignored in a frenzy of speed mania. As Spivak points out in response to a quip that she was a kind of Luddite, this is not to deny the workers word processors, or the comforts of capuccinos, but to remind the capuccino-drinking worker and the word-processing critic the 'actual price-in-exploitation of the machine producing coffee and words' (Spivak 1987:167). Capuccinos for all is certainly a slogan I would adopt, but it is also important to work against the reality that we now have only capuccinos for some. The internet is not about universal access yet, the fruits of advanced capitalist production, science, medicine, central heating, air-conditioning, entertainment and 200 TV (and still nothing to watch) channels have yet to be delivered to all – and indeed, by the logic of capitalism cannot be delivered to all, thus 'we' [all of us] will have to take them. You know the routine here, get out the flags.

7. See Hutnyk, John [forthcoming] 'Copper, Connectivity, Anthropology and the Mines' in the *Journal of Redistributive Justice – JRJ*.

8. I tried to show some of this in *The Rumour of Calcutta* (Hutnyk 1996).

9. Derrida once told an American student looking for a thesis topic to consider the telephone in literature, in Proust for example, and then ask 'the question of the effects of the most advanced telematics on whatever would still remain of literature'. He seems surprised when she replied that she still loved literature. He says: 'So do I' (Derrida 1980/1987:204). Carrie Clanton is currently conducting PhD research in anthropology at Goldsmiths College on the recording technologies used by ghost hunting groups in Brighton, England. I am indebted to her for spooky discussions on this theme.

10. No need to rehearse these debates, see Hutnyk 1996: ch. 1. He was a Nazi.

11. A cursory reading of activity on various usenet discussions of Derrida and Deconstruction suggests that these tos and fros dominate such lists.

12. Reading Derrida with communists in Calcutta was influential here, see Hutnyk 1996 and 2000a, but also Spivak's work, especially 'Supplementing Marx' (Spivak 1995a). Spivak's other important discussion of Derrida's recent efforts to say 'hello' to Marx – 'Ghostwriting' (Spivak 1995b) – is crucially important. I would direct the reader to that instructive text,

especially for its discussion of the Ghost Dance and the Algerian writer Assia Djebar. I took up some of the lessons Spivak provides in 'Ghostwriting' when discussing Clifford's reversing misreading of Marx on exchange in the previous section.

## 4   Spectres

1. Obviously a 'bad' allusion to Derrida's excellent article 'Of an Apocalyptic Tone Recently Taken in Philosophy', which is an inspiration for this writing.

2. In the public presentations of this paper these ten words were covered at a swift and breathless speed, and as a part-parody of this performance at the end I offered my own ten bullet points – but of course these make no sense outside a party formation/organisation capable of 'winning' and not just taking over; the process of *rapprochement* under way in many countries deserves comment, though not here. To the extent that efforts in this direction take up questions of international solidarity and struggle I am particularly interested, as too often Marxist politics does not travel. On *rapprochement*, in the UK several experiments have been under way, including that initiated by the Association of Communist Workers (ACW), and the Indian Workers' Association (IWA-GB); the Red Action and Revolutionary Communist Group-inspired Independent Working Class Association (IWCA); and that initiated by the Provisional Committee of the Communist Party of Great Britain (CPGB), accommodating various ex-CPGB and Trotskyite fragments. The extraordinary gymnastics of the Trotskyite sects are well glossed in all their chaotic alphabet code by the Spartacist League as:

> Posturing as an alternative to liquidationism is the Leninist-Trotskyist Tendency (LTT) who are hosting a conference on 'revolutionary regroupment' aimed at picking up disaffected groups from the disintegrating USec [United Secretariat of the Fourth International]. The particular consummation of this intention is to be a fusion with the ex-USec members now in the Committee for Revolutionary Regroupment as well as with elements of the Liaison Committee of Militants for a Revolutionary Communist International (LCM-RCI), a split from Workers Power's 'international' tendency of roughly the same name with a few less initials.
>
> (Spartacist League pamphlet, *Revolutionary Regroupment or Centrist Alchemy?*, February 1997)

Discussion groups interested in the 'circulation of political struggles' on the web and sponsored by groups like Subversion in Manchester and Aufheben in Brighton, as well as the various 'Conference[s] of Socialist Economists', should also be counted. The Socialist Alliance experiment has not yet completely collapsed, but seems mortally wounded by Socialist Workers' Party sectarianism. See the *Weekly Worker* for reports.

3. See Steve Wright's *Storming Heaven* for an excellent account of the history of autonomist Marxism in Italy (2000). The 'planetary work machine' was to be the name of a volume of essays on class recomposition worldwide,

and for which I prepared a long study of work practices and planning in Malaysia's Multimedia Super Corridor. A short version of that paper was published as Hutnyk (1999).

4. Saul Goode's PhD dissertation in anthropology at Goldsmiths College deals with the *sans-papiers* movement in a Parisian suburb and the struggle over the 'list'.

5. Rather less optimistically, the razor-wire camps of the Bush–Blair war on terror show the nether side of travel in ever more brutal forms. I have written about the refinement of concentration camp technology for detention of asylum seekers and dissidents in the *Weekly Worker* (no. 489, 17 July 2003). Available at: <http://www.cpgb.org.uk/worker/489/ detention.html>.

6. In *Postcard* Derrida's meditation on the post carries a more sinister and even paranoid tone and evokes the spectral forces of the cops as invasive communications experts:

I no longer know to whom I am speaking, nor about what. The difficulty I would have in sorting out this *courrier* with the aim of publication is due, among other perils, to this one: you know that I do not believe in propriety, property, and above all not in the form that it takes according to the opposition public/private ... This opposition doesn't work, neither for psychoanalysis ... nor for the post (the postcard is neither private nor public), nor even for the police (they leave us, whatever the regime, only the choice between several police forces .. and when a pp (public police) doesn't accost you in the street, another pp (private parallel police) plugs its microphones into your bed, seizes your mail.

(Derrida 1980/1987:185)

7. Who, it turns out, might have, maybe, somewhere, hidden, according to unnamed intelligence, attempted to buy materials for weapons related programme activities. Of course this rogue departure on the part of the former US client now justifies revenge, the hunt for him and his doubles, the killing of his sons and the brutal occupation of Iraq. See Gore Vidal's *Perpetual War for Perpetual Peace* (2002) for commentary on US policy outside 'the Homeland'.

8. See also *Dis-Orienting Rhythms: The Politics of the New Asian Dance Music* (Sharma et al. 1996).

## 5  Struggles

1. A term used by various sections of the British Left to refer, sometimes approvingly, to those who would follow the letter of Trotsky's recommendation on how to deal with fascists:

The tactical, or if you will 'technical' task was quite simple – grab every fascist or every isolated group of fascists by their collars, acquaint them with the pavement a few times, strip them of their fascist insignia and documents, and without carrying things any further, leave them with their fright and a few black and blue marks.

(From the pamphlet *Ultraleft Tactics in Fighting the Fascists*, March 1934)

Somehow I suspect Derrida would not go so far. See my discussion of this in terms of anti-racist self-defence (Hutnyk 2000a).

2. See Joel Kovel's *Red Hunting in the Promised Land* (1994) for documentation of the millions killed in the US-led Cold War – Korea, Vietnam, Nicaragua, etc. – for the crime of wanting to live with their own choices.

3. See the forthcoming collection of Althusser's early writings, including his Master's thesis on the dialectic in Hegel, which complicates any notion of the break in Marx by positing also a break in Althusser – the text is to be called *The Specter of Hegel*. Mind that I do not want to insist that there is an early and late Derrida, but if there is, one was paralysed before the party, the other speaks to Freud (obliquely) about Marx and Shakespeare (but this is not nothing, of course – too strong).

4. My debt here is to (ex) members of Left Alliance, especially Ben Ross and Angie Mitropoulis, but also Cass Bennett, Hazel Blunden, Lucy Blamey, Damien Lawson, Marcus Strom, Vanessa Chan, Melanie Hood, Chris Francis and others (<//red salute.learn-to-like-it>).

5. See Hutnyk, John (forthcoming) 'The Wind-up Radio and Other Small-scale Tricks' in *Journal of Redistributive Justice – JRJ*.

6. Nick Thoburn's text *Deleuze, Marx and Politics* (2003) deals extensively with this.

7. The texts Derrida critiques are Schmitt (1932/1976) and Schmitt (1963). Michael Dutton has recently excavated the terrain of this point with regard to Chinese studies, Mao badges (trinketisation), the work unit, (re)education and the opening lines of Mao's *Selected Works*, vol. 1 (important in the next section). His paper presented at Goldsmiths College on 17 October 2003, is forthcoming.

8. We will see in Chapter 8 that Maoist revolutionary tactics were directed to imperialism as such in order to forge alliances across difference within 'common struggle' (Mao 1928/1975, vol. 1:93). It might also be worth noting here that support for a Maoism that does not reduce 'Third World' struggles to exotic t-shirt emblems and fantasy idealism, but rather acknowledges sharp and difficult practicalities (in the jungle) is preferable to most forms of 'academic' Maoism. That a boys' own adventure ('brothers') seems to prevail here is possibly quite typical of Parisian theory at the time.

## PART 3   TALES FROM THE RAJ

## 6   On Empire

1. I am particularly interested to evaluate theoretical pronouncements about hybridity – as will be seen at the end of Part 3 – in relation to really existing political problems. As part of a book called *Diaspora and Hybridity*, written with Virinder Kalra and Raminder Kaur, I have detailed my concerns much more extensively, see Kalra et al. (2004).

2. Consider for example the attempted recruitment of Sandline International, a UK based private mercenary army, by the PNG government in the hope of ending the war on Bouganville initiated after islanders forced the closure of the exploitative RTZ copper mine (see Moody 1991).

3. Confirmation that Hardt and Negri are wrong on the advent of the Raj can be found in one of Marx's less known comments, where he writes of the financial burdens accepted by England after the 1857 revolt for the purpose of 'securing the monopoly of the Indian market to the Manchester free traders' (*New York Daily Tribune* 30 April 1859). I am indebted to the work of Irfan Habib for pointing out this otherwise ignored reference – not included, for example, in Marx and Engels' *On Colonialism*, prepared by Progress Publishers. See Habib (1999:65).

## 8   The Chapatti Story

1. I presented this chapatti story at the UCL Anthropology Department seminar in January 2004. Strange fossils lined up at the back of the room.
2. This probably also explains why the First World cultural studies scholar no longer invokes Mao, no matter how 'activist' that scholar imagines themselves to be. It's not the 1960s any more.
3. A discussion of hybridity in the texts of Subaltern Studies is not just a project of historical commentary – the implications for contemporary struggles are there to be drawn by readers. Ambivalence about hybridity is perhaps a key – that in cultural studies' contemporary pronouncements hybridity is most often found in the glamour domains of youth music and the cultural industries (especially hip-hop and its commercial cultural spin-offs) should alert us to a vacation from politics. Brian Alleyne's insightful study *Radicals against Race* makes the point that cultural studies has been fascinated with popular culture to the relative neglect 'more "dated" forms of resistance such as trade union activity' (2002:8). His study addresses issues of activism and organisation, and the problematic relations between a white Left interested in recruitment and a political education project dedicated to a shared political struggle that builds a wide basis of support to enable participants to 'engage in their own battles' (2002:93). Notably the term 'hybridity' does not appear in Alleyne's index – highly unusual for a text in this era.
4. In India this 'mutiny' is known, significantly, as the Indian War of Independence of 1857, and features in an extensive museum display in Delhi's Red Fort. For a convenient and entertaining alternative reading of this event, see the play *The Great Rebellion (Mahavidroha)* by Utpal Dutt (1986), but for the most impressive versioning – where the chapatti story discussed here also features – see Mahasweta Devi's text *The Queen of Jhansi* (1956/2000). Here Devi makes a case that the British had 'no clue' (1956/2000:70) of the extent of Indian resentment at their rule, and shows how the Rani of Jhansi was certainly justified, after a long train of grievances, in joining the revolt against the Raj. Disregard of Hindu law, confiscation of lands, introduction of slaughterhouses and other unclean practices within Jhansi city (1956/2000:69); futile wars in Afghanistan, forced road-building programmes of no local benefit, floggings and murders without investigation or redress; slaughter of Santhals: 'There were millions of small incidents building up ... the earth of Chhotanagpur and Rajmahal turned red with the blood of thousands of Santhals who dared to brave [British] guns with their bows and arrows. Can such blood-soaked soil ever bear the fruits of the earth?' (1956/2000:76). The circulation of chapattis from one village to another

signals that 'It's time for the British rule to end' (1956/2000:77) but the greased bullets were only the ostensible cause of 'mutiny'. The war lasted at least two years.

5. We might add a note on ambivalence as some sort of kin to contradiction or dialectics – artfully, Gyan Prakash responds to criticisms made by O'Hanlon and Washbrook (2000), that, as a 'deconstructionist' and a Marxist, he wants to ride two beasts in quite incommensurate directions. By pointing to the British denigration of Indian horsemanship that kept Western-educated Bengalis out of the Civil Service, Prakash, with a nod to Bhabha, shows how such an excuse for exclusion is about the management of ambivalences that threaten the polarity of coloniser and colonised (Prakash 2000:221). Rather than running off in two directions, however, the competent equestrian will tame both horses.

6. It is clearly the case that the Marxist notion of dialectics relies more upon flux movement and flow than the orthodox Hegelian and tripartite presentation of thesis, antithesis and synthesis may imply.

## PART 4   BATAILLE'S WARS: SURREALISM, MARXISM, FASCISM

### 9   Librarian

1. The Surrealists engaged in anti-colonial activity before 1925 but it was only with issue 5 of *La Revolution Surrealiste* that they began to use a Marxist vocabulary writing in opposition to the imperialist Riff war in Morocco (Lewis 1990:32–5).

2. *Blue of Noon* opens with a few pages from the unpublished and destroyed earlier book *WC*, and it is set in the Savoy Hotel, London. Is it worth travelling to the foyer of that luxurious hotel to read these pages, as a kind of perverted tourist appreciation? And to participate perhaps, if you can afford the extortionate tariff for a room, in an orgiastic diversion something like that therein described as passing between the characters Troppman, Dirty, the doorman and the maid. Vomit, then leave.

3. Richardson, in the intro to Bataille 1994, says a similar comment 'too many fucking idealists' was contained in Bataille's letter of reply to the meeting invitation, claiming this as his first written criticism of Surrealism (in Bataille 1994:4).

4. Bataille was criticised by Sartre for telling us about laughter but not making anyone laugh. Surya and Lotringer have both commented on this. They point out that were he to write of an orgasm Sartre would not then expect to come (Lotringer introduction to Bataille 1945/1992:xiv).

5. In the final volume of the trilogy *The Accursed Share*, he writes: 'I am not overly concerned about the legitimacy of the results that I borrowed, as judiciously as I could, from the history of religions, from sociology, from political economy or from psychoanalysis ...' (Bataille 1976/1991:201).

### 10   Activist

1. Bataille also side-steps the rather 'simple-minded' practice which condemns on false grounds: 'If one wishes to judge communism, it is

necessary to begin by noting the differences between the development Marx forecast and the facts subsequent to that development' (Bataille 1976/1991:265).

2. And he then curiously begins a comparison of the treatment of a beggar in London with the outcaste in Bengal. What the significance of the Bengali example achieves here is separate from, but cannot be separated from, the ways Bengal, India, Calcutta continue to serve as a limit experience, as the polarity on the other end of the scale from London. As I have said in *The Rumour of Calcutta* I tried to contextualise this hierarchy by reading the history of Empire up to the present day from a centre in Calcutta – through which the wealth of India flowed – rather than from the moribund finance capital and retirement home for Raj officials that was colonial London (Hutnyk 1996).

## 11   Anthropologist

1. Charity is 'only the expression of the cowardice of the modern upper classes, who no longer have the force to recognise the results of their own destructive acts' (Bataille 1997:177).

2. For that matter, Surrealism as a whole has been similarly stalled and sanitised. Why did the 2002 Tate Modern Surrealism exhibition cleanse the movement of any political content? Desire for a communist future was fundamental to Surrealism, but went almost without mention in 2002. What this amounts to is a systematic 'cretinisation' [a good Surrealist and Marxist word]. A way of blocking meanings from circulation, the disqualification of revolutionary spirit through sanctioned ignorance (Spivak 1999).

## 12   Provocateur

1. For an extended critique of charity see the last chapter of *The Rumour of Calcutta* (Hutnyk 1996).

2. Black Panther Party journalist Mumia Abu-Jamal was charged with killing a cop in 1978 and still writes today from death row. An international campaign to secure his release has produced much information, some of which can be found on <http://www.mumia2000.org/>.

3. The detention centre in France that Blair and Home Office Minister Blunkett forced into closure. Blunkett himself has been particularly rabid on issues of asylum – challenging even allocations of lottery money – charity after all – to the NCADC (National Coalition of Anti-Deportation Campaigns) as part of his no sympathy Fortress UK regimen. Apparently the Minister had decided the NCADC website went beyond its brief and strayed into 'political' matters (*The Guardian* 12 August 2002).

4. Woomera is a former weapons testing area and US spy base in the South Australian desert, land appropriated from the Kukutha people, the US facility was transformed into a high security prison for primarily Afghani and Iraqi refugees. Some of whom were able to escape after solidarity actions by activists outside the camp over Easter 2002.

5. Kamunting is the detention centre which houses the Malaysian internees held under the notorious Internal Security Act (ISA) of Mahathir Mohammed. Originally a British law contrived to deal with the communist

insurgency of the 1940s and 1950s, the Malaysian state took it over and have used it to stifle dissent, holding opposition leaders and suspected militants for two years without trial or charge. In July 2002 there were 113 in detention. Opposition youth leader Tian Chua served time under ISA from 2001 to 2003.

6. The tabloid British newspaper *The Mirror* was among the few to take a fighting stand on the issue of Guantanamo when its front page headline commemorated the 200th day of incarceration for those held by the US without charge, trial, lawyers of rights with the banner headline, NO JUSTICE.

## Conclusion: The Cultivation of Capital Studies

1. In this I am influenced by the inspired work of Reed (2000).
2. He also writes that:

> Where ideology is no longer added to things as a vindication or complement … a critique that operates with the unequivocal causal relation of superstructure and infrastructure is wide of the mark. In a total society all things are equidistant from the centre.
>
> (Adorno 1966/1973:268)

3. On the theme of coppers and electronic surveillance, Derrida suggests that accelerating technics is even sufficient to undo the power of totalitarian states. Given a certain density of telephones, he says, 'police control is no longer possible' (Derrida and Stiegler 2002:72) – though this was a TV interview, and perhaps said in haste.
4. Again, in an interview of 1987 not published until 2002, Derrida repeats that when he hears the 'Internationale' he 'may sing along and tears come to my eyes', a condition he names as 'viscerally left wing' (2002:39).
5. It is perhaps too easy to play games with the temporal here, but as Derrida was always strangely prone to time-travel, I am amused to find this prescient item where, in *Anti-During*, Engels mocks the 'childish pastime of alternately writing and canceling a – from which nothing eventuates but the silliness of the person who adopts such a tedious procedure' (1947:173).
6. I am reading the harrowing reports of Ewa Jasiewicz from Iraq as I write, where the chaos in Baghdad that ranges from lack of basic supplies like electricity and water, to widespread rape, looting, danger and death on the streets at checkpoints, and at the hands of military patrols operating under cover of darkness, is characterised as 'a fall-out of the fact that the owners and funders of the Occupation apparatus are focused on economic reconstruction (exploitation) and not civilian infrastructure or social security' (email: 9 September 2003).
7. Atticus Che Narain of Goldsmiths College is conducting PhD research in Guyana on indenture and its meanings in the context of diaspora and locality.
8. The two-step described here has been pointed out before. Already in 1924 the Comintern argued that fascism and social democracy were 'two sides of a single instrument of capitalist dictatorship' (Radek 1923:559–600).

9. This is a paraphrase of Marx in *Grundrisse* (1858/1973:510). See Hutnyk (2000b).

10. COPEX is a trade fair for repressive police technologies from batons and stunguns to the new capsicum sprays and goo-guns.

11. What chance for an evaluation of Blairism here? New Labour's record is pitiful on prisons, asylum and immigration law, arms sales, corporate favours, rail privatisation and fat-cat cream-offs, war on Afghanistan and Iraq, new and unprecedented civil rights curtailments, failure to address institutional racism and police crime. At the same time, the failure of the left to organise effectively against these measures means we perhaps deserve much of what we get. The disarray of the Left is the fault of the Left of course – however much factors such as shifting bourgeois class alliances and betrayals might be counted as mitigating factors, there are really no excuses – the Left is also its own worst enemy.

12. Arthur Craven, interviewing André Gide, asked: 'Monsieur Gide, where are we with regard to time?' To which Gide replied, apparently with no malice intended: 'Fifteen minutes before six' (reported in Breton 1929/1972:x). It is getting late.

13. Samir Amin is *the* theorist of polarisation:

> The overall dynamic of accumulation on the periphery is governed by exports, whereas in the more articulated centres, production of the means of production is linked to production of goods for local consumption … [Amin links] the driving force of production for export to the increasing inequality of income distribution in the periphery. This brought to light a whole range of distortions as symptoms of modern underdevelopment, including impoverishment of the peasants and enhancement of the landowners; preference for investment in light industry; markedly low wages in relation to productivity; disarticulation of the economy; and the juxtaposition of economic 'miracles' with areas of devastation.
>
> (Amin 1994:59)

14. The take-up of the new technologies is of course uneven as well, with more phone lines and internet connections *per capita* in the West the obvious outcome of differential access, and one which is not mitigated by some trickle-down effect or by computer aid gifts of obsolete machines to Third World NGOs. Surprising as it may seem, the majority of the people on the planet still do not have a mobile phone, personal organiser, broadband or DVD player, and will not have such items any time soon.

15. On solidarity and the co-constitution of 'here' and 'there': at the fifth congress of the Comintern, Nguyen Ai Quoc (Ho Chi Minh) described the neglect of imperialism on the part of metropolitan communists as something that rendered all their efforts futile, as they were trying to 'kill the serpent by beating its tail'. He continued:

> All of you know that at present the poison and vital capacity of the imperialist viper are concentrated in the colonies rather than the metropolitan countries. The colonies provide raw materials for its factories.

The colonies supply soldiers for its army. The colonies will serve it as a mainstay of counter-revolution. And yet you, in speaking of the revolution, neglect the colonies.

(In Carrère d'Encausse and Schram 1969:199–200)

Lenin was more concise: 'internationalism consists of deeds and not phrases, not expressions of solidarity, not resolutions' (Lenin 1917 'The Crisis has Matured' in Žižek 2002).

16. 'Sanctioned ignorance' and 'transnational literacy' are the terms from Spivak that I have used most often and most freely. Her work in general offers the indefatigable guide for the one who wants to pursue the necessary task of fighting for redistributive justice (see in particular Spivak 1999, 2003).

17. Michael Taussig has worried relentlessly at the public secret over many years. His Columbia diary, written under duress of curfew and terror, animates and contextualises my theoretical concerns (see Taussig 2003).

18. With Virinder Kalra I have tried to develop a critique of representation that engages here with visibility and politics. See the special issue of *Postcolonial Studies* we edited together (vol. 1, no. 3, 1999). His work carries this politics further, as the sign on the front of the bus used to say.

# References

Adorno, Theodor 1951/1974 *Minima Moralia*. London: Verso.

Adorno, Theodor 1966/1973 *Negative Dialectics*. London: Routledge.

Adorno, Theodor 1998 *Critical Models: Interventions and Catchwords*. New York: Columbia University Press.

Adorno, Theodor 2000 *Introduction to Sociology (Lectures 1968)*. Cambridge: Polity.

Agamben, Giorgio 1998 *Homo Sacer*, trans. Daniel Heller-Roazen. Stanford, CA: Stanford University Press.

Agamben, Giorgio 2000 *Means without End*. Minneapolis: University of Minnesota Press.

Ahmad, Aijaz 1992 *In Theory: Classes, Nations, Literatures*. Verso: London.

Alleyne, Brian 2002 *Radicals against Race*. Oxford: Berg.

Amin, Samir 1994 *Re-reading the Post-war Period: An Intellectual Itinerary*. New York: Monthly Review Press.

Anderson, Perry 1976 *Considerations on Western Marxism*. London: New Left Books.

Ardener, Edwin 1985 'Social Anthropology and the Decline of Modernism', in Joanna Overing (ed.) *Reason and Morality*. London: Tavistock Publications.

Babcock, Barbara 1993 'Feminism/Pretexts: Fragments, Questions and Reflections', *Anthropological Quarterly* 66(2):59–66.

Balibar, Etienne 1994 *Masses, Classes, Ideas: Studies on Politics and Philosophy Before and After Marx*. New York: Routledge.

Banerjee, Sumanta 1984 *India's Simmering Revolution: The Naxalite Uprising*. London: Zed Books.

Bard, Alexander and Jan Söderqvist 2002 *Netocracy*. London: Pearson Education.

Bataille, Georges 1928/2001 *The Story of the Eye*. Harmondsworth: Penguin.

Bataille, Georges 1943/1988 *Inner Experience*. New York: State University of New York Press.

Bataille, Georges 1944/1988 *Guilty*. San Francisco: The Lapis Press.

Bataille, Georges 1945/1992 *On Nietzsche*. New York: Paragon House.

Bataille, Georges 1949/1988 *The Accursed Share, Volume 1: Consumption*. New York: Zone Books.

Bataille, Georges 1957/1985 *Literature and Evil*. London: Marion Boyars.

Bataille, Georges 1957/1986 *Blue of Noon*. London: Marion Boyars.

Bataille, Georges 1976/1991 *The Accursed Share, Vols 2 and 3: Eroticism and Sovereignty*. New York: Zone Books.

Bataille, Georges 1985 *Visions of Excess: Selected Writings 1927–1939*. Minneapolis: University of Minnesota Press.

Bataille, Georges 1994 *The Absence of Myth: Writings on Surrealism*. London: Verso.

Bataille, Georges 1997 *The Bataille Reader*. Oxford: Blackwell.

Bataille, Georges 2001 *The Unfinished System of Non-knowledge*. Minneapolis: University of Minnesota Press.

Bataille, Georges et al. 1995 *Encyclopaedia Acephale*. London: Atlas Press.

Baudrillard, Jean 1976/1993 *Symbolic Exchange and Death*. London: Sage.

Behar, Ruth and Deborah Gordon (eds) 1995 *Women Writing Culture*. Berkeley: California University Press.

Benjamin, Walter 1999 *The Arcades Project*. Cambridge, MA: Harvard University Press.

Benninton, Geoffrey and Jacques Derrida 1991/1993 *Jacques Derrida*. Chicago: University of Chicago Press.

Bhabha, Homi 1994 *The Location of Culture*. London: Routledge.

Bhabha, Homi 1996 'Culture's In-between', in Stuart Hall and Paul du Gay (eds) *Questions of Cultural Identity*. London: Sage, pp. 53–60.

Bois, Yve-Alain and Rosalind E. Krauss 1997 *Formless: A User's Guide*. New York: Zone Books.

Bonefeld, Werner 1992 'Social Constitution and the Form of the Capitalist State', in Werner Bonefeld, Richard Gunn and Kosmas Psychopedis (eds) *Open Marxism: Dialectics and History*. London: Pluto Press, pp. 93–132.

Bonefeld, Werner, Richard Gunn and Kosmas Psychopedis 1992 'Introduction', in *Open Marxism: Dialectics and History*. London: Pluto Press, pp. ix–xx.

Boon, James 1983 'Functionalists Write Too: Frazer/Malinowski and the Semiotics of the Monograph', *Semiotica* 4.

Brah, Avtar 1996 *Cartographies of Diaspora: Contesting Identities*. London: Routledge.

Breton, André 1929/1972 *Manifestos of Surrealism*, trans. Richard Seaver and Helen R. Lane. Ann Arbor: Michigan University Press.

Carrère d'Encausse, Hélène and Stuart Schram 1968 *Marxism and Asia*. London: Allen Lane.

Cesura 1982 unsourced manuscript.

Clifford, James 1982 *Person and Myth: Maurice Leenhardt in the Melanesian World*. Berkeley: University of California Press.

Clifford, James 1986 'On Ethnographic Self-fashioning: Conrad and Malinowski', in T.C. Heller, M. Sonsa and D.E. Welbery (eds) *Reconstructing Individualism: Autonomy, Individuality and the Self in Western Thought*. Stanford, CA: Stanford University Press.

Clifford, James 1988 *The Predicament of Culture: Twentieth-century Ethnography, Literature and Art*. Cambridge, MA: Harvard University Press.

Clifford, James 1989 'Notes on Travel and Theory', *Inscriptions* 5:177–88.

Clifford, James 1990 'Notes on (Field)Notes', in Roger Sanjek (ed.) *Fieldnotes: The Makings of Anthropology*. Ithaca, NY: Cornell University Press, pp. 47–70.

Clifford, James 1991 'Response', *Social Analysis* 29:145–58.

Clifford, James 1997 *Routes: Travel and Translation in the Late Twentieth Century*. Cambridge, MA: Harvard University Press.

Clifford, James and George Marcus (eds) 1986 *Writing Culture: The Poetics and Politics of Ethnography*. Berkeley: University of California Press.

Davis, Mike 1990 *City of Quartz: Excavating the Future in Los Angeles*. New York: Vintage Books.

Deleuze, Gilles and Félix Guattari 1972/1983 *Anti-Oedipus: Capitalism and Schizophrenia*. London: Athlone Press.

Deleuze, Gilles and Félix Guattari 1980/1987 *Mille Plateaux: Capitalism and Schizophrenia*. Minneapolis: University of Minnesota Press.

Derrida, Jacques 1967/1976 *Of Grammatology*, trans. and introduction by Gayatri Chakravorty Spivak. Baltimore, MD: Johns Hopkins University Press.

Derrida, Jacques 1967/1978 *Writing and Difference*. London: Routledge and Kegan Paul.

Derrida, Jacques 1972/1982 *Margins of Philosophy*. Chicago: University of Chicago Press/Sussex: Harvester Press.

Derrida, Jacques 1980/1987 *The Post Card: From Socrates to Freud and Beyond*, trans. with an introduction and additional notes by Alan Bass. Chicago: University of Chicago Press.

Derrida, Jacques 1981 *Positions*, trans. and annotated by Alan Bass. Chicago: University of Chicago Press.

Derrida, Jacques 1983 'The Time of a Thesis: Punctuations', in Alan Montefiore (ed.) *Philosophy in France Today*. Cambridge: Cambridge University Press.

Derrida, Jacques 1984 'Of an Apocalyptic Tone Recently Adopted in Philosophy', *Oxford Literary Review* 6(2):3–37.

Derrida, Jacques 1987/1992 'Mochloss; or, The Conflict of the Faculties', in Richard Rand (ed.) *Logomachia: The Conflict of the Faculties*. Lincoln: University of Nebraska Press.

Derrida, Jacques 1988 *Limited Inc*. Evanston, IL: Northwestern University Press.

Derrida, Jacques 1990/1992 *The Other Heading: Reflections on Today's Europe*, trans. Pascale-Anne Brault and Michael B. Naas, introduction by Michael B. Naas. Bloomington, IN: Indiana University Press.

Derrida, Jacques 1991/1992 *Given Time: Counterfeit Money*, trans. Peggy Kamuf. Chicago: University of Chicago Press.

Derrida, Jacques 1992 'Force of Law: The "Mystical Foundations of Authority"', in Drucilla Cornell, Michel Rosenfeld and David Gray Carlson (eds) *Deconstruction and the Possibility of Justice*. New York: Routledge, pp. 3–67.

Derrida, Jacques 1993 'Back from Moscow, in the USSR', in Mark Poster (ed.) *Politics, Theory and Contemporary Culture*. New York: Columbia University Press.

Derrida, Jacques 1993/1994 *Spectres of Marx: The State of the Debt, the Work of Mourning and the New International*. New York: Routledge.

Derrida, Jacques 1994/1997 *The Politics of Friendship*. London: Verso.

Derrida, Jacques 1995/1996 *Archive Fever: A Freudian Impression*. Chicago: University of Chicago Press.

Derrida, Jacques 1999 'Marx and Sons', in Michael Sprinkler (ed.) *Ghostly Demarcations: A Symposium on Jacques Derrida's 'Spectres of Marx'*. London: Verso, pp. 213–69.

Derrida, Jacques 2000 *Of Hospitality*. Stanford, CA: Stanford University Press.

Derrida, Jacques 2002 *Negotiations: Interventions and Interviews 1971–2001*. Stanford, CA: Stanford University Press.

Derrida, Jacques and Michael Sprinkler 1993 'Politics and Friendship: An Interview', in E. Ann Kaplan and Michael Sprinkler (eds) *The Althusserian Legacy*. New York: Verso, pp. 183–232.

Derrida, Jacques and Bernard Stiegler 2002 *Echographies of Television*. Cambridge: Polity.

Devi, Mahasweta 1956/2000 *The Queen of Jhansi*. Calcutta: Seagull Books.

Devi, Mahasweta 1997a *Breast Stories*, trans. Gayatri Chakravorty Spivak. Calcutta: Seagull Books.

Devi, Mahasweta 1997b *Mother of 1084*, trans. Shamik Bandyopadhyay. Calcutta: Seagull Books.

Dorfman, Ariel and Armand Mattelart 1971 *How to Read Donald Duck: Imperialist Ideology in the Disney Comic*. New York: International General.

Douglas, Ian R. 1997 'Power Dreaming of a Fast Globe' unpublished paper.

Dube, Suarabh 1998 'Travelling Light: Missionary Musings, Colonial Cultures and Anthropological Anxieties', in Raminder Kaur and John Hutnyk (eds) *Travelworlds: Journeys in Contemporary Cultural Politics*. London: Zed Books.

Dutt, Utpal 1986 *The Great Rebellion 1857 (Mahavidroha)*. Calcutta: Seagull Books.

Dutton, Michael 1998 *Streetlife China*. Cambridge: Cambridge University Press.

Dworkin, Dennis 1997 *Cultural Marxism in Postwar Britain: History, the New Left and the Origins of Cultural Studies*. Durham, NC: Duke University Press.

Eisenstein, Sergei 1995 *Beyond the Stars: The Memoirs of Sergei Eisenstein*. Calcutta: Seagull Books.

Engels, Friedrich 1947 *Anti-During*. Moscow: Progress Press.

Feuerbach, Ludwig 1841/1972 'The Essence of Christianity', in *The Fiery Brook*. New York: Doubleday.

Fortunati, Leopoldina 1981/1995 *The Arcane of Reproduction: Housework, Prostitution, Labour and Capital*. New York: Autonomedia.

Foucault, Michel 1962 *Death and the Labyrinth: The World of Raymond Roussel*. New York: Doubleday.

Freud, Sigmund 1900/1976 *The Interpretation of Dreams*. Harmondsworth: Penguin.

Gasché, Rudolph 1994 *Inventions of Difference: On Jacques Derrida*. Cambridge, MA: Harvard University Press.

Geertz, Clifford 1973 *The Interpretation of Cultures*. New York: Basic Books.

Geertz, Clifford 1988 *Works and Lives: The Anthropologist as Author*. Stanford, CA: Stanford University Press.

Geertz, Clifford 1995 *After the Fact: Two Countries, Four Decades, One Anthropologist*. Cambridge, MA: Harvard University Press.

Gellner, Ernest 1985 'Malinowski Go Home', *Anthropology Today* 1:5–7.

Genet, Jean 1986/1989 *Prisoner of Love*. London: Picador.

Gibson-Graham, J.K., Stephen A. Resnick and Richard D. Wolff 2000 *Class and its Others*. Minneapolis: University of Minnesota Press.

Gilroy, Paul 1993 *The Black Atlantic: Modernity and Double Consciousness*. London: Routledge.

Gledhill, John 1994 *Power and its Disguises*. London: Pluto Press (1st edn of Gledhill 2000).

Gledhill, John 2000 *Power and its Disguises: Anthropological Perspectives on Politics*. London: Pluto Press.

Guattari, Félix and Antonio Negri 1990 *Communists Like Us*. New York: Semiotext(e).

Guha, Ranajit 1983 *Elementary Aspects of Peasant Insurgency*. Delhi: Oxford University Press.

Habermas, Jürgen 1987 *The Philosophical Discourse of Modernity*. Cambridge: Polity Press.

Habib, Irfan 1999 'The Reading of History', in Prakesh Karat (ed.) *A World to Win*. New Delhi: Left Word Books, pp. 48–67.

Hanfi, Zawar 1972 *The Fiery Brook: Selected Writings of Ludwig Feuerbach*. New York: Anchor Books.

Hardt, Michael and Antonio Negri 1994 *The Labour of Dionysius*. Minneapolis: University of Minnesota Press.

Hardt, Michael and Antonio Negri 2000 *Empire*. Cambridge, MA: Harvard University Press.

Healy, Michael 1986 'The Redness of Tomatoes', *Arena* 77:81–5.

Heidegger, Martin 1971 *On the Way to Language*. New York: Harper and Row.

Holland, Eugene 1997 'Derrida's Marx versus Deleuze's', *South Atlantic Quarterly* July.

Hollier, Denis 1988 *The College of Sociology*. Minneapolis: University of Minnesota Press.

Hollier, Denis 1989 *Against Architecture: The Writings of Georges Bataille*. Cambridge, MA: MIT Press.

Holmes, David 1990 Article in *Arena* 89.

hooks, bell 1995 *Killing Rage, Ending Racism*. Harmondsworth: Penguin.

Hutnyk, John 1987 'The Authority of Style', *Social Analysis* 21:59–79.

Hutnyk, John 1988 'Castaway Anthropology: Malinowski's Tropical Writings', *Antithesis* 2(1):43–54.

Hutnyk, John 1989 'Clifford Geertz as a Cultural System', *Social Analysis* 25:91–107.

Hutnyk, John 1996 *The Rumour of Calcutta: Tourism, Charity and the Poverty of Representation*. London: Zed Books.

Hutnyk, John 1997a 'derrida@marx.archive', *Space and Culture* 2:95–122.

Hutnyk, John 1997b *derrida@marx.archive* Manchester: Department of Anthropology, University of Manchester.

Hutnyk, John 1998a 'Adorno at Womad: South Asian Crossovers and the Limits of Hybridity-talk', *Postcolonial Studies* 1(3):401–26.

Hutnyk, John 1998b 'Clifford's Ethnographica', *Critique of Anthropology* 18(4):339–78.

Hutnyk, John 1998c 'Argonauts of Western Pessimism: Jim Clifford's Ethnographica', in Steve Clarke (ed.) *Travel Writing and Empire*. London: Zed Books.

Hutnyk, John 1999 'Semifeudal Cybercolonialism: Technocratic Dreamtime in Malaysia', in J. Bosma et al. (eds) *Readme! Filtered by Nettime: Ascii Culture and the Revenge of Knowledge*. New York: Autonomedia, pp. 315–21.

Hutnyk, John 2000a *Critique of Exotica: Music, Politics and the Culture Industry*. London: Pluto Press.

Hutnyk, John 2000b 'Capital Calcutta Coins, Maps, Monuments', in David Bell and Azzadine Haddour (eds) *City Visions*. London: Longman.

Hutnyk, John 2000c 'The Right to Difference is a Fundamental Human Right: Against the Motion', contribution to GDAT debate No. 10, with S. Corry, I. Jean-Klein, R. Wilson, in P. Wade (ed.) *The Right to Difference is a Fundamental Human Right*. Manchester: Manchester University Press, pp. 40–52.

Hutnyk, John 2002a 'Jungle Studies', *Futures* 34(1):15–32.

Hutnyk, John 2002b 'Tales from the Raj', *Rethinking Marxism* 13(3/4): 119–36.

Hutnyk, John 2003 'Bataille's Wars: Surrealism, Marxism, Fascism', *Critique of Anthropology* 23(3):264–88.

Kalra, Virinder, John Hutnyk and Raminder Kaur 2004 *Diaspora and Hybridity*. London: Sage.

Kaplan, Caren 1996 *Questions of Travel: Postmodern Discourses of Displacement*. Durham, NC: Duke University Press.

Kaur, Raminder and John Hutnyk 1999 *Travel Worlds: Journeys in Contemporary Cultural Politics*. London: Zed Books.

Koepping, Klaus Peter 1983 *Adolf Bastian and the Psychic Unity of Mankind: The Foundation of Anthropology in Nineteenth-century Germany*. St Lucia: University of Queensland Press.

Koepping, Klaus Peter 1989 'Mind, Body, Text: Not Quite Satirical Reflections on the Trickster', *Criticism, Heresy and Interpretation* 2:37–76.

Köpping, Klaus-Peter 2002 *Shattering Frames: Transgressions and Transformations in Anthropological Discourse and Practice*. Berlin: Dietrich Reimer Verlag.

Kovel, Joel 1994 *Red Hunting in a Promised Land*. New York: Basic Books.

Krader, Lawrence 1974 *The Ethnological Notebooks of Karl Marx: Studies of Morgan, Phear, Maine, Lubbock*. Assan: Van Gorcum.

Kratz, Corinne A. 1994 'On Telling/Selling a Book by its Cover', *Cultural Anthropology* 9(2):179–200.

Kuan-Hsing Chen 1998 'The Decolonizing Question', *Trajectories: Inter-Asia Cultural Studies*. London: Routledge, pp. 1–53.

Kuper, Adam 1991 *The Invention of Primitive Society: Transformations of an Illusion*. London: Routledge.

Lacoue-Labarthe, Philippe and Jean-Luc Nancy 1997 *Retreating the Political*. London: Routledge.

Land, Nick 1992 *The Thirst for Annihilation*. London: Routledge.

Laporte, Dominique 1978/2000 *History of Shit*. Cambridge, MA: MIT Press.

Leiris, Michel 1966/1989 *Brisées: Broken Branches*. San Francisco: North Point Press.

Lenin, Vladimir I. 1917/2000 *Imperialism: The Highest Stage of Capitalism*. New Delhi: Leftword Books.

Lévi-Strauss, Claude 1955 *Tristes Tropiques*. London: Jonathan Cape.

Lévi-Strauss, Claude 1987 *An Introduction to the Work of Marcel Mauss*. London: Routledge.

Lewis, Helena 1990 *Dada Turns Red: The Politics of Surrealism*. Edinburgh: Edinburgh University Press.

Leyda, Jay and Zina Voynov 1982 *Eisenstein at Work*. New York: Random House.

Malinowski, Bronislaw 1922 *Argonauts of the Western Pacific: An Account of Native Enterprise and Adventure in the Archipelagos of Melanesian New Guinea*. London: Routledge.

Malinowski, Bronislaw 1929a 'Practical Anthropology', *Africa* 11(1):22–38.

Malinowski, Bronislaw 1929b *The Sexual Life of Savages in North-western Melanesia*. Honolulu: University Press of the Pacific.

Malinowski, Bronislaw 1930 'The Rationalisation of Anthropology and its Administration', *Africa* 111(4):405–30.

Malinowski, Bronislaw 1935 *Coral Gardens and their Magic*, 2 vols. London: George Allen and Unwin.

Malinowski, Bronislaw 1967 *A Diary in the Strict Sense of the Term*. London: Routledge.

Mao Zedong 1928/1975 'The Struggle in the ChingKong Mountains', *Selected Works*, vol. 1. Peking: Foreign Languages Press, pp. 73–104.

Mao Zedong 1937/1975 'On Contradiction', *Selected Works*, vol. 1. Peking: Foreign Languages Press, pp. 311–47.

Marcus, George 1988 'Parody and the Parodic in Polynesian Cultural History', *Cultural Anthropology* 3(1):68–76.

Marcus, George 1995 'Ethnography in/of the World System: The Emergence of Multi-sited Ethnography', *Annual Review of Anthropology* 24:95–140.

Marcus, George and Michael Fischer 1986 *Anthropology as Cultural Critique: An Experimental Moment in the Human Sciences*. Chicago: University of Chicago Press.

Marcus, Julie 1991 'Something Critical about Clifford', *Social Analysis* 29.

Marx, Karl 1847 *The Poverty of Philosophy* <http://csf.Colorado.EDU/psn/marx/Admin>.

Marx, Karl 1857–58 *Pre-capitalist Economic Formations* <http://csf.Clorado.EDU/psn/marx/Admin>.

Marx, Karl 1858/1973 *Grundrisse*. Harmondsworth: Penguin.

Marx, Karl 1867/1967 *Capital: A Critique of Political Economy, Vol. 1: The Process of Capitalist Production*, edited by F. Engels, trans. S. Moore and E. Aveling. New York: International Publishers.

Marx, Karl 1867/1976 *Value Studies by Marx*. London: New Park Publications.

Marx, Karl 1871 *The Civil War in France*. Moscow: Progress Publishers.

Marx, Karl 1890/1975 *Das Kapital*. Berlin: Dietz Verlag.

Marx, Karl 1893/1974 *Capital, Vol. 2*. Moscow: Progress Publishers.

Marx, Karl 1898/1950 'Wages, Prices and Profit', in K. Marx and F. Engels, *Selected Works, Vol. 1*. Moscow: Progress Press, pp. 361–405.

Marx, Karl 1947 *Notes on Indian History*. Moscow: Progress Publishers.

Marx, Karl 1968 *Selected Works* London: Lawrence and Wishart.

Marx, Karl and Friedrich Engels 1848/1952 *Manifesto of the Communist Party*. Moscow: Progress Publishers.

Marx, Karl and Friedrich Engels 1848/1970 *Manifest der Kommunistischen Partei*. Berlin: Dietz Verlag.

Marx, Karl and Friedrich Engels 1975 *Marx and Engels Collected Works (MECW)*. Moscow: Foreign Languages Publishing House.

Marx, Karl and Friedrich Engels 1990–2004 *Gesamtausgabe* (MEGA-Stiftung Berlin e.V). Berlin: Akademie Verlag GmbH.

Massumi, Brian 2002 *Parables for the Virtual*. Durham, NC: Duke University Press.

Mauss, Marcel 1926/2000 *The Gift*. New York: Norton.

McQuire 1990 'But, Who, Derrida?', *Arena* 90:130–63.

McQuire, Scott 1995 *Art, Culture and Power*. Waurn Ponds: Deakin University.

McQuire, Scott 1997a *Visions of Modernity: Representation, Memory, Time and Space in the Age of the Camera*. London: Sage.

McQuire, Scott 1997b 'The Uncanny Home: Or Living On-line with Others', in Peter Droege (ed.) *Intelligent Environments: Spatial Aspects of the Information Revolution*. Amsterdam: Elsevier.

McQuire, Scott 2003 'From Glass Architecture to *Big Brother*: Scenes from a Cultural History of Transparency', *Cultural Studies Review* 9(1):103–23.

Miller, Daniel 1987 *Material Culture and Mass Consumption*. Oxford: Blackwell.

Miller, Daniel 1994 *Modernity – An Ethnographic Approach: Dualism and Mass Consumption in Trinidad*. Oxford: Berg.

Miller, Daniel 1995 'Consumption and Commodities', *Annual Review of Anthropology* 24:141–61.

Miller, Donald F. 1992 *The Reason of Metaphor: A Study in Politics*. New Delhi: Sage.

Moody, Roger 1991 *Plunder*. London: Partizans.

Mulvaney, D.J. and J.H. Calaby 1985 *'So Much that is New': Baldwin Spencer 1860–1929, A Biography*. Melbourne: Melbourne University Press.

Mulvaney, John, Howard Morphy and Alison Petch (eds) 1997 *My Dear Spencer: The Letters of F.J. Gillen to Baldwin Spencer*. Melbourne: Hyland House.

Nancy, Jean-Luc 1991 *The Inoperative Community*. Minneapolis: University of Minnesota Press.

Negri, Antonio 1991 *Marx Beyond Marx: Lessons in the Grundrisse*. New York: Autonomedia.

Negri, Antonio 1999 *Insurgencies: Constituent Power and the Modern State*. Minneapolis: University of Minnesota Press.

Newton, Esther 1993 'My Best Informant's Dress: The Erotic in Fieldwork', *Cultural Anthropology* 8(1):3–23.

Nugent, Stephen 1991 'Tell Me about Your Trope', *Social Analysis* 29:130–5.

Nugent, Stephen 1993 *Amazonian Caboclo Society: An Essay on Invisibility and Peasant Economy*. Oxford: Berg.

Nugent, Stephen and Cris Shore 1997 *Anthropology and Cultural Studies*. London: Pluto Press.

O'Hanlon, Michael 1993 *Paradise: Portraying the New Guinea Highlands*. London: British Museum Press.

O'Hanlon, Rosalind and David Washbrook 2000 'After Orientalism: Culture, Criticism and Politics in the Third World', in Vinayak Chaturvedi (ed.) *Mapping Subaltern Studies and the Postcolonial*. London: Verso, pp. 191–219.

Ong, Aiwa 1999 *Flexible Citizenship: The Cultural Logics of Transnationality*. Durham, NC: Duke University Press.

Pershits, A. 1980 *Ethnographic Reconstruction of the History of Primitive Society in Soviet and Western Anthropology*, edited by Ernest Gellner. London: Duckworth.

Phipps, Peter 1998 'Tourists and Terrorists', in Raminder Kaur and John Hutnyk (eds) *Travelworlds: Journeys in Contemporary Cultural Politics*. London: Zed Books.

Prakash, Gyan 2000 'Can the Subaltern Ride? A Reply to O'Hanlon and Washbrook', in Vinayak Chaturvedi (ed.) *Mapping Subaltern Studies and the Postcolonial*. London: Verso, pp. 220–38.

Price, Sally and Jean Jamin 1988 'A Conversation with Michel Leiris', *Current Anthropology* 29(1):157–74.

Pynchon, Thomas 1990 *Vineland*. London: Secker and Warburg.

Rabinow, Paul 1977 *Reflections of Fieldwork in Morocco*. Berkeley: University of California Press.

Radek, K. 1923 'International Fascism and the Communist International', *Inprecorr* 3(53, 26 July):599–600.

Rapport, Nigel 1990 'Surely Everything has Already been Said about Malinowski's Diary!', *Anthropology Today* 6(1):6–9.

Reed, Adolf Jr 2000 *Class Notes: Posing as Politics and Other Thoughts on the American Scene*. New York: The New Press.

Resnick, Stephen A. and Richard D. Wolff 1995 'Lessons from the USSR', in Bernd Magnus and Stephen Cullenberg (eds) *Whither Marxism? Global Crises in International Perspective*. New York: Routledge.

Richardson, Michael 1994 *Georges Bataille*. London: Routledge.

Richardson, Michael and Krzysztof Fijalkowski (eds) 2001 *Surrealism against the Current*. London: Pluto Press.

Richardson, Miles 1975 'Anthropologist – the Myth Teller', *American Ethnologist* 2:517–33.

Ronell, Avital 1989 *The Telephone Book: Technology, Schizophrenia, Electric Speech*. Lincoln: University of Nebraska Press.

Ronell, Avital 2002 *Stupidity*. Champaign: University of Illinois Press.

Ross, Dan 1992 Unpublished Honours thesis, Department of Political Science, University of Melbourne.

Roswell, Nicholas 1996 'The Case of the Closed Book', *Australian Magazine* May:12–20.

Ryan, Michael 1982 *Marxism and Deconstruction*. Baltimore, MD: Johns Hopkins University Press.

Schippers, Thomas K. 1995 'A History of Paradoxes: Anthropologies of Europe', in Han F. Vermeulan and Arturo Alvarez Roldán (eds) *Fieldwork and Footnotes: Studies in the History of European Anthropology*. London: Routledge, pp. 234–47.

Schmitt, Carl 1932/1976 *The Concept of the Political*. New Jersey: Rutgers University Press.

Schmitt, Carl 1963 *Theorie des Partisans, Zwishenbermerkung zum Begriff des Politischen*. Berlin: Drucker and Humbolt.

Shanin, Teodor (ed.) 1983 *Late Marx and the Russian Road*. New York: Monthly Review Press.

Sharma, Sanjay, John Hutnyk and Ashwani Sharma 1996 *Dis-Orienting Rhythms: The Politics of the New Asian Dance Music*. London: Zed Books.

Spivak, Gayatri Chakravorty 1985 'Scattered Speculations on the Question of Value', *Diacritics* winter:73–93.

Spivak, Gayatri Chakravorty 1987 *In Other Worlds: Essays in Cultural Politics*. New York: Methuen.

Spivak, Gayatri Chakravorty 1993 *Outside in the Teaching Machine*. New York: Routledge.

Spivak, Gayatri Chakravorty 1995a 'Supplementing Marx', in Bernd Magnus and Stephen Cullenberg (eds) *Whither Marxism? Global Crises in International Perspective*. New York: Routledge.

Spivak, Gayatri Chakravorty 1995b 'Ghostwriting', in *Diacritics* 25(summer): manuscript version.

Spivak, Gayatri Chakravorty 1996 *The Spivak Reader*, edited by Donna Landry and Gerald Maclean. New York: Routledge.

Spivak, Gayatri Chakravorty 1999 *A Critique of Postcolonial Reason: Toward a History of the Vanishing Present*. Cambridge, MA: Harvard University Press.

Spivak, Gayatri Chakravorty 2000a 'The New Subaltern: A Silent Interview', in Vinayak Chaturvedi (ed.) *Mapping Subaltern Studies and the Postcolonial*. London: Verso, pp. 324–40.

Spivak, Gayatri Chakravorty 2000b 'Thinking Cultural Questions in "Pure" Literary Terms', in Paul Gilroy, Lawrence Grossberg and Angela McRobbie (eds) *Without Guarantees: In Honour of Stuart Hall*. London: Verso, pp. 335–57.

Spivak, Gayatri Chakravorty 2003 *Death of a Discipline*. New York: Columbia University Press.

Srinivas, M.N. 1962 *Caste in Modern India and Other Essays*. Bombay: Media Promoters and Publishers.

Stagl, Justin 1996 'Nicolai Nicolayevich Miklouho-Maclay: Or, The Dilemma of the Ethnographer in the Pre-colonial Situation', *History and Anthropology* 9(2–3):255–65.

Stagl, Justin and Christopher Pinney 1996 'Introduction: From Travel Writing to Ethnography', *History and Anthropology* 9(2–3):121–4.

Stocking, George W. Jr 1985 'Anthropology and the Science of the Irrational: Malinowski's Encounter with Freudian Psychoanalysis', in G.W. Stocking (ed.) *Malinowski, Rivers, Benedict and Others: Essays on Culture and Personality*. Madison: University of Wisconsin Press.

Stocking, George W. Jr 1991 'Maclay, Kubary, Malinowski: Archetypes from the Dreamtime of Anthropology', in George W. Stocking (ed.) *Colonial Situations: Essays on the Contextualization of Ethnographic Knowledge*. Madison: University of Wisconsin Press.

Strathern, Marilyn 1987 'Out of Context: The Persuasive Fictions of Anthropology', *Current Anthropology* 28:

Strathern, Marilyn 1991 'Or, Rather, on Not Collecting Clifford', *Social Analysis* 29:88–95.

Surya, Michel 1992/2002 *Georges Bataille*. London: Verso.

Swedenbourg, Ted 1995 'With Genet in the Palestinian Field', in Carolyn Nordstrom and Antonius Robben (eds) *Fieldwork under Fire: Contemporary Studies of Violence and Survival*. Berkeley: University of California Press.

Taussig, Michael 1980 *The Devil and Commodity Fetishism in South America*. Chapel Hill: University of North Carolina Press.

Taussig, Michael 1987 *Shamanism, Colonialism and the Wild Man: A Study in Terror and Healing*. Chicago: University of Chicago Press.

Taussig, Michael 1999 *Defacement*. Stanford, CA: Stanford University Press.

Taussig, Michael 2003 *Law in the Lawless Land*. New York: The New Press.

Thoburn, Nicholas 2003 *Deleuze, Marx and Politics*. London: Routledge.

Thornton, Robert 1985 'Imagine Yourself Set Down … : Mach, Frazer, Conrad, Malinowski and the Role of the Imagination in Ethnography', *Anthropology Today* 1:7–14.

Thrift, Nigel 1996 *Spatial Formations*. London: Sage.

Trinh T. Minh-ha and Anamaria Morelli 1996 'The Undone Interval', in Iain Chambers and Linda Curtis (eds) *The Post-colonial Question*. London: Routledge, pp. 3–16.

Uberoi, J.P.S. 1962 *The Politics of the Kula Ring: An Analysis of the Findings of Bronislaw Malinowski*. Manchester: Manchester University Press.

Vermeulan, Han F. 1995 'Origins and Institutionalisation of Ethnography and Ethnology in Europe and the USA, 1771–1845', in Han F. Vermeulan and Arturo Alvarez Roldán (eds) *Fieldwork and Footnotes, Studies in the History of European Anthropology*. London: Routledge, pp. 39–60.

Vidal, Gore 2002 *Perpetual War for Perpetual Peace*. New York: Nation Books.

Wade, Peter 1993 'Sexuality and Masculinity in Fieldwork among Columbian Blacks', in Diane Bell, Pat Caplan and Jahan Karim Wazir (eds) *Gendered Fields: Women, Men and Ethnography*. London: Routledge.

Wayne, Helena (ed.) 1995 *The Story of a Marriage, Vols 1 and 2: The Letters of Bronislaw Malinowski and Elsie Masson*. London: Routledge.

Weiner, Annette B. 1977 'Review of "Trobriand Cricket" ', *Man* 79:506–7.

Weiner, Annette B. 1988 *The Trobrianders of Papua New Guinea*. New York: Holt Rinehart and Winston.

Whitten Jr, Norman E. 1991 'Pretext of a Modernist Predicament', *Social Analysis* 29:96–109.

Wright, Steve 2000 *Storming Heaven*. London: Pluto Press.

Young, Michael 1979 *The Ethnography of Malinowski: The Trobriand Islands, 1915–1918*. London: Routledge and Kegan Paul.

Young, Michael 1984 'The Intensive Study of a Restricted Area, or, Why Did Malinowski Go to the Trobriand Islands?' *Oceania* 55(1):1–26.

Žižek, Slavoj 2002 *Revolution at the Gates*. London: Verso.

# Index